W9-ARY-775

About the Authors

Stephen G. Kochan is the owner of TechFitness, a technology-based fitness company. Prior to that, he was president and CEO of Pipeline Associates, a company specializing in color printing software. Mr. Kochan is the author of several best-selling books on Unix and C programming, including the best-selling *Programming in C*. He also acted as Series Editor for the Hayden Unix System Library.

Patrick Wood is the CTO of the New Jersey location of Electronics for Imaging. He was a member of the technical staff at Bell Laboratories when he met Mr. Kochan in 1985. Together they founded Pipeline Associates, Inc., a Unix consulting firm, where he was the Vice President. They coauthored *Exploring the Unix System, Unix System Security, Topics in C Programming,* and *Unix Shell Programming.*

Dedication

To my father, Harry Wood
—Patrick Wood

To Gregory, Linda, and Julia for giving meaning to my life
—Stephen G. Kochan

We Want to Hear from You!

As the reader of this book, *you* are our most important critic and commentator. We value your opinion and want to know what we're doing right, what we could do better, what areas you'd like to see us publish in, and any other words of wisdom you're willing to pass our way.

You can email or write me directly to let me know what you did or didn't like about this book—as well as what we can do to make our books stronger.

Please note that I cannot help you with technical problems related to the topic of this book, and that due to the high volume of mail I receive, I might not be able to reply to every message.

When you write, please be sure to include this book's title and author as well as your name and phone or email address. I will carefully review your comments and share them with the author and editors who worked on the book.

Email: feedback@samspublishing.com

Mail: Mark Taber
           Associate Publisher
           Sams Publishing
           800 East 96th Street
           Indianapolis, IN 46240 USA

Reader Services

For more information about this book or others from Sams Publishing, visit our Web site at www.samspublishing.com. Type the ISBN (excluding hyphens) or the title of the book in the Search box to find the book you're looking for.

1

Introduction

It's no secret that the Unix operating system has emerged as a standard operating system. For programmers who have been using Unix for many years now, this came as no surprise: The Unix system provides an elegant and efficient environment for program development. After all, this is what Dennis Ritchie and Ken Thompson strived for when they developed Unix at Bell Laboratories in the late 1960s.

One of the strongest features of the Unix system is its wide collection of programs. More than 200 basic commands are distributed with the standard operating system. These commands (also known as *tools*) do everything from counting the number of lines in a file, to sending electronic mail, to displaying a calendar for any desired year.

But the real strength of the Unix system comes not entirely from this large collection of commands but also from the elegance and ease with which these commands can be combined to perform far more sophisticated functions.

To further this end, and also to provide a consistent buffer between the user and the guts of the Unix system (the *kernel*), the shell was developed. The *shell* is simply a program that reads in the commands you type and converts them into a form more readily understood by the Unix system. It also includes some fundamental programming constructs that let you make decisions, loop, and store values in variables.

The standard shell distributed with Unix and Linux systems derives from AT&T's distribution, which evolved from a version originally written by Stephen Bourne at Bell Labs. Since then, the IEEE created standards based on the Bourne shell and the other more recent shells. The current version of this standard as of this revision is the Shell and Utilities volume of IEEE Std 1003.1-2001, also known as the POSIX standard. This shell is what we propose to teach you about in this book.

The examples in this book were tested on both SunOS 5.7 running on a Sparcstation Ultra-30 and on Silicon Graphics IRIX 6.5 running on an Octane; some examples were also run on Red Hat Linux 7.1 and Cygwin. All examples, except some Bash examples in Chapter 15, were run using the Korn shell, although many were also run with Bash.

Many Unix systems are still around that have Bourne shell derivatives and utilities not compliant with the POSIX standard. We'll try to note this throughout the text wherever possible; however, there are so many different versions of Unix from so many different vendors that it's simply not possible to mention every difference. If you do have an older Unix system that doesn't supply a POSIX-compliant shell, there's still hope. We'll list resources at the end of this book where you can obtain free copies of three different POSIX-compliant shells.

Because the shell offers an interpreted programming language, programs can be written, modified, and debugged quickly and easily. We turn to the shell as our first choice of programming language. After you become adept at programming in the shell, you too may turn to it first.

This book assumes that you are familiar with the fundamentals of the Unix system; that is, that you know how to log in; how to create files, edit them, and remove them; and how to work with directories. But in case you haven't used the Unix system for a while, we'll examine the basics in Chapter 2, "A Quick Review of the Basics." Besides the basic file commands, filename substitution, I/O redirection, and pipes are also reviewed in Chapter 2.

Chapter 3, "What Is the Shell?," reveals what the shell really is. You'll learn about what happens every time you log in to the system, how the shell program gets started, how it parses the command line, and how it executes other programs for you. A key point made in Chapter 3 is that the shell is just a program; nothing more, nothing less.

Chapter 4, "Tools of the Trade," provides tutorials on tools useful in writing shell programs. Covered in this chapter are `cut`, `paste`, `sed`, `grep`, `sort`, `tr`, and `uniq`. Admittedly, the selection is subjective, but it does set the stage for programs that we'll develop throughout the remainder of the book. Also in Chapter 4 is a detailed discussion of regular expressions, which are used by many Unix commands such as `sed`, `grep`, and `ed`.

Chapters 5 through 10 teach you how to put the shell to work for writing programs. You'll learn how to write your own commands; use variables; write programs that accept arguments; make decisions; use the shell's `for`, `while`, and `until` looping commands; and use the `read` command to read data from the terminal or from a file. Chapter 6, "Can I Quote You on That?," is devoted entirely to a discussion on one of the most intriguing (and often confusing) aspects of the shell: the way it interprets quotes.

By this point in the book, all the basic programming constructs in the shell will have been covered, and you will be able to write shell programs to solve your particular problems.

Chapter 11, "Your Environment," covers a topic of great importance for a real understanding of the way the shell operates: the *environment*. You'll learn about local and exported variables; subshells; special shell variables such as HOME, PATH, and CDPATH; and how to set up your `.profile` file.

Chapter 12, "More on Parameters," and Chapter 13, "Loose Ends," tie up some loose ends, and Chapter 14, "Rolo Revisited," presents a final version of a phone directory program called `rolo` that is developed throughout the book.

Chapter 15, "Interactive and Nonstandard Shell Features," discusses features of the shell that either are not formally part of the IEEE POSIX standard shell (but are available in most Unix and Linux shells) or are mainly used interactively instead of in programs.

Appendix A, "Shell Summary," summarizes the features of the IEEE POSIX standard shell.

Appendix B, "For More Information," lists references and resources, including the Web sites where different shells can be downloaded.

The philosophy this book uses is to teach by example. Properly chosen examples do a far superior job at illustrating how a particular feature is used than ten times as many words. The old "A picture is worth..." adage seems to apply just as well to examples. You are encouraged to type in each example and test it on your system, for only by doing can you become adept at shell programming. You also should not be afraid to experiment. Try changing commands in the program examples to see the effect, or add different options or features to make the programs more useful or robust.

At the end of most chapters you will find exercises. These can be used as assignments in a classroom environment or by yourself to test your progress.

This book teaches the IEEE POSIX standard shell. Incompatibilities with earlier Bourne shell versions are noted in the text, and these tend to be minor.

Acknowledgments from the first edition of this book: We'd like to thank Tony Iannino and Dick Fritz for editing the manuscript. We'd also like to thank Juliann Colvin for performing her usual wonders copy editing this book. Finally, we'd like to thank Teri Zak, our acquisitions editor, and posthumously Maureen Connelly, our production editor. These two were not only the best at what they did, but they also made working with them a real pleasure.

For the first revised edition of this book, we'd like to acknowledge the contributions made by Steven Levy and Ann Baker, and we'd like to also thank the following people from Sams: Phil Kennedy, Wendy Ford, and Scott Arant.

For the second revised edition of this book, we'd like to thank Kathryn Purdum, our acquisitions editor, Charlotte Clapp, our project editor, and Geneil Breeze, our copy editor.

2

A Quick Review of the Basics

This chapter provides a review of the Unix system, including the file system, basic commands, filename substitution, I/O redirection, and pipes.

Some Basic Commands

Displaying the Date and Time: The date Command

The date command tells the system to print the date and time:

```
$ date
Sat Jul 20 14:42:56 EDT 2002
$
```

date prints the day of the week, month, day, time (24-hour clock, the system's time zone), and year. Throughout this book, whenever we use **boldface type like this**, it's to indicate what you, the user, types in. Normal face type like this is used to indicate what the Unix system prints. *Italic type* is used for comments in interactive sequences.

Every Unix command is ended with the pressing of the Enter key. Enter says that you are finished typing things in and are ready for the Unix system to do its thing.

Finding Out Who's Logged In: The who Command

The who command can be used to get information about all users currently logged in to the system:

```
$ who
pat        tty29    Jul 19 14:40
ruth       tty37    Jul 19 10:54
steve      tty25    Jul 19 15:52
$
```

Here, three users are logged in: pat, ruth, and steve. Along with each user id, the *tty* number of that user and the day and time that user logged in is listed. The tty number is a unique identification number the Unix system gives to each terminal or network device that a user has logged into.

The who command also can be used to get information about yourself:

```
$ who am i
pat        tty29    Jul 19 14:40
$
```

who and who am i are actually the same command: who. In the latter case, the am and i are *arguments* to the who command.

Echoing Characters: The echo **Command**

The echo command prints (or *echoes*) at the terminal whatever else you happen to type on the line (there are some exceptions to this that you'll learn about later):

```
$ echo this is a test
this is a test
$ echo why not print out a longer line with echo?
why not print out a longer line with echo?
$ echo
                              A blank line is displayed
$ echo one          two     three          four   five
one two three four five
$
```

You will notice from the preceding example that echo squeezes out extra blanks between words. That's because on a Unix system, the words are important; the blanks are merely there to separate the words. Generally, the Unix system ignores extra blanks (you'll learn more about this in the next chapter).

Working with Files

The Unix system recognizes only three basic types of files: *ordinary* files, *directory* files, and *special* files. An ordinary file is just that: any file on the system that contains data, text, program instructions, or just about anything else. Directories are described later in this chapter. As its name implies, a special file has a special meaning to the Unix system and is typically associated with some form of I/O.

A filename can be composed of just about any character directly available from the keyboard (and even some that aren't) provided that the total number of characters contained in the name is not greater than 255. If more than 255 characters are specified, the Unix system simply ignores the extra characters.[1]

The Unix system provides many tools that make working with files easy. Here we'll review many basic file manipulation commands.

Listing Files: The `ls` Command

To see what files you have stored in your directory, you can type the `ls` command:

```
$ ls
READ_ME
names
tmp
$
```

This output indicates that three files called READ_ME, names, and tmp are contained in the current directory. (Note that the output of `ls` may vary from system to system. For example, on many Unix systems `ls` produces multicolumn output when sending its output to a terminal; on others, different colors may be used for different types of files. You can always force single-column output with the -1 option.)

Displaying the Contents of a File: The `cat` Command

You can examine the *contents* of a file by using the `cat` command. The argument to `cat` is the name of the file whose contents you want to examine.

```
$ cat names
Susan
Jeff
Henry
Allan
Ken
$
```

---

[1]*Modern Unix and Microsoft Windows systems support long filenames; however, some older Unix and Windows systems only allow much shorter filenames.*

Counting the Number of Words in a File: The wc Command

With the wc command, you can get a count of the total number of lines, words, and characters of information contained in a file. Once again, the name of the file is needed as the argument to this command:

```
$ wc names
        5       5       27 names
$
```

The wc command lists three numbers followed by the filename. The first number represents the number of lines contained in the file (5), the second the number of words contained in the file (in this case also 5), and the third the number of characters contained in the file (27).

Command Options

Most Unix commands allow the specification of *options* at the time a command is executed. These options generally follow the same format:

-*letter*

That is, a command option is a minus sign followed immediately by a single letter. For example, to count just the number of lines contained in a file, the option -l (that's the letter l) is given to the wc command:

```
$ wc -l names
        5 names
$
```

To count just the number of characters in a file, the -c option is specified:

```
$ wc -c names
       27 names
$
```

Finally, the -w option can be used to count the number of words contained in the file:

```
$ wc -w names
        5 names
$
```

Some commands require that the options be listed before the filename arguments. For example, sort names -r is acceptable, whereas wc names -l is not. Let's generalize by saying that command options should *precede* filenames on the command line.

Making a Copy of a File: The cp Command

To make a copy of a file, the cp command is used. The first argument to the command is the name of the file to be copied (known as the *source file*), and the second argument is the name of the file to place the copy into (known as the *destination file*). You can make a copy of the file names and call it saved_names as follows:

```
$ cp names saved_names
$
```

Execution of this command causes the file named names to be copied into a file named saved_names. As with many Unix commands, the fact that a command prompt was displayed after the cp command was typed indicates that the command executed successfully.

Renaming a File: The mv Command

A file can be renamed with the mv command. The arguments to the mv command follow the same format as the cp command. The first argument is the name of the file to be renamed, and the second argument is the new name. So, to change the name of the file saved_names to hold_it, for example, the following command would do the trick:

```
$ mv saved_names hold_it
$
```

When executing an mv or cp command, the Unix system does not care whether the file specified as the second argument already exists. If it does, the contents of the file will be lost.[2] For example, if a file called old_names exists, executing the command

```
cp names old_names
```

would copy the file names to old_names, destroying the previous contents of old_names in the process. Similarly, the command

```
mv names old_names
```

would rename names to old_names, even if the file old_names existed prior to execution of the command.

---

[2]*Assuming that you have the proper permission to write to the file.*

Removing a File: The `rm` Command

To remove a file from the system, you use the `rm` command. The argument to `rm` is simply the name of the file to be removed:

```
$ rm hold_it
$
```

You can remove more than one file at a time with the `rm` command by simply specifying all such files on the command line. For example, the following would remove the three files `wb`, `collect`, and `mon`:

```
$ rm wb collect mon
$
```

Working with Directories

Suppose that you had a set of files consisting of various memos, proposals, and letters. Further suppose that you had a set of files that were computer programs. It would seem logical to group this first set of files into a directory called `documents`, for example, and the latter set of files into a directory called `programs`. Figure 2.1 illustrates such a directory organization.

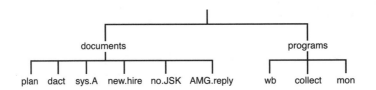

FIGURE 2.1   Example directory structure.

The file directory `documents` *contains* the files `plan`, `dact`, `sys.A`, `new.hire`, `no.JSK`, and `AMG.reply`. The directory `programs` contains the files `wb`, `collect`, and `mon`. At some point, you may decide to further categorize the files in a directory. This can be done by creating subdirectories and then placing each file into the appropriate subdirectory. For example, you might want to create subdirectories called `memos`, `proposals`, and `letters` inside your `documents` directory, as shown in Figure 2.2.

`documents` contains the subdirectories `memos`, `proposals`, and `letters`. Each of these directories in turn contains two files: `memos` contains `plan` and `dact`; `proposals` contains `sys.A` and `new.hire`; and `letters` contains `no.JSK` and `AMG.reply`.

Although each file in a given directory must have a unique name, files contained in different directories do not. So, for example, you could have a file in your `programs` directory called `dact`, even though a file by that name also exists in the `memos` subdirectory.

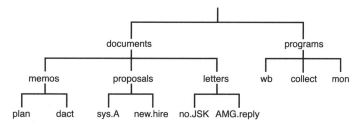

FIGURE 2.2   Directories containing subdirectories.

The Home Directory and Pathnames

The Unix system always associates each user of the system with a particular directory. When you log in to the system, you are placed automatically into a directory called your *home* directory.

Although the location of users' home directories can vary from one Unix version to the next, and even one user to the next, let's assume that your home directory is called `steve` and that this directory is actually a subdirectory of a directory called `users`. Therefore, if you had the directories `documents` and `programs`, the overall directory structure would actually look something like Figure 2.3. A special directory known as / (pronounced *slash*) is shown at the top of the directory tree. This directory is known as the *root*.

Whenever you are "inside" a particular directory (called your *current working* directory), the files contained within that directory are immediately accessible. If you want to access a file from another directory, you can either first issue a command to "change" to the appropriate directory and then access the particular file, or you can specify the particular file by its pathname.

A pathname enables you to uniquely identify a particular file to the Unix system. In the specification of a pathname, successive directories along the path are separated by the slash character /. A pathname that *begins* with a slash character is known as a *full* pathname because it specifies a complete path from the root. So, for example, the pathname `/users/steve` identifies the directory `steve` contained under the directory `users`. Similarly, the pathname `/users/steve/documents` references the directory `documents` as contained in the directory `steve` under `users`. As a final example, the pathname `/users/steve/documents/letters/AMG.reply` identifies the file `AMG.reply` contained along the appropriate directory path.

To help reduce some of the typing that would otherwise be required, Unix provides certain notational conveniences. Pathnames that do not begin with a slash character are known as *relative* pathnames. The path is relative to your current working directory. For example, if you just logged in to the system and were placed into your home directory `/users/steve`, you could directly reference the directory `documents` simply by typing `documents`. Similarly, the relative pathname `programs/mon` could be typed to access the file `mon` contained inside your `programs` directory.

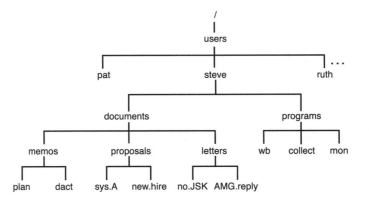

FIGURE 2.3   Hierarchical directory structure.

By convention, the directory name `..` always references the directory that is one level higher. For example, after logging in and being placed into your home directory `/users/steve`, the pathname `..` would reference the directory `users`. And if you had issued the appropriate command to change your working directory to `documents/letters`, the pathname `..` would reference the `documents` directory, `../..` would reference the directory `steve`, and `../proposals/new.hire` would reference the file `new.hire` contained in the `proposals` directory. Note that in this case, as in most cases, there is usually more than one way to specify a path to a particular file.

Another notational convention is the single period `.`, which always refers to the current directory.

Now it's time to examine commands designed for working with directories.

Displaying Your Working Directory: The `pwd` Command

The `pwd` command is used to help you "get your bearings" by telling you the name of your current working directory.

Recall the directory structure from Figure 2.3. The directory that you are placed in after you log in to the system is called your home directory. You can assume from Figure 2.3 that the home directory for the user `steve` is `/users/steve`. Therefore, whenever `steve` logs in to the system, he will automatically be placed inside this directory. To verify that this is the case, the `pwd` (print working directory) command can be issued:

```
$ pwd
/users/steve
$
```

The output from the command verifies that steve's current working directory is /users/steve.

Changing Directories: The cd Command

You can change your current working directory by using the cd command. This command takes as its argument the name of the directory you want to change to.

Let's assume that you just logged in to the system and were placed inside your home directory, /users/steve. This is depicted by the arrow in Figure 2.4.

You know that two directories are directly "below" steve's home directory: documents and programs. In fact, this can be verified at the terminal by issuing the ls command:

```
$ ls
documents
programs
$
```

The ls command lists the two directories documents and programs the same way it listed other ordinary files in previous examples.

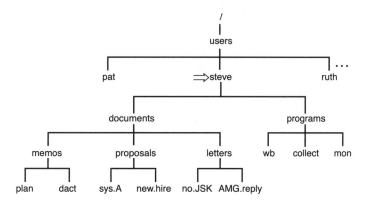

FIGURE 2.4   Current working directory is steve.

To change your current working directory, issue the cd command, followed by the name of the directory to change to:

```
$ cd documents
$
```

After executing this command, you will be placed inside the documents directory, as depicted in Figure 2.5.

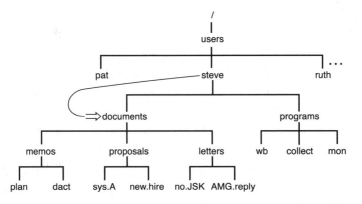

FIGURE 2.5   `cd documents`.

You can verify at the terminal that the working directory has been changed by issuing the pwd command:

```
$ pwd
/users/steve/documents
$
```

The easiest way to get one level up in a directory is to issue the command

```
cd ..
```

because by convention .. always refers to the directory one level up (known as the *parent* directory; see Figure 2.6).

```
$ cd ..
$ pwd
/users/steve
$
```

If you wanted to change to the letters directory, you could get there with a single cd command by specifying the relative path documents/letters (see Figure 2.7):

```
$ cd documents/letters
$ pwd
/users/steve/documents/letters
$
```

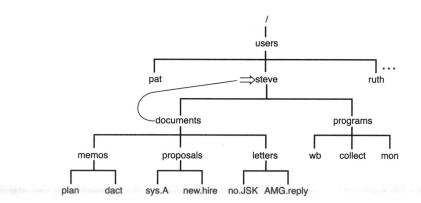

FIGURE 2.6   `cd ..`

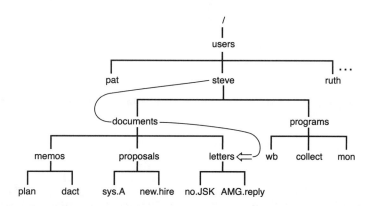

FIGURE 2.7   `cd documents/letters`.

You can get back up to the home directory by using a single `cd` command to go up two directories as shown:

```
$ cd ../..
$ pwd
/users/steve
$
```

Or you can get back to the home directory using a full pathname rather than a relative one:

```
$ cd /users/steve
$ pwd
/users/steve
$
```

Finally, there is a third way to get back to the home directory that is also the easiest. Typing the command cd *without* an argument *always* places you back into your home directory, no matter where you are in your directory path:

```
$ cd
$ pwd
/users/steve
$
```

More on the ls Command

When you type the ls command, the files contained in the current working directory are listed. But you can also use ls to obtain a list of files in other directories by supplying an argument to the command. First let's get back to your home directory:

```
$ cd
$ pwd
/users/steve
$
```

Now let's take a look at the files in the current working directory:

```
$ ls
documents
programs
$
```

If you supply the name of one of these directories to the ls command, you can get a list of the contents of that directory. So, you can find out what's contained in the documents directory simply by typing the command ls documents:

```
$ ls documents
letters
memos
proposals
$
```

To take a look at the subdirectory memos, you follow a similar procedure:

```
$ ls documents/memos
dact
plan
$
```

If you specify a nondirectory file argument to the ls command, you simply get that filename echoed back at the terminal:

```
$ ls documents/memos/plan
documents/memos/plan
$
```

An option to the ls command enables you to determine whether a particular file is a directory, among other things. The -l option (the letter l) provides a more detailed description of the files in a directory. If you were currently in steve's home directory as indicated in Figure 2.6, the following would illustrate the effect of supplying the -l option to the ls command:

```
$ ls -l
total 2
drwxr-xr-x    5 steve     DP3725       80 Jun 25 13:27 documents
drwxr-xr-x    2 steve     DP3725       96 Jun 25 13:31 programs
$
```

The first line of the display is a count of the total number of *blocks* (1,024 bytes) of storage that the listed files use. Each successive line displayed by the ls -l command contains detailed information about a file in the directory. The first character on each line tells whether the file is a directory. If the character is d, it is a directory; if it is -, it is an ordinary file; finally, if it is b, c, l, or p, it is a special file.

The next nine characters on the line tell how every user on the system can access the *particular* file. These *access modes* apply to the file's owner (the first three characters), other users in the same *group* as the file's owner (the next three characters), and finally to all other users on the system (the last three characters). They tell whether the user can read from the file, write to the file, or execute the contents of the file.

The ls -l command lists the *link* count (see "Linking Files: The ln Command," later in this chapter), the owner of the file, the group owner of the file, how large the file is (that is, how many characters are contained in it), and when the file was last modified. The information displayed last on the line is the filename itself.

```
$ ls -l programs
total 4
-rwxr-xr-x    1 steve     DP3725      358 Jun 25 13:31 collect
-rwxr-xr-x    1 steve     DP3725     1219 Jun 25 13:31 mon
-rwxr-xr-x    1 steve     DP3725       89 Jun 25 13:30 wb
$
```

The dash in the first column of each line indicates that the three files collect, mon, and wb are ordinary files and not directories.

Creating a Directory: The mkdir **Command**

To create a directory, the mkdir command must be used. The argument to this command is simply the name of the directory you want to make. For example, assume that you are still working with the directory structure depicted in Figure 2.7 and that you want to create a new directory called misc *on the same level* as the directories documents and programs. If you were currently in your home directory, typing the command mkdir misc would achieve the desired effect:

```
$ mkdir misc
$
```

Now if you execute an ls command, you should get the new directory listed:

```
$ ls
documents
misc
programs
$
```

The directory structure now appears as shown in Figure 2.8.

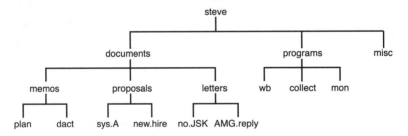

FIGURE 2.8   Directory structure with newly created misc directory.

Copying a File from One Directory to Another

The cp command can be used to copy a file from one directory into another. For example, you can copy the file wb from the programs directory into a file called wbx in the misc directory as follows:

```
$ cp programs/wb misc/wbx
$
```

Because the two files are contained in different directories, it is not even necessary that they be given different names:

```
$ cp programs/wb misc/wb
$
```

When the destination file has the same name as the source file (in a different directory, of course), it is necessary to specify only the destination directory as the second argument:

```
$ cp programs/wb misc
$
```

When this command gets executed, the Unix system recognizes that the second argument is the name of a directory and copies the source file into that directory. The new file is given the same name as the source file. You can copy more than one file into a directory by listing the files to be copied before the name of the destination directory. If you were currently in the programs directory, the command

```
$ cp wb collect mon ../misc
$
```

would copy the three files wb, collect, and mon into the misc directory, under the same names.

To copy a file from another directory into your current one and give it the same name, use the fact that the current directory can always be referenced as '.':

```
$ pwd
/users/steve/misc
$ cp ../programs/collect .
$
```

The preceding command copies the file collect from the directory ../programs into the current directory (/users/steve/misc).

Moving Files Between Directories

You recall that the mv command can be used to rename a file. However, when the two arguments to this command reference different directories, the file is actually moved from the first directory into the second directory. For example, first change from the home directory to the documents directory:

```
$ cd documents
$
```

Suppose that now you decide that the file plan contained in the memos directory is really a proposal and not a memo. So you want to move it from the memos directory into the proposals directory. The following would do the trick:

```
$ mv memos/plan proposals/plan
$
```

As with the `cp` command, if the source file and destination file have the same name, only the name of the destination directory need be supplied.

```
$ mv memos/plan proposals
$
```

Also like the `cp` command, a group of files can be simultaneously moved into a directory by simply listing all files to be moved before the name of the destination directory:

```
$ pwd
/users/steve/programs
$ mv wb collect mon ../misc
$
```

This would move the three files `wb`, `collect`, and `mon` into the directory `misc`. You can also use the `mv` command to change the name of a directory. For example, the following renames the directory `programs` to `bin`.

```
$ mv programs bin
$
```

Linking Files: The `ln` Command

In simplest terms, the `ln` command provides an easy way for you to give more than one name to a file. The general form of the command is

ln *from to*

This links the file *from* to the file *to*.

Recall the structure of `steve`'s `programs` directory from Figure 2.8. In that directory, he has stored a program called `wb`. Suppose that he decides that he'd also like to call the program `writeback`. The most obvious thing to do would be to simply create a copy of `wb` called `writeback`:

```
$ cp wb writeback
$
```

The drawback with this approach is that now twice as much disk space is being consumed by the program. Furthermore, if `steve` ever changes `wb`, he may forget to make a new copy of `writeback`, resulting in two different copies of what he thinks is the same program.

By linking the file `wb` to the new name, these problems are avoided:

```
$ ln wb writeback
$
```

Now instead of two copies of the file existing, only one exists with two different names: `wb` and `writeback`. The two files have been logically linked by the Unix system. As far as you're concerned, it appears as though you have two *different* files. Executing an `ls` command shows the two files separately:

```
$ ls
collect
mon
wb
writeback
$
```

Look what happens when you execute an `ls -l`:

```
$ ls -l
total 5
-rwxr-xr-x   1 steve      DP3725       358 Jun 25 13:31 collect
-rwxr-xr-x   1 steve      DP3725      1219 Jun 25 13:31 mon
-rwxr-xr-x   2 steve      DP3725        89 Jun 25 13:30 wb
-rwxr-xr-x   2 steve      DP3725        89 Jun 25 13:30 writeback
$
```

The number right before `steve` is 1 for `collect` and `mon` and 2 for `wb` and `writeback`. This number is the number of links to a file, normally 1 for nonlinked, nondirectory files. Because `wb` and `writeback` are linked, this number is 2 for these files. This implies that you can link to a file more than once.

You can remove either of the two linked files at any time, and the other will not be removed:

```
$ rm writeback
$ ls -l
total 4
-rwxr-xr-x   1 steve      DP3725       358 Jun 25 13:31 collect
-rwxr-xr-x   1 steve      DP3725      1219 Jun 25 13:31 mon
-rwxr-xr-x   1 steve      DP3725        89 Jun 25 13:30 wb
$
```

Note that the number of links on `wb` went from 2 to 1 because one of its links was removed.

Most often, ln is used to link files between directories. For example, suppose that pat wanted to have access to steve's wb program. Instead of making a copy for himself (subject to the same problems described previously) or including steve's programs directory in his PATH (described in detail in Chapter 11, "Your Environment"), he can simply link to the file from his own program directory; for example:

```
$ pwd
/users/pat/bin                        pat's program directory
$ ls -l
total 4
-rwxr-xr-x    1 pat      DP3822     1358 Jan 15 11:01 lcat
-rwxr-xr-x    1 pat      DP3822      504 Apr 21 18:30 xtr
$ ln /users/steve/wb .                link wb to pat's bin
$ ls -l
total 5
-rwxr-xr-x    1 pat      DP3822     1358 Jan 15 11:01 lcat
-rwxr-xr-x    2 steve    DP3725       89 Jun 25 13:30 wb
-rwxr-xr-x    1 pat      DP3822      504 Apr 21 18:30 xtr
$
```

Note that steve is still listed as the owner of wb, even though the listing came from pat's directory. This makes sense, because really only one copy of the file exists—and it's owned by steve.

The only stipulation on linking files is that for ordinary links, the files to be linked together must reside on the same *file system*. If they don't, you'll get an error from ln when you try to link them. (To determine the different file systems on your system, execute the df command. The first field on each line of output is the name of a file system.)

To create links to files on different file systems (or perhaps on different networked systems), you can use the -s option to the ln command. This creates a *symbolic* link. Symbolic links behave a lot like regular links, except that the symbolic link points to the original file; if the original file is removed, the symbolic link no longer works. Let's see how symbolic links work with the previous example:

```
$ rm wb
$ ls -l
total 4
-rwxr-xr-x    1 pat      DP3822     1358 Jan 15 11:01 lcat
-rwxr-xr-x    1 pat      DP3822      504 Apr 21 18:30 xtr
$ ln -s /users/steve/wb ./symwb              Symbolic link to wb
$ ls -l
```

```
total 5
-rwxr-xr-x    1 pat       DP3822      1358 Jan 15 11:01 lcat
lrwxr-xr-x    1 pat       DP3822        15 Jul 20 15:22 symwb -> /users/steve/wb
-rwxr-xr-x    1 pat       DP3822       504 Apr 21 18:30 xtr
$
```

Note that pat is listed as the owner of symwb, and the file type is l, which indicates a symbolic link. The size of the symbolic link is 15 (the file actually contains the string /users/steve/wb), but if we attempt to access the contents of the file, we are presented with the contents of its symbolic link, /users/steve/wb:

```
$ wc symwb
        5      9        89 symwb
$
```

The -L option to the ls command can be used with the -l option to get a detailed list of information on the file the symbolic link points to:

```
$ ls -Ll
total 5
-rwxr-xr-x    1 pat       DP3822      1358 Jan 15 11:01 lcat
-rwxr-xr-x    2 steve     DP3725        89 Jun 25 13:30 wb
-rwxr-xr-x    1 pat       DP3822       504 Apr 21 18:30 xtr
$
```

Removing the file that a symbolic link points to invalidates the symbolic link (because symbolic links are maintained as filenames), although the symbolic link continues to stick around:

```
$ rm /users/steve/wb             Assume pat can remove this file
$ ls -l
total 5
-rwxr-xr-x    1 pat       DP3822      1358 Jan 15 11:01 lcat
lrwxr-xr-x    1 pat       DP3822        15 Jul 20 15:22 wb -> /users/steve/wb
-rwxr-xr-x    1 pat       DP3822       504 Apr 21 18:30 xtr
$ wc wb
Cannot open wb: No such file or directory
$
```

This type of file is called a *dangling symbolic link* and should be removed unless you have a specific reason to keep it around (for example, if you intend to replace the removed file).

One last note before leaving this discussion: The `ln` command follows the same general format as `cp` and `mv`, meaning that you can link a bunch of files at once into a directory using the format

`ln` *files directory*

Removing a Directory: The `rmdir` Command

You can remove a directory with the `rmdir` command. The stipulation involved in removing a directory is that no files be contained in the directory. If there *are* files in the directory when `rmdir` is executed, you will not be allowed to remove the directory. To remove the directory `misc` that you created earlier, the following could be used:

```
$ rmdir /users/steve/misc
$
```

Once again, the preceding command works only if no files are contained in the `misc` directory; otherwise, the following happens:

```
$ rmdir /users/steve/misc
rmdir: /users/steve/misc not empty
$
```

If this happens and you still want to remove the `misc` directory, you would first have to remove all the files contained in that directory before reissuing the `rmdir` command.

As an alternate method for removing a directory and the files contained in it, you can use the `-r` option to the `rm` command. The format is simple:

`rm -r` *dir*

where *dir* is the name of the directory that you want to remove. `rm` removes the indicated directory and *all* files (including directories) in it.

Filename Substitution

The Asterisk

One powerful feature of the Unix system that is actually handled by the shell is *filename substitution*. Let's say that your current directory has these files in it:

```
$ ls
chapt1
chapt2
```

```
chapt3
chapt4
$
```

Suppose that you want to print their contents at the terminal. Well, you could take advantage of the fact that the cat command allows you to specify more than one filename at a time. When this is done, the contents of the files are displayed one after the other:

```
$ cat chapt1 chapt2 chapt3 chapt4
    . . .
$
```

But you can also type in

```
$ cat *
    . . .
$
```

and get the same results. The shell automatically *substitutes* the names of all the files in the current directory for the *. The same substitution occurs if you use * with the echo command:

```
$ echo *
chapt1 chapt2 chapt3 chapt4
$
```

Here the * is again replaced with the names of all the files contained in the current directory, and the echo command simply displays them at the terminal.

Any place that * appears on the command line, the shell performs its substitution:

```
$ echo * : *
chapt1 chapt2 chapt3 chapt4 : chapt1 chapt2 chapt3 chapt4
$
```

The * can also be used in combination with other characters to limit the filenames that are substituted. For example, let's say that in your current directory you have not only chapt1 through chapt4 but also files a, b, and c:

```
$ ls
a
b
c
chapt1
chapt2
```

```
chapt3
chapt4
$
```

To display the contents of just the files beginning with chapt, you can type in

```
$ cat chapt*
    .
    .
    .
$
```

The chapt* matches any filename that *begins* with chapt. All such filenames matched are substituted on the command line.

The * is not limited to the end of a filename; it can be used at the beginning or in the middle as well:

```
$ echo *t1
chapt1
$ echo *t*
chapt1 chapt2 chapt3 chapt4
$ echo *x
*x
$
```

In the first echo, the *t1 specifies all filenames that end in the characters t1. In the second echo, the first * matches everything up to a t and the second everything after; thus, all filenames containing a t are printed. Because there are no files ending with x, no substitution occurs in the last case. Therefore, the echo command simply displays *x.

Matching Single Characters

The asterisk (*) matches *zero* or more characters, meaning that x* matches the file x as well as x1, x2, xabc, and so on. The question mark (?) matches exactly one character. So cat ? prints all files with one-character names, just as cat x? prints all files with two-character names beginning with x.

```
$ ls
a
aa
aax
alice
```

```
b
bb
c
cc
report1
report2
report3
$ echo ?
a b c
$ echo a?
aa
$ echo ??
aa bb cc
$ echo ??*
aa aax alice bb cc report1 report2 report3
$
```

In the preceding example, the ?? matches two characters, and the * matches zero or more up to the end. The net effect is to match all filenames of two or more characters.

Another way to match a single character is to give a list of the characters to use in the match inside square brackets [ ]. For example, [abc] matches *one* letter a, b, or c. It's similar to the ?, but it allows you to choose the characters that will be matched. The specification [0-9] matches the characters 0 *through* 9. The only restriction in specifying a *range* of characters is that the first character must be alphabetically less than the last character, so that [z-f] is not a valid range specification.

By mixing and matching ranges and characters in the list, you can perform some complicated substitutions. For example, [a-np-z]* matches all files that start with the letters a through n *or* p through z (or more simply stated, any lowercase letter but o).

If the first character following the [is a !, the sense of the match is inverted. That is, any character is matched *except* those enclosed in the brackets. So

[!a-z]

matches any character except a lowercase letter, and

*[!o]

matches any file that doesn't end with the lowercase letter o.

Table 2.1 gives a few more examples of filename substitution.

TABLE 2.1   Filename Substitution Examples

Command	Description
echo a*	Print the *names* of the files beginning with a
cat *.c	Print all files ending in .c
rm *.*	Remove all files containing a period
ls x*	List the names of all files beginning with x
rm *	Remove *all* files in the current directory (Note: Be careful when you use this.)
echo a*b	Print the names of all files beginning with a and ending with b
cp ../programs/* .	Copy all files from ../programs into the current directory
ls [a-z]*[!0-9]	List files that begin with a lowercase letter and don't end with a digit

Standard Input/Output and I/O Redirection

Standard Input and Standard Output

Most Unix system commands take input from your terminal and send the resulting output back to your terminal. A command normally reads its input from a place called *standard input*, which happens to be your terminal by default. Similarly, a command normally writes its output to *standard output*, which is also your terminal by default. This concept is depicted in Figure 2.9.

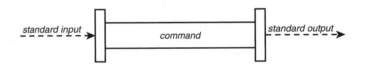

FIGURE 2.9   Typical Unix command.

Recall that executing the who command results in the display of the currently logged-in users. More formally, the who command writes a list of the logged-in users to standard output. This is depicted in Figure 2.10.

If a sort command is executed *without* a filename argument, the command takes its input from standard input. As with standard output, this is your terminal by default.

When entering data to a command from the terminal, the *Ctrl* and *d* keys (denoted *Ctrl+d* in this text) must be simultaneously pressed after the last data item has been entered. This tells the command that you have finished entering data. As an example, let's use the sort command to sort the following four names: Tony,

Barbara, Harry, Dick. Instead of first entering the names into a file, we'll enter them directly from the terminal:

```
$ sort
Tony
Barbara
Harry
Dick
Ctrl+d
Barbara
Dick
Harry
Tony
$
```

```
                                                    ai     tty01  Sep 12  07:30
                                                    oko    tty36  Sep 12  13:32
                              who                   pat    tty21  Sep 12  10:10
                                                    ruth   tty24  Sep 12  13:07
                                                    steve  tty25  Sep 12  13:03
```

FIGURE 2.10   who command.

Because no filename was specified to the sort command, the input was taken from standard input, the terminal. After the fourth name was typed in, the *Ctrl* and *d* keys were pressed to signal the end of the data. At that point, the sort command sorted the four names and displayed the results on the standard output device, which is also the terminal. This is depicted in Figure 2.11.

The wc command is another example of a command that takes its input from standard input if no filename is specified on the command line. So the following shows an example of this command used to count the number of lines of text entered from the terminal:

```
$ wc -l
This is text that
is typed on the
```

```
standard input device.
Ctrl+d
        3
$
```

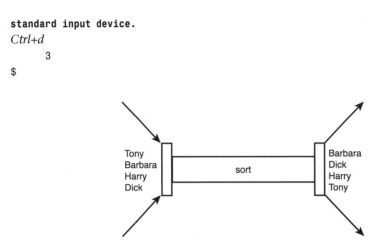

FIGURE 2.11   sort command.

Note that the *Ctrl+d* that is used to terminate the input is not counted as a separate line by the wc command. Furthermore, because no filename was specified to the wc command, only the count of the number of lines (3) is listed as the output of the command. (Recall that this command normally prints the name of the file directly after the count.)

Output Redirection

The output from a command normally intended for standard output can be easily diverted to a file instead. This capability is known as *output redirection*.

If the notation > *file* is appended to *any* command that normally writes its output to standard output, the output of that command will be written to *file* instead of your terminal:

```
$ who > users
$
```

This command line causes the who command to be executed and its output to be written into the file users. Notice that no output appears at the terminal. This is because the output has been *redirected* from the default standard output device (the terminal) into the specified file:

```
$ cat users
oko    tty01  Sep 12 07:30
ai     tty15  Sep 12 13:32
ruth   tty21  Sep 12 10:10
pat    tty24  Sep 12 13:07
```

```
steve tty25  Sep 12 13:03
$
```

If a command has its output redirected to a file and the file already contains some data, that data will be lost. Consider this example:

```
$ echo line 1 > users
$ cat users
line 1
$ echo line 2 >> users
$ cat users
line 1
line 2
$
```

The second echo command uses a different type of output redirection indicated by the characters >>. This character pair causes the standard output from the command to be *appended* to the specified file. Therefore, the previous contents of the file are not lost, and the new output simply gets added onto the end.

By using the redirection append characters >>, you can use cat to append the contents of one file onto the end of another:

```
$ cat file1
This is in file1.
$ cat file2
This is in file2.
$ cat file1 >> file2              Append file1 to file2
$ cat file2
This is in file2.
This is in file1.
$
```

Recall that specifying more than one filename to cat results in the display of the first file followed immediately by the second file, and so on:

```
$ cat file1
This is in file1.
$ cat file2
This is in file2.
$ cat file1 file2
This is in file1.
This is in file2.
$ cat file1 file2 > file3          Redirect it instead
```

```
$ cat file3
This is in file1.
This is in file2.
$
```

Now you can see where the cat command gets its name: When used with more than one file, its effect is to *catenate* the files together.

Incidentally, the shell recognizes a special format of output redirection. If you type

> *file*

not preceded by a command, the shell creates an empty (that is, zero character length) *file* for you. If *file* previously exists, its contents will be lost.

Input Redirection

Just as the output of a command can be redirected to a file, so can the input of a command be redirected from a file. And as the greater-than character > is used for output redirection, the less-than character < is used to redirect the input of a command. Of course, only commands that normally take their input from standard input can have their input redirected from a file in this manner.

To redirect the input of a command, you type the < character followed by the name of the file that the input is to be read from. So, for example, to count the number of lines in the file users, you know that you can execute the command wc -l users:

```
$ wc -l users
      2 users
$
```

Or, you can count the number of lines in the file by redirecting the standard input of the wc command from the file users:

```
$ wc -l < users
      2
$
```

Note that there is a difference in the output produced by the two forms of the wc command. In the first case, the name of the file users is listed with the line count; in the second case, it is not. This points out the subtle distinction between the execution of the two commands. In the first case, wc knows that it is reading its input from the file users. In the second case, it only knows that it is reading its input from standard input. The shell redirects the input so that it comes from the file users and not the terminal (more about this in the next chapter). As far as wc is concerned, it doesn't know whether its input is coming from the terminal or from a file!

Pipes

As you will recall, the file users that was created previously contains a list of all the users currently logged in to the system. Because you know that there will be one line in the file for each user logged in to the system, you can easily determine the *number* of users logged in by simply counting the number of lines in the users file:

```
$ who > users
$ wc -l < users
      5
$
```

This output would indicate that currently five users were logged in. Now you have a command sequence you can use whenever you want to know how many users are logged in.

Another approach to determine the number of logged-in users bypasses the use of a file. The Unix system allows you to effectively connect two commands together. This connection is known as a *pipe*, and it enables you to take the output from one command and feed it directly into the input of another command. A pipe is effected by the character |, which is placed between the two commands. So to make a pipe between the who and wc -l commands, you simply type who | wc -l:

```
$ who | wc -l
      5
$
```

The pipe that is effected between these two commands is depicted in Figure 2.12.

When a pipe is set up between two commands, the standard output from the first command is connected directly to the standard input of the second command. You know that the who command writes its list of logged-in users to standard output. Furthermore, you know that if no filename argument is specified to the wc command, it takes its input from standard input. Therefore, the list of logged-in users that is output from the who command automatically becomes the input to the wc command. Note that you never see the output of the who command at the terminal because it is piped directly into the wc command. This is depicted in Figure 2.13.

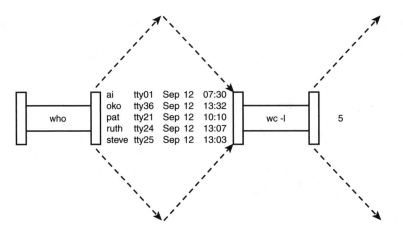

FIGURE 2.12   Pipeline process: who | wc -l.

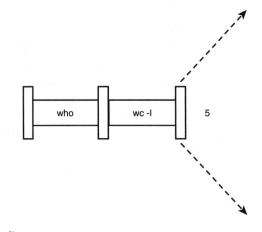

FIGURE 2.13   Pipeline process.

A pipe can be made between *any* two programs, provided that the first program writes its output to standard output, and the second program reads its input from standard input.

As another example of a pipe, suppose that you wanted to count the number of files contained in your directory. Knowledge of the fact that the ls command displays one line of output per file enables you to use the same type of approach as before:

```
$ ls | wc -l
    10
$
```

The output indicates that the current directory contains 10 files.

It is also possible to form a pipeline consisting of more than two programs, with the output of one program feeding into the input of the next.

Filters

The term *filter* is often used in Unix terminology to refer to any program that can take input from standard input, perform some operation on that input, and write the results to standard output. More succinctly, a filter is any program that can be used between two other programs in a pipeline. So in the previous pipeline, wc is considered a filter. ls is not because it does not read its input from standard input. As other examples, cat and sort are filters, whereas who, date, cd, pwd, echo, rm, mv, and cp are not.

Standard Error

In addition to standard input and standard output, there is another place known as *standard error*. This is where most Unix commands write their error messages. And as with the other two "standard" places, standard error is associated with your terminal by default. In most cases, you never know the difference between standard output and standard error:

```
$ ls n*                          List all files beginning with n
n* not found
$
```

Here the "not found" message is actually being written to standard error and not standard output by the ls command. You can verify that this message is not being written to standard output by redirecting the ls command's output:

```
$ ls n* > foo
n* not found
$
```

So, you still get the message printed out at the terminal, even though you redirected standard output to the file foo.

The preceding example shows the *raison d'être* for standard error: so that error messages will still get displayed at the terminal even if standard output is redirected to a file or piped to another command.

You can also redirect standard error to a file by using the notation

command 2> *file*

No space is permitted between the 2 and the >. Any error messages normally intended for standard error will be diverted into the specified *file*, similar to the way standard output gets redirected.

```
$ ls n* 2> errors
$ cat errors
n* not found
$
```

More on Commands

Typing More Than One Command on a Line

You can type more than one command on a line provided that you separate each command with a semicolon. For example, you can find out the current time and also your current working directory by typing in the date and pwd commands on the same line:

```
$ date; pwd
Sat Jul 20 14:43:25 EDT 2002
/users/pat/bin
$
```

You can string out as many commands as you want on the line, as long as each command is delimited by a semicolon.

Sending a Command to the Background

Normally, you type in a command and then wait for the results of the command to be displayed at the terminal. For all the examples you have seen thus far, this waiting time is typically short—maybe a second or two. However, you may have to run commands that require many seconds or even minutes to execute. In those cases, you'll have to wait for the command to finish executing before you can proceed further *unless you execute the command in the background.*

If you type in a command followed by the ampersand character &, that command will be sent to the background for execution. This means that the command will no longer tie up your terminal, and you can then proceed with other work. The standard output from the command will still be directed to your terminal; however, in most cases the standard input will be dissociated from your terminal. If the command does try to read any input from standard input, it will be stopped and will wait for you to bring it to the foreground (we'll discuss this in more detail in Chapter 15, "Interactive and Nonstandard Shell Features").[3]

---

[3]*Note that the capability to stop a command when it reads from standard input may be missing on non-Unix implementations of the shell or on older shells that do not conform to the POSIX standard. On these implementations, any read from standard input will get an end-of-file condition as if Ctrl+d were typed.*

```
$ sort data > out &          Send the sort to the background
[1] 1258                     Process id
$ date                       Your terminal is immediately available to do other work
Sat Jul 20 14:45:09 EDT 2002
$
```

When a command is sent to the background, the Unix system automatically displays two numbers. The first is called the command's *job number* and the second the *process id.* In the preceding example, 1 was the job number and 1258 the process id. The job number is used by some shell commands that you'll learn more about in Chapter 15. The process id uniquely identifies the command that you sent to the background and can be used to obtain status information about the command. This is done with the ps command.

The ps Command

The ps command gives you information about the processes running on the system. ps without any options prints the status of just your processes. If you type in ps at your terminal, you'll get a few lines back describing the processes you have running:

```
$ ps
   PID   TTY   TIME COMMAND
   195    01   0:21 sh         The shell
  1353    01   0:00 ps         This ps command
  1258    01   0:10 sort       The previous sort
$
```

The ps command prints out four columns of information: PID, the process id; TTY, the terminal number that the process was run from; TIME, the amount of computer time in minutes and seconds that process has used; and COMMAND, the name of the process. (The sh process in the preceding example is the shell that was started when you logged in, and it has used 21 seconds of computer time.) Until the command is finished, it shows up in the output of the ps command as a running process. Process number 1353 in the preceding example is the ps command that was typed in, and 1258 is the sort from the preceding example.

When used with the -f option, ps prints out more information about your processes, including the *parent* process id (PPID), the time the processes started (STIME), and the command arguments:

```
$ ps -f
     UID   PID  PPID  C    STIME TTY      TIME COMMAND
   steve   195     1  0 10:58:29 tty01    0:21 -sh
   steve  1360   195 43 14:54:48 tty01    0:01 ps -f
```

```
    steve   1258   195  0 14:45:04 tty01    3:17 sort data
$
```

Command Summary

Table 2.2 summarizes the commands reviewed in this chapter. In this table, *file* refers to a file, *file(s)* to one or more files, *dir* to a directory, and *dir(s)* to one or more directories.

TABLE 2.2   Command Summary

Command	Description
cat *file(s)*	Display contents of *file(s)* or standard input if not supplied
cd *dir*	Change working directory to *dir*
cp *file$_1$ file$_2$*	Copy *file$_1$* to *file$_2$*
cp *file(s) dir*	Copy *file(s)* into *dir*
date	Display the date and time
echo *args*	Display *args*
ln *file$_1$ file$_2$*	Link *file$_1$* to *file$_2$*
ln *file(s) dir*	Link *file(s)* into *dir*
ls *file(s)*	List *file(s)*
ls *dir(s)*	List files in *dir(s)* or in current directory if *dir(s)* is not specified
mkdir *dir(s)*	Create directory *dir(s)*
mv *file$_1$ file$_2$*	Move *file$_1$* to *file$_2$* (simply rename it if both reference the same directory)
mv *file(s) dir*	Move *file(s)* into directory *dir*
ps	List information about active processes
pwd	Display current working directory path
rm *file(s)*	Remove *files(s)*
rmdir *dir(s)*	Remove empty directory *dir(s)*
sort *file(s)*	Sort lines of *file(s)* or standard input if not supplied
wc *file(s)*	Count the number of lines, words, and characters in *file(s)* or standard input if not supplied
who	Display who's logged in

Exercises

1. Given the following files in your current directory:

```
$ ls
feb96
jan12.02
jan19.02
```

```
jan26.02
jan5.02
jan95
jan96
jan97
jan98
mar98
memo1
memo10
memo2
memo2.sv
$
```

What would be the output from the following commands?

```
echo *                          echo *[!0-9]

echo m[a-df-z]*                 echo [A-Z]*

echo jan*                       echo *.*

echo ?????                      echo *02

echo jan?? feb?? mar??          echo [fjm][ae][bnr]*
```

2. What is the effect of the following command sequences?

```
ls | wc -l                      rm ???

who | wc -l                     mv progs/* /users/steve/backup

ls *.c | wc -l                  rm *.o

who | sort                      cd; pwd

cp memo1 ..                     plotdata 2>errors &
```

3

What Is the Shell?

In this chapter you'll learn what the shell is and what it does.

The Kernel and the Utilities

The Unix system is itself logically divided into two pieces: the *kernel* and the *utilities* (see Figure 3.1).

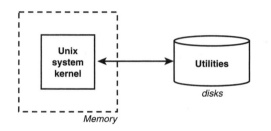

FIGURE 3.1 The Unix system.

The kernel is the heart of the Unix system and resides in the computer's memory from the time the computer is turned on and *booted* until the time it is shut down.

The utilities, on the other hand, reside on the computer's disk and are only brought into memory as requested. Virtually every command you know under the Unix system is classified as a utility; therefore, the program resides on the disk and is brought into memory only when you request that the command be executed. So, for example, when you execute the date command, the Unix system loads the program called date from the computer's disk into memory and initiates its execution.

The shell, too, is a utility program. It is loaded into memory for execution whenever you log in to the system.

In fact, it's worth learning the precise sequence of events that occurs when the first shell on a terminal or window starts up.

The Login Shell

A terminal is connected to a Unix system through a direct wire, modem, or network. In the first case, as soon as you turn on the terminal (and press the Enter key a couple of times if necessary), you should get a `login:` message on your screen. In the second case, you must first dial the computer's number and get connected before the `login:` message appears. In the last case, you may connect over the network via a program such as `ssh`, `telnet`, or `rlogin`, or you may use some kind of networked windowing system (for example, X Window System) to start up a terminal emulation program (for example, xterm).

For each physical terminal port on a system, a program called `getty` will be active. This is depicted in Figure 3.2.

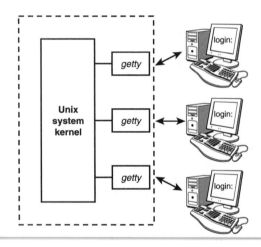

FIGURE 3.2   The `getty` process.

The Unix system—more precisely a program called `init`—automatically starts up a `getty` program on each terminal port whenever the system is allowing users to log in. `getty` determines the baud rate, displays the message `login:` at its assigned terminal, and then just waits for someone to type in something. As soon as someone types in some characters followed by Enter, the `getty` program disappears; but before it goes away, it starts up a program called `login` to finish the process of logging in (see Figure 3.3). It also gives `login` the characters you typed in at the terminal— characters that presumably represent your login name.

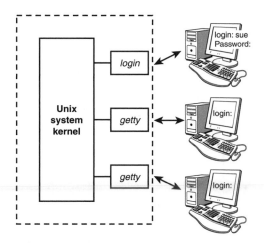

FIGURE 3.3   login started on sue's terminal.

When login begins execution, it displays the string Password: at the terminal and then waits for you to type your password. After you have typed it, login then proceeds to verify your login name and password against the corresponding entry in the file /etc/passwd. This file contains one line for each user of the system. That line specifies, among other things, the login name, home directory, and program to start up when that user logs in.[1] The last bit of information (the program to start up) is stored after the *last* colon of each line. If nothing follows the last colon, the *standard* shell /usr/bin/sh is assumed by default. The following three lines show typical lines from /etc/passwd for three users of the system: sue, pat, and bob:

```
sue:*:15:47::/users/sue:
pat:*:99:7::/users/pat:/usr/bin/ksh
bob:*:13:100::/users/data:/users/data/bin/data_entry
```

After login checks the password you typed in against the one stored in /etc/shadow, it then checks for the name of a program to execute. In most cases, this will be /usr/bin/sh, /usr/bin/ksh, or /bin/bash. In other cases, it may be a special custom-designed program. The main point here is that you can set up a login account to automatically run any program whatsoever whenever someone logs in to it. The shell just happens to be the program most often selected.

---

[1]*The file's name (passwd) derives from a time when encrypted versions of the users' passwords were stored in this file along with other user information. The encrypted passwords are no longer stored in /etc/passwd but for security reasons are now kept in the /etc/shadow file, which is not readable by normal users.*

So login initiates execution of the standard shell on sue's terminal after validating her password (see Figure 3.4).

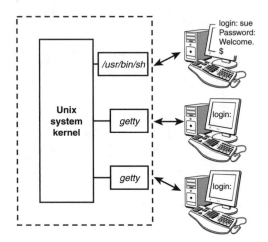

FIGURE 3.4   login executes /usr/bin/sh.

According to the other entries from /etc/passwd shown previously, pat gets the program ksh stored in /usr/bin (this is the Korn shell), and bob gets the program data_entry (see Figure 3.5).

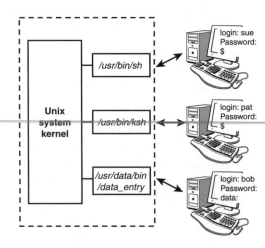

FIGURE 3.5   Three users logged in.

The init program starts up other programs similar to getty for networked connections. For example, sshd, telnetd, and rlogind are started to service logins via ssh, telnet, and rlogin, respectively. Instead of being tied directly to a specific, physical terminal or modem line, these programs connect users' shells to *pseudo ttys*. These are devices that emulate terminals over network connections. You can see this whether you're logged in to your system over a network or on an X Windows screen:

```
$ who
phw      pts/0    Jul 20 17:37      Logged in with rlogin
$
```

Typing Commands to the Shell

When the shell starts up, it displays a command prompt—typically a dollar sign $—at your terminal and then waits for you to type in a command (see Figure 3.6, Steps 1 and 2). Each time you type in a command and press the Enter key (Step 3), the shell analyzes the line you typed and then proceeds to carry out your request (Step 4). If you ask it to execute a particular program, the shell searches the disk until it finds the named program. When found, the shell asks the kernel to initiate the program's execution and then the shell "goes to sleep" until the program has finished (Step 5). The kernel copies the specified program into memory and begins its execution. This copied program is called a *process*; in this way, the distinction is made between a program that is kept in a file on the disk and a process that is in memory doing things.

If the program writes output to standard output, it will appear at your terminal unless redirected or piped into another command. Similarly, if the program reads input from standard input, it will wait for you to type in input unless redirected from a file or piped from another command (Step 6).

When the command finishes execution, control once again returns to the shell, which awaits your next command (Steps 7 and 8).

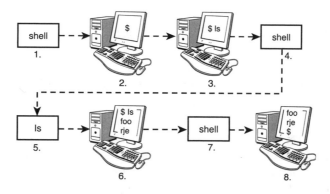

FIGURE 3.6   Command cycle.

Note that this cycle continues as long as you're logged in. When you log off the system, execution of the shell then terminates and the Unix system starts up a new getty (or rlogind, and so on) at the terminal and waits for someone else to log in. This cycle is illustrated in Figure 3.7.

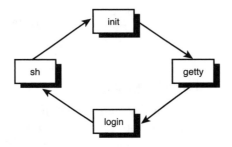

FIGURE 3.7   Login cycle.

It's important for you to recognize that the shell is just a program. It has no special privileges on the system, meaning that anyone with the capability and devotion can create his own shell program. This is in fact the reason why various flavors of the shell exist today, including the older Bourne shell, developed by Stephen Bourne; the Korn shell, developed by David Korn; the "Bourne again shell," mainly used on Linux systems; and the C shell, developed by Bill Joy.

The Shell's Responsibilities

Now you know that the shell analyzes each line you type in and initiates execution of the selected program. But the shell also has other responsibilities, as outlined in Figure 3.8.

Program Execution

The shell is responsible for the execution of all programs that you request from your terminal.

Each time you type in a line to the shell, the shell analyzes the line and then determines what to do. As far as the shell is concerned, each line follows the same basic format:

program-name arguments

The line that is typed to the shell is known more formally as the *command line*. The shell scans this command line and determines the name of the program to be executed and what arguments to pass to the program.

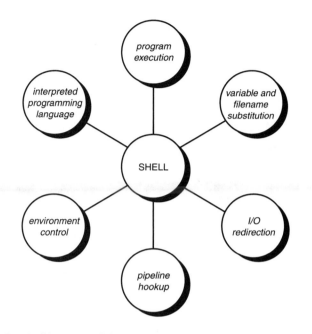

FIGURE 3.8 The shell's responsibilities.

The shell uses special characters to determine where the program name starts and ends, and where each argument starts and ends. These characters are collectively called *whitespace characters*, and are the space character, the horizontal tab character, and the end-of-line character, known more formally as the *newline character*. Multiple occurrences of whitespace characters are simply ignored by the shell. When you type the command

```
mv tmp/mazewars games
```

the shell scans the command line and takes everything from the start of the line to the first whitespace character as the name of the program to execute: mv. The set of characters up to the next whitespace character is the first argument to mv: tmp/mazewars. The set of characters up to the next whitespace character (known as a word to the shell)—in this case, the newline—is the second argument to mv: games. After analyzing the command line, the shell then proceeds to execute the mv command, giving it the two arguments tmp/mazewars and games (see Figure 3.9).

FIGURE 3.9 Execution of mv with two arguments.

As mentioned, multiple occurrences of whitespace characters are ignored by the shell. This means that when the shell processes this command line:

```
echo            when   do          we      eat?
```

it passes four arguments to the echo program: when, do, we, and eat? (see Figure 3.10).

FIGURE 3.10   Execution of echo with four arguments.

Because echo takes its arguments and simply displays them at the terminal, separating each by a space character, the output from the following becomes easy to understand:

```
$ echo          when   do          we      eat?
when do we eat?
$
```

The fact is that the echo command never sees those blank spaces; they have been "gobbled up" by the shell. When we discuss quotes in Chapter 6, "Can I Quote You on That?," you'll see how you can include blank spaces in arguments to programs.

We mentioned earlier that the shell searches the disk until it finds the program you want to execute and then asks the Unix kernel to initiate its execution. This is true most of the time. However, there are some commands that the shell knows how to execute itself. These built-in commands include cd, pwd, and echo. So before the shell goes searching the disk for a command, the shell first determines whether it's a built-in command, and if it is, the shell executes the command directly.

Variable and Filename Substitution

Like any other programming language, the shell lets you assign values to variables. Whenever you specify one of these variables on the command line, preceded by a dollar sign, the shell substitutes the value assigned to the variable at that point. This topic is covered in complete detail in Chapter 5, "And Away We Go."

The shell also performs filename substitution on the command line. In fact, the shell scans the command line looking for filename substitution characters *, ?, or [...]

before determining the name of the program to execute and its arguments. Suppose
that your current directory contains the files as shown:

```
$ ls
mrs.todd
prog1
shortcut
sweeney
$
```

Now let's use filename substitution for the echo command:

```
$ echo *              List all files
mrs.todd prog1 shortcut sweeney
$
```

How many arguments do you think were passed to the echo program, one or four?
Because we said that the shell is the one that performs the filename substitution, the
answer is four. When the shell analyzes the line

```
echo *
```

it recognizes the special character * and substitutes on the command line the names
of all files in the current directory (it even alphabetizes them for you):

```
echo mrs.todd prog1 shortcut sweeney
```

Then the shell determines the arguments to be passed to the command. So echo
never sees the asterisk. As far as it's concerned, four arguments were typed on the
command line (see Figure 3.11).

FIGURE 3.11   Execution of echo.

I/O Redirection

It is the shell's responsibility to take care of input and output redirection on the
command line. It scans the command line for the occurrence of the special redirection characters <, >, or >> (also << as you'll learn in Chapter 13, "Loose Ends").

When you type the command

```
echo Remember to tape Law and Order > reminder
```

the shell recognizes the special output redirection character > and takes the next word on the command line as the name of the file that the output is to be redirected to. In this case, the file is reminder. If reminder already exists and you have write access to it, the previous contents are lost (if you don't have write access to it, the shell gives you an error message).

Before the shell starts execution of the desired program, it redirects the standard output of the program to the indicated file. As far as the program is concerned, it never knows that its output is being redirected. It just goes about its merry way writing to standard output (which is normally your terminal, you'll recall), unaware that the shell has redirected it to a file.

Let's take another look at two nearly identical commands:

```
$ wc -l users
      5 users
$ wc -l < users
      5
$
```

In the first case, the shell analyzes the command line and determines that the name of the program to execute is wc and it is to be passed two arguments: -l and users (see Figure 3.12).

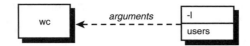

FIGURE 3.12   Execution of wc -l users.

When wc begins execution, it sees that it was passed two arguments. The first argument, -l, tells it to count the number of lines. The second argument specifies the name of the file whose lines are to be counted. So wc opens the file users, counts its lines, and then prints the count together with the filename at the terminal.

Operation of wc in the second case is slightly different. The shell spots the input redirection character < when it scans the command line. The word that follows on the command line is the name of the file input is to be redirected from. Having "gobbled up" the < users from the command line, the shell then starts execution of the wc program, redirecting its standard input from the file users and passing it the single argument -l (see Figure 3.13).

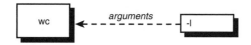

FIGURE 3.13   Execution of wc -l < users.

When wc begins execution this time, it sees that it was passed the single argument -l. Because no filename was specified, wc takes this as an indication that the number of lines appearing on standard input is to be counted. So wc counts the number of lines on standard input, unaware that it's actually counting the number of lines in the file users. The final tally is displayed at the terminal—without the name of a file because wc wasn't given one.

The difference in execution of the two commands is important for you to understand. If you're still unclear on this point, review the preceding section.

Pipeline Hookup

Just as the shell scans the command line looking for redirection characters, it also looks for the pipe character |. For each such character that it finds, it connects the standard output from the command preceding the | to the standard input of the one following the |. It then initiates execution of both programs.

So when you type

```
who | wc -l
```

the shell finds the pipe symbol separating the commands who and wc. It connects the standard output of the former command to the standard input of the latter, and then initiates execution of both commands. When the who command executes, it makes a list of who's logged in and writes the results to standard output, unaware that this is not going to the terminal but to another command instead.

When the wc command executes, it recognizes that no filename was specified and counts the lines on standard input, unaware that standard input is not coming from the terminal but from the output of the who command.

Environment Control

The shell provides certain commands that let you customize your environment. Your environment includes your home directory, the characters that the shell displays to prompt you to type in a command, and a list of the directories to be searched whenever you request that a program be executed. You'll learn more about this in Chapter 11, "Your Environment."

Interpreted Programming Language

The shell has its own built-in programming language. This language is *interpreted*, meaning that the shell analyzes each statement in the language one line at a time and then executes it. This differs from programming languages such as C and FORTRAN, in which the programming statements are typically compiled into a machine-executable form before they are executed.

Programs developed in interpreted programming languages are typically easier to debug and modify than compiled ones. However, they usually take much longer to execute than their compiled equivalents.

The shell programming language provides features you'd find in most other programming languages. It has looping constructs, decision-making statements, variables, and functions, and is procedure-oriented. Modern shells based on the IEEE POSIX standard have many other features including arrays, data typing, and built-in arithmetic operations.

4

Tools of the Trade

This chapter provides detailed descriptions of some commonly used shell programming tools. Covered are cut, paste, sed, tr, grep, uniq, and sort. The more proficient you become at using these tools, the easier it will be to write shell programs to solve your problems. In fact, that goes for all the tools provided by the Unix system.

Regular Expressions

Before getting into the tools, you need to learn about *regular expressions*. Regular expressions are used by several different Unix commands, including ed, sed, awk, grep, and, to a more limited extent, vi. They provide a convenient and consistent way of specifying *patterns* to be matched.

The shell recognizes a limited form of regular expressions when you use filename substitution. Recall that the asterisk (*) specifies zero or more characters to match, the question mark (?) specifies any single character, and the construct [...] specifies any character enclosed between the brackets. The regular expressions recognized by the aforementioned programs are far more sophisticated than those recognized by the shell. Also be advised that the asterisk and the question mark are treated differently by these programs than by the shell.

Throughout this section, we assume familiarity with a line-based editor such as ex or ed. See Appendix B, "For More Information," for more information on these editors.

Matching Any Character: The Period (.)

A period in a regular expression matches any single character, no matter what it is. So the regular expression

```
r.
```

specifies a pattern that matches an r followed by any single character.

The regular expression

```
.x.
```

matches an x that is surrounded by any two characters, not necessarily the same.

The ed command

```
/ ... /
```

searches forward in the file you are editing for the first line that contains any three characters surrounded by blanks:

```
$ ed intro
248
1,$p                        Print all the lines
The Unix operating system was pioneered by Ken
Thompson and Dennis Ritchie at Bell Laboratories
in the late 1960s.  One of the primary goals in
the design of the Unix system was to create an
environment that promoted efficient program
development.
/ ... /                     Look for three chars surrounded by blanks
The Unix operating system was pioneered by Ken
/                           Repeat last search
Thompson and Dennis Ritchie at Bell Laboratories
1,$s/p.o/XXX/g              Change all p.os to XXX
1,$p                        Let's see what happened
The Unix operating system was XXXneered by Ken
ThomXXXn and Dennis Ritchie at Bell Laboratories
in the late 1960s.  One of the primary goals in
the design of the Unix system was to create an
environment that XXXmoted efficient XXXgram
development.
```

In the first search, ed started searching from the beginning of the file and found the characters " was " in the first line that matched the indicated pattern. Repeating the search (recall that the ed command / means to repeat the last search), resulted in the display of the second line of the file because " and " matched the pattern. The substitute command that followed specified that all occurrences of the character p, followed by any single character, followed by the character o were to be replaced by the characters XXX.

Matching the Beginning of the Line: The Caret (^)

When the caret character ^ is used as the first character in a regular expression, it matches the beginning of the line. So the regular expression

```
^George
```

matches the characters George *only if they occur at the beginning of the line.*

```
$ ed intro
248
/^the/                          Find the line that starts with the
the design of the Unix system was to create an
1,$s/^/>>/                      Insert >> at the beginning of each line
1,$p
>>The Unix operating system was pioneered by Ken
>>Thompson and Dennis Ritchie at Bell Laboratories
>>in the late 1960s.  One of the primary goals in
>>the design of the Unix system was to create an
>>environment that promoted efficient program
>>development.
```

The preceding example shows how the regular expression ^ can be used to match just the beginning of the line. Here it is used to insert the characters >> at the start of each line. A command such as

```
1,$s/^/     /
```

is commonly used to insert spaces at the start of each line (in this case five spaces would be inserted).

Matching the End of the Line: The Dollar Sign ($)

Just as the ^ is used to match the beginning of the line, so is the dollar sign $ used to match the end of the line. So the regular expression

```
contents$
```

matches the characters contents *only if they are the last characters on the line.* What do you think would be matched by the regular expression .$?

Would this match a period character that ends a line? No. This matches any single character at the end of the line (including a period) recalling that the period matches any character. So how do you match a period? In general, if you want to match any of the characters that have a special meaning in forming regular expressions, you must precede the character by a backslash (\) to remove that special meaning. So the regular expression

```
\.$
```

matches any line that ends in a period, and the regular expression

```
^\.
```

matches any line that starts with one (good for searching for `nroff` commands in your text).

```
$ ed intro
248
/\.$/                            Search for a line that ends with a period
development.
1,$s/$/>>/                       Add >> to the end of each line
1,$p
The Unix operating system was pioneered by Ken>>
Thompson and Dennis Ritchie at Bell Laboratories>>
in the late 1960s.  One of the primary goals in>>
the design of the Unix system was to create an>>
environment that promoted efficient program>>
development.>>
1,$s/..$//                       Delete the last two characters from each line
1,$p
The Unix operating system was pioneered by Ken
Thompson and Dennis Ritchie at Bell Laboratories
in the late 1960s.  One of the primary goals in
the design of the Unix system was to create an
environment that promoted efficient program
development.
```

It's worth noting that the regular expression

```
^$
```

matches any line that contains *no* characters (such a line can be created in ed by simply pressing Enter while in insert mode). This regular expression is to be distinguished from one such as

```
^ $
```

which matches any line that consists of a single space character.

Matching a Choice of Characters: The [...] Construct

Suppose that you are editing a file and want to search for the first occurrence of the characters the. In ed, this is easy: You simply type the command

```
/the/
```

This causes ed to search forward in its buffer until it finds a line containing the indicated string of characters. The first line that matches will be displayed by ed:

```
$ ed intro
248
/the/                           Find line containing the
in the late 1960s.  One of the primary goals in
```

Notice that the first line of the file also contains the word the, except it starts a sentence and so begins with a capital T. You can tell ed to search for the first occurrence of the *or* The by using a regular expression. Just as in filename substitution, the characters [and] can be used in a regular expression to specify that one of the enclosed characters is to be matched. So, the regular expression

```
[tT]he
```

would match a lower- or uppercase t followed immediately by the characters he:

```
$ ed intro
248
/[tT]he/                        Look for the or The
The Unix operating system was pioneered by Ken
/                               Continue the search
in the late 1960s.  One of the primary goals in
/                               Once again
the design of the Unix system was to create an
1,$s/[aeiouAEIOU]//g            Delete all vowels
1,$p
Th nx prtng systm ws pnrd by Kn
Thmpsn nd Dnns Rtch t Bll Lbrtrs
```

```
n th lt 1960s. n f th prmry gls n
th dsgn f th nx systm ws t crt n
nvrnmnt tht prmtd ffcnt prgrm
dvlpmnt.
```

A range of characters can be specified inside the brackets. This can be done by separating the starting and ending characters of the range by a dash (-). So, to match any
digit character 0 through 9, you could use the regular expression

`[0123456789]`

or, more succinctly, you could simply write

`[0-9]`

To match an uppercase letter, you write

`[A-Z]`

And to match an upper- or lowercase letter, you write

`[A-Za-z]`

Here are some examples with ed:

```
$ ed intro
248
/[0-9]/                          Find a line containing a digit
in the late 1960s. One of the primary goals in
/^[A-Z]/                         Find a line that starts with an uppercase letter
The Unix operating system was pioneered by Ken
/                                Again
Thompson and Dennis Ritchie at Bell Laboratories
1,$s/[A-Z]/*/g                   Change all uppercase letters to *s
1,$p
*he *nix operating system was pioneered by *en
*hompson and *ennis *itchie at *ell *aboratories
in the late 1960s. *ne of the primary goals in
the design of the *nix system was to create an
environment that promoted efficient program
development.
```

As you'll learn shortly, the asterisk is a special character in regular expressions.
However, you don't need to put a backslash before the asterisk in the replacement

string of the substitute command. In general, regular expression characters such as *, ., [...], $, and ^ are only meaningful in the search string and have no special meaning when they appear in the replacement string.

If a caret (^) appears as the first character after the left bracket, the sense of the match is *inverted*.[1] For example, the regular expression

```
[^A-Z]
```

matches any character *except* an uppercase letter. Similarly,

```
[^A-Za-z]
```

matches any nonalphabetic character.

```
$ ed intro
248
1,$s/[^a-zA-Z]//g              Delete all nonalphabetic characters
1,$p
TheUnixoperatingsystemwaspioneeredbyKen
ThompsonandDennisRitchieatBellLaboratories
InthelatesOneoftheprimarygoalsin
ThedesignoftheUnixsystemwastocreatean
Environmentthatpromotedefficientprogram
development
```

Matching Zero or More Characters: The Asterisk (*)

You know that the asterisk is used by the shell in filename substitution to match zero or more characters. In forming regular expressions, the asterisk is used to match zero or more occurrences of the *preceding* character in the regular expression (which may itself be another regular expression).

So, for example, the regular expression

```
X*
```

matches zero, one, two, three, ... capital X's. The expression

```
XX*
```

matches one or more capital X's, because the expression specifies a single X followed by zero or more X's. A similar type of pattern is frequently used to match the occurrence of one or more blank spaces.

---

[1] *Recall that the shell uses the ! for this purpose.*

```
$ ed lotsaspaces
85
1,$p
This        is   an example   of a
file   that  contains       a  lot
of   blank spaces
```
                                                         Change multiple blanks to single blanks
```
1,$s/  */ /g
1,$p
This is an example of a
file that contains a lot
of blank spaces
```

The ed command

```
1,$s/  */ /g
```

told ed to substitute all occurrences of a space followed by zero or more spaces with a single space.

The regular expression

```
.*
```

is often used to specify zero or more occurrences of *any* characters. Bear in mind that a regular expression matches the *longest* string of characters that match the pattern. Therefore, used by itself, this regular expression always matches the *entire* line of text.

As another example of the combination of . and *, the regular expression

```
e.*e
```

matches all the characters from the first e on a line to the last one.

```
$ ed intro
248
1,$s/e.*e/+++/
1,$p
Th+++n
Thompson and D+++S
in th+++ primary goals in
th+++ an
+++nt program
d+++nt.
```

Here's an interesting regular expression. What do you think it matches?

```
[A-Za-z][A-Za-z]*
```

That's right, this matches any alphabetic character followed by zero or more alphabetic characters. This is pretty close to a regular expression that matches words.

```
$ ed intro
248
1,$s/[A-Za-z][A-Za-z]*/X/g
1,$p
X X X X X X X
X X X X X X X
X X X 1960X.  X X X X X
X X X X X X X X X
X X X X X
X.
```

The only thing it didn't match in this example was 1960. You can change the regular expression to also consider a sequence of digits as a word:

```
$ ed intro
248
1,$s/[A-Za-z0-9][A-Za-z0-9]*/X/g
1,$p
X X X X X X X
X X X X X X X
X X X X.  X X X X X
X X X X X X X X X
X X X X X
X.
```

We could expand on this somewhat to consider hyphenated words and contracted words (for example, don't), but we'll leave that as an exercise for you. As a point of note, if you want to match a dash character inside a bracketed choice of characters, you must put the dash immediately after the left bracket (and after the inversion character ^ if present) or immediately before the right bracket]. So the expression

```
[-0-9]
```

matches a single dash or digit character.

If you want to match a right bracket character, it must appear after the opening left bracket (and after the ^ if present). So

```
[]a-z]
```

matches a right bracket or a lowercase letter.

Matching a Precise Number of Characters: \{...\}

In the preceding examples, you saw how to use the asterisk to specify that *one* or more occurrences of the preceding regular expression are to be matched. For instance, the regular expression

```
XX*
```

means match at least one consecutive X. Similarly,

```
XXX*
```

means match at least *two* consecutive X's. There is a more general way to specify a precise number of characters to be matched: by using the construct

\{*min,max*\}

where *min* specifies the minimum number of occurrences of the preceding regular expression to be matched, and *max* specifies the maximum. For example, the regular expression

```
X\{1,10\}
```

matches from one to ten consecutive X's. As stated before, whenever there is a choice, the largest pattern is matched; so if the input text contains eight consecutive X's at the beginning of the line, that is how many will be matched by the preceding regular expression. As another example, the regular expression

```
[A-Za-z]\{4,7\}
```

matches a sequence of alphabetic letters from four to seven characters long.

```
$ ed intro
248
1,$s/[A-Za-z]\{4,7\}/X/g
1,$p
The X Xng X was Xed by Ken
Xn and X X at X XX
in the X 1960s.  One of the X X in
the X of the X X was to X an
```

```
XX X Xd Xnt X
XX.
```

A few special cases of this special construct are worth noting. If only one number is enclosed between the braces, as in

```
\{10\}
```

that number specifies that the preceding regular expression must be matched *exactly* that many times. So

```
[a-zA-Z]\{7\}
```

matches exactly seven alphabetic characters; and

```
.\{10\}
```

matches exactly ten characters (no matter what they are):

```
$ ed intro
248
1,$s/^.\{10\}//          Delete the first 10 chars from each line
1,$p
perating system was pioneered by Ken
nd Dennis Ritchie at Bell Laboratories
e 1960s. One of the primary goals in
 of the Unix system was to create an
t that promoted efficient program
t.
1,$s/.\{5\}$//          Delete the last 5 chars from each line
1,$p
perating system was pioneered b
nd Dennis Ritchie at Bell Laborat
e 1960s. One of the primary goa
 of the Unix system was to crea
t that promoted efficient pr
t.
```

Note that the last line of the file didn't have five characters when the last substitute command was executed; therefore, the match failed on that line and thus was left alone (recall that we specified that *exactly* five characters were to be deleted).

If a single number is enclosed in the braces, followed immediately by a comma, then at *least* that many occurrences of the previous regular expression must be matched. So

```
+\{5,\}
```

matches at least five consecutive plus signs. Once again, if more than five exist, the largest number is matched.

```
$ ed intro
248
1,$s/[a-zA-Z]\{6,\}/X/g          Change words at least 6 letters long to X
1,$p
The Unix X X was X by Ken
X and X X at Bell X
in the late 1960s. One of the X goals in
the X of the Unix X was to X an
X that X X X
X.
```

Saving Matched Characters: \(...\)

It is possible to capture the characters matched within a regular expression by enclosing the characters inside backslashed parentheses. These captured characters are stored in "registers" numbered 1 through 9.

For example, the regular expression

`^\(.\)`

matches the first character on the line, whatever it is, and stores it into register 1. To retrieve the characters stored in a particular register, the construct \n is used, where n is from 1–9.

So the regular expression

`^\(.\)\1`

matches the first character on the line and stores it in register 1. Then the expression matches whatever is stored in register 1, as specified by the \1. The net effect of this regular expression is to match the first two characters on a line *if they are both the same character*. Go over this example if it doesn't seem clear.

The regular expression

`^\(.\).*\1$`

matches all lines in which the first character on the line (^.) is the same as the last character on the line (\1$). The .* matches all the characters in-between.

Successive occurrences of the \(...\) construct get assigned to successive registers. So when the following regular expression is used to match some text

^\(...\)\(...\)

the first three characters on the line will be stored into register 1, and the next three characters into register 2.

When using the substitute command in ed, a register can also be referenced as part of the replacement string:

```
$ ed phonebook
114
1,$p
Alice Chebba     973-555-2015
Barbara Swingle 201-555-9257
Liz Stachiw      212-555-2298
Susan Goldberg  201-555-7776
Tony Iannino     973-555-1295
1,$s/\(.*\)     \(.*\)/\2 \1/          Switch the two fields
1,$p
973-555-2015 Alice Chebba
201-555-9257 Barbara Swingle
212-555-2298 Liz Stachiw
201-555-7776 Susan Goldberg
973-555-1295 Tony Iannino
```

The names and the phone numbers are separated from each other in the phonebook file by a single tab character. The regular expression

\(.*\)   \(.*\)

says to match all the characters up to the first tab (that's the character between the) and the \) and assign them to register 1, and to match all the characters that follow the tab character and assign them to register 2. The replacement string

\2 \1

specifies the contents of register 2, followed by a space, followed by the contents of register 1.

So when ed applies the substitute command to the first line of the file:

Alice Chebba   973-555-2015

it matches everything up to the tab (Alice Chebba) and stores it into register 1, and everything after the tab (973-555-2015) and stores it into register 2. Then it substitutes the characters that were matched (the entire line) with the contents of register 2 (973-555-2015) followed by a space, followed by the contents of register 1 (Alice Chebba):

973-555-2015 Alice Chebba

As you can see, regular expressions are powerful tools that enable you to match complex patterns. Table 4.1 summarizes the special characters recognized in regular expressions.

TABLE 4.1   Regular Expression Characters

Notation	Meaning	Example	Matches
.	*any* character	a..	a followed by any two characters
^	beginning of line	^wood	wood only if it appears at the beginning of the line
$	end of line	x$	x only if it is the last character on the line
		^INSERT$	a line containing just the characters INSERT
		^$	a line that contains *no* characters
*	zero or more occurrences of previous regular expression	x*	zero or more consecutive x's
		xx*	one or more consecutive x's
		.*	zero or more characters
		w.*s	w followed by zero or more characters followed by an s
[*chars*]	any character in *chars*	[tT]	lower- or uppercase t
		[a-z]	lowercase letter
		[a-zA-Z]	lower- or uppercase letter
[^*chars*]	any character *not* in *chars*	[^0-9]	any nonnumeric character
		[^a-zA-Z]	any nonalphabetic character
\{*min*,*max*\}	at least *min* and at most *max* occurrences of previous regular expressions	x\{1,5\}	at least 1 and at and at most 5 x's
		[0-9]\{3,9\}	anywhere from 3 to 9 successive digits
		[0-9]\{3\}	exactly 3 digits
		[0-9]\{3,\}	at least 3 digits

TABLE 4.1   Continued

Notation	Meaning	Example	Matches
\(...\)	store characters matched between parentheses in next register (1-9)	^\(.\)	first character on line and stores it in register 1
		^\(.\)\1	first and second characters on the line if they're the same

cut

This section teaches you about a useful command known as cut. This command comes in handy when you need to extract (that is, "cut out") various fields of data from a data file or the output of a command. The general format of the cut command is

cut -c*chars file*

where *chars* specifies what characters you want to extract from each line of *file*. This can consist of a single number, as in -c5 to extract character 5; a comma-separated list of numbers, as in -c1,13,50 to extract characters 1, 13, and 50; or a dash-separated range of numbers, as in -c20-50 to extract characters 20 through 50, inclusive. To extract characters to the end of the line, you can omit the second number of the range; so

cut -c5- data

extracts characters 5 through the end of the line from each line of data and writes the results to standard output.

If *file* is not specified, cut reads its input from standard input, meaning that you can use cut as a filter in a pipeline.

Let's take another look at the output from the who command:

```
$ who
root      console Feb 24 08:54
steve     tty02   Feb 24 12:55
george    tty08   Feb 24 09:15
dawn      tty10   Feb 24 15:55
$
```

As shown, currently four people are logged in. Suppose that you just want to know the names of the logged-in users and don't care about what terminals they are on or when they logged in. You can use the cut command to cut out just the usernames from the who command's output:

```
$ who | cut -c1-8                 Extract the first 8 characters
root
steve
george
dawn
$
```

The -c1-8 option to cut specifies that characters 1 through 8 are to be extracted from each line of input and written to standard output.

The following shows how you can tack a sort to the end of the preceding pipeline to get a sorted list of the logged-in users:

```
$ who | cut -c1-8 | sort
dawn
george
root
steve
$
```

If you wanted to see what terminals were currently being used, you could cut out just the tty numbers field from the who command's output:

```
$ who | cut -c10-16
console
tty02
tty08
tty10
$
```

How did you know that who displays the terminal identification in character positions 10 through 16? Simple! You executed the who command at your terminal and *counted* out the appropriate character positions.[2]

You can use cut to extract as many different characters from a line as you want. Here, cut is used to display just the username and login time of all logged-in users:

```
$ who | cut -c1-8,18-
root      Feb 24 08:54
```

---

[2]*On some versions of the Unix system, this field starts in character position 12 and not 10.*

```
steve     Feb 24 12:55
george    Feb 24 09:15
dawn      Feb 24 15:55
$
```

The option -c1-8,18- says "extract characters 1 through 8 (the username) and also characters 18 through the end of the line (the login time)."[3]

The -d and -f Options

The cut command as described previously is useful when you need to extract data from a file or command provided that file or command has a fixed format.

For example, you could use cut on the who command because you know that the usernames are *always* displayed in character positions 1–8, the terminal in 10–16, and the login time in 18–29. Unfortunately, not all your data will be so well organized! For instance, take a look at the file /etc/passwd:

```
$ cat /etc/passwd
root:*:0:0:The Super User:/:/usr/bin/ksh
cron:*:1:1:Cron Daemon for periodic tasks:/:
bin:*:3:3:The owner of system files:/:
uucp:*:5:5::/usr/spool/uucp:/usr/lib/uucp/uucico
asg:*:6:6:The Owner of Assignable Devices:/:
steve:*:203:100::/users/steve:/usr/bin/ksh
other:*:4:4:Needed by secure program:/:
$
```

/etc/passwd is the master file that contains the usernames of all users on your computer system. It also contains other information such as your user id number, your home directory, and the name of the program to start up when you log in. Getting back to the cut command, you can see that the data in this file does not align itself the same way who's output does. So getting a list of all the possible users of your system cannot be done using the -c option to cut.

One nice thing about the format of /etc/passwd, however, is that fields are delimited by a colon character. So although each field may not be the same length from one line to the next, you know that you can "count colons" to get the same field from each line.

The -d and -f options are used with cut when you have data that is delimited by a particular character. The format of the cut command in this case becomes

cut -d*dchar* -f*fields file*

---

[3]*Again, on some systems the login time field starts in column 25.*

where *dchar* is the character that delimits each field of the data, and *fields* specifies the fields to be extracted from *file*. Field numbers start at 1, and the same type of formats can be used to specify field numbers as was used to specify character positions before (for example, -f1,2,8, -f1-3, -f4-).

So to extract the names of all users of your system from /etc/passwd, you could type the following:

```
$ cut -d: -f1 /etc/passwd          Extract field 1
root
cron
bin
uucp
asg
steve
other
$
```

Given that the home directory of each user is in field 6, you can associate each user of the system with his or her home directory as shown:

```
$ cut -d: -f1,6 /etc/passwd        Extract fields 1 and 6
root:/
cron:/
bin:/
uucp:/usr/spool/uucp
asg:/
steve:/users/steve
other:/
$
```

If the cut command is used to extract fields from a file and the -d option is not supplied, cut uses the tab character as the default field delimiter.

The following depicts a common pitfall when using the cut command. Suppose that you have a file called phonebook that has the following contents:

```
$ cat phonebook
Alice Chebba      973-555-2015
Barbara Swingle   201-555-9257
Jeff Goldberg     201-555-3378
Liz Stachiw       212-555-2298
Susan Goldberg    201-555-7776
Tony Iannino      973-555-1295
$
```

If you just want to get the names of the people in your phone book, your first impulse would be to use cut as shown:

```
$ cut -c1-15 phonebook
Alice Chebba     97
Barbara Swingle
Jeff Goldberg    2
Liz Stachiw      212
Susan Goldberg
Tony Iannino     97
$
```

Not quite what you want! This happened because the name is separated from the phone number by a tab character and not blank spaces in the phonebook file. And as far as cut is concerned, tabs count as a single character when using the -c option. So cut extracts the first 15 characters from each line in the previous example, giving the results as shown.

Given that the fields are separated by tabs, you should use the -f option to cut instead:

```
$ cut -f1 phonebook
Alice Chebba
Barbara Swingle
Jeff Goldberg
Liz Stachiw
Susan Goldberg
Tony Iannino
$
```

Much better! Recall that you don't have to specify the delimiter character with the -d option because cut assumes that a tab character is the delimiter by default.

But how do you know in advance whether fields are delimited by blanks or tabs? One way to find out is by trial and error as shown previously. Another way is to type the command

sed -n 1 *file*

at your terminal. If a tab character separates the fields, \t will be displayed instead of the tab:

```
$ sed -n 1 phonebook
Alice Chebba\t973-555-2015
Barbara Swingle\t201-555-9257
```

```
Jeff Goldberg\t201-555-3378
Liz Stachiw\t212-555-2298
Susan Goldberg\t201-555-7776
Tony Iannino\t973-555-1295
$
```

The output verifies that each name is separated from each phone number by a tab character. sed is covered in more detail shortly.

paste

The paste command is sort of the inverse of cut: Instead of breaking lines apart, it puts them together. The general format of the paste command is

paste *files*

where corresponding lines from each of the specified *files* are "pasted" together to form single lines that are then written to standard output. The dash character - can be used in *files* to specify that input is from standard input.

Suppose that you have a set of names in a file called names:

```
$ cat names
Tony
Emanuel
Lucy
Ralph
Fred
$
```

Suppose that you also have a file called numbers that contains corresponding phone numbers for each name in names:

```
$ cat numbers
(307) 555-5356
(212) 555-3456
(212) 555-9959
(212) 555-7741
(212) 555-0040
$
```

You can use paste to print the names and numbers side-by-side as shown:

```
$ paste names numbers          Paste them together
Tony    (307) 555-5356
Emanuel (212) 555-3456
```

```
Lucy     (212) 555-9959
Ralph    (212) 555-7741
Fred     (212) 555-0040
$
```

Each line from names is displayed with the corresponding line from numbers, separated by a tab.

The next example illustrates what happens when more than two files are specified:

```
$ cat addresses
55-23 Vine Street, Miami
39 University Place, New York
17 E. 25th Street, New York
38 Chauncey St., Bensonhurst
17 E. 25th Street, New York
$ paste names addresses numbers
Tony    55-23 Vine Street, Miami         (307) 555-5356
Emanuel 39 University Place, New York    (212) 555-3456
Lucy    17 E. 25th Street, New York      (212) 555-9959
Ralph   38 Chauncey St., Bensonhurst     (212) 555-7741
Fred    17 E. 25th Street, New York      (212) 555-0040
$
```

The -d Option

If you don't want the fields separated by tab characters, you can specify the -d option with the format

-d*chars*

where *chars* is one or more characters that will be used to separate the lines pasted together. That is, the first character listed in *chars* will be used to separate lines from the first file that are pasted with lines from the second file; the second character listed in *chars* will be used to separate lines from the second file from lines from the third, and so on.

If there are more files than there are characters listed in *chars*, paste "wraps around" the list of characters and starts again at the beginning.

In the simplest form of the -d option, specifying just a single delimiter character causes that character to be used to separate *all* pasted fields:

```
$ paste -d'+' names addresses numbers
Tony+55-23 Vine Street, Miami+(307) 555-5356
Emanuel+39 University Place, New York+(212) 555-3456
```

```
Lucy+17 E. 25th Street, New York+(212) 555-9959
Ralph+38 Chauncey St., Bensonhurst+(212) 555-7741
Fred+17 E. 25th Street, New York+(212) 555-0040
```

It's always safest to enclose the delimiter characters in single quotes. The reason why will be explained shortly.

The -s Option

The -s option tells paste to paste together lines from the same file, not from alternate files. If just one file is specified, the effect is to merge all the lines from the file together, separated by tabs, or by the delimiter characters specified with the -d option.

```
$ paste -s names        Paste all lines from names
Tony    Emanuel Lucy    Ralph   Fred
$ ls | paste -d' ' -s -  Paste ls's output, use space as delimiter
addresses intro lotsaspaces names numbers phonebook
$
```

In the preceding example, the output from ls is piped to paste, which merges the lines (-s option) from standard input (-), separating each field with a space (-d' ' option). Of course, you'll recall from Chapter 2, "A Quick Review of the Basics," that the command

```
echo *
```

would have worked just as well (and is certainly more straightforward).

sed

sed is a program used for editing data. It stands for *stream editor*. Unlike ed, sed cannot be used interactively. However, its commands are similar. The general form of the sed command is

sed *command file*

where *command* is an ed-style command applied to *each* line of the specified *file*. If no file is specified, standard input is assumed. As sed applies the indicated command to each line of the input, it writes the results to standard output.

Recall the file intro from previous examples:

```
$ cat intro
The Unix operating system was pioneered by Ken
Thompson and Dennis Ritchie at Bell Laboratories
```

```
in the late 1960s. One of the primary goals in
the design of the Unix system was to create an
environment that promoted efficient program
development.
$
```

Suppose that you want to change all occurrences of "Unix" in the text to "UNIX." This can be easily done in sed as follows:

```
$ sed 's/Unix/UNIX/' intro        Substitute Unix with UNIX
The UNIX operating system was pioneered by Ken
Thompson and Dennis Ritchie at Bell Laboratories
in the late 1960s. One of the primary goals in
the design of the UNIX system was to create an
environment that promoted efficient program
development.
$
```

For now, get into the habit of enclosing your sed command in a pair of single quotes. Later, you'll know when the quotes are necessary and when to use double quotes instead.

The sed command s/Unix/UNIX/ is applied to every line of intro. Whether or not the line gets changed by the command, it gets written to standard output all the same. Note that sed makes no changes to the original input file. To make the changes permanent, you must redirect the output from sed into a temporary file and then move the file back to the old one:

```
$ sed 's/Unix/UNIX/' intro > temp    Make the changes
$ mv temp intro                      And now make them permanent
$
```

Always make sure that the correct changes were made to the file before you over-write the original; a cat of temp could have been included between the two commands shown previously to ensure that the sed succeeded as planned.

If your text included more than one occurrence of "Unix" on a line, the preceding sed would have changed just the first occurrence on each line to "UNIX." By appending the *global* option g to the end of the s command, you can ensure that multiple occurrences of the string on a line will be changed. In this case, the sed command would read

```
$ sed 's/Unix/UNIX/g' intro > temp
```

Suppose that you wanted to extract just the usernames from the output of who. You already know how to do that with the cut command:

```
$ who | cut -c1-8
root
ruth
steve
pat
$
```

Alternatively, you can use sed to delete all the characters from the first blank space (that marks the end of the username) through the end of the line by using a regular expression in the edit command:

```
$ who | sed 's/ .*$//'
root
ruth
steve
pat
$
```

The sed command says to substitute a blank space followed by any characters up to the end of the line (.*$) with *nothing* (//); that is, delete the characters from the first blank to the end of the line from each line of the input.

The -n Option

We pointed out that sed always writes each line of input to standard output, whether or not it gets changed. Sometimes, however, you'll want to use sed just to extract some lines from a file. For such purposes, use the -n option. This option tells sed that you don't want it to print any lines unless explicitly told to do so. This is done with the p command. By specifying a line number or range of line numbers, you can use sed to selectively print lines of text. So, for example, to print just the first two lines from a file, the following could be used:

```
$ sed -n '1,2p' intro          Just print the first 2 lines
The UNIX operating system was pioneered by Ken
Thompson and Dennis Ritchie at Bell Laboratories
$
```

If, instead of line numbers, you precede the p command with a string of characters enclosed in slashes, sed prints just those lines from standard input that contain those characters. The following example shows how sed can be used to display just the lines that contain a particular string:

```
$ sed -n '/UNIX/p' intro        Just print lines containing UNIX
The UNIX operating system was pioneered by Ken
the design of the UNIX system was to create an
$
```

Deleting Lines

To delete entire lines of text, use the d command. By specifying a line number or range of numbers, you can delete specific lines from the input. In the following example, sed is used to delete the first two lines of text from intro:

```
$ sed '1,2d' intro        Delete lines 1 and 2
in the late 1960s. One of the primary goals in
the design of the UNIX system was to create an
environment that promoted efficient program
development.
$
```

Remembering that by default sed writes all lines of the input to standard output, the remaining lines in text—that is, lines 3 through the end—simply get written to standard output.

By preceding the d command with a string of text, you can use sed to delete all lines that contain that text. In the following example, sed is used to delete all lines of text containing the word UNIX:

```
$ sed '/UNIX/d' intro        Delete all lines containing UNIX
Thompson and Dennis Ritchie at Bell Laboratories
in the late 1960s. One of the primary goals in
environment that promoted efficient program
development.
$
```

The power and flexibility of sed goes far beyond what we've shown here. sed has facilities that enable you to loop, build text in a buffer, and combine many commands into a single editing script. Table 4.2 shows some more examples of sed commands.

TABLE 4.2   sed Examples

sed Command	Description
sed '5d'	Delete line 5
sed '/[Tt]est/d'	Delete all lines containing Test or test
sed -n '20,25p' text	Print only lines 20 through 25 from text

TABLE 4.2   Continued

sed Command	Description
sed '1,10s/unix/UNIX/g' intro	Change unix to UNIX wherever it appears in the first 10 lines of intro
sed '/jan/s/-1/-5/'	Change the first -1 to -5 on all lines containing jan
sed 's/...//' data	Delete the first three characters from each line of data
sed 's/...$//' data	Delete the last 3 characters from each line of data
sed -n 'l' text	Print all lines from text, showing nonprinting characters as \nn (where nn is the octal value of the character), and tab characters as \t

tr

The tr filter is used to translate characters from standard input. The general form of the command is

tr *from-chars to-chars*

where *from-chars* and *to-chars* are one or more single characters. Any character in *from-chars* encountered on the input will be translated into the corresponding character in *to-chars*. The result of the translation is written to standard output.

In its simplest form, tr can be used to translate one character into another. Recall the file intro from earlier in this chapter:

```
$ cat intro
The UNIX operating system was pioneered by Ken
Thompson and Dennis Ritchie at Bell Laboratories
in the late 1960s. One of the primary goals in
the design of the UNIX system was to create an
environment that promoted efficient program
development.
$
```

The following shows how tr can be used to translate all letter e's to x's:

```
$ tr e x < intro
Thx UNIX opxrating systxm was pionxxrxd by Kxn
```

```
Thompson and Dxnnis Ritchix at Bxll Laboratorixs
in thx latx 1960s. Onx of thx primary goals in
thx dxsign of thx UNIX systxm was to crxatx an
xnvironmxnt that promotxd xfficixnt program
dxvxlopmxnt.
$
```

The input to `tr` must be redirected from the file `intro` because `tr` always expects its input to come from standard input. The results of the translation are written to standard output, leaving the original file untouched. Showing a more practical example, recall the pipeline that you used to extract the usernames and home directories of everyone on the system:

```
$ cut -d: -f1,6 /etc/passwd
root:/
cron:/
bin:/
uucp:/usr/spool/uucp
asg:/
steve:/users/steve
other:/
$
```

You can translate the colons into tab characters to produce a more readable output simply by tacking an appropriate `tr` command to the end of the pipeline:

```
$ cut -d: -f1,6 /etc/passwd | tr : '    '
root    /
cron    /
bin     /
uucp    /usr/spool/uucp
asg     /
steve   /users/steve
other   /
$
```

Enclosed between the single quotes is a tab character (even though you can't see it—just take our word for it). It must be enclosed in quotes to keep it from the shell and give `tr` a chance to see it.

The octal representation of a character can be given to `tr` in the format

nnn

where *nnn* is the octal value of the character. For example, the octal value of the tab character is 11. If you are going to use this format, be sure to enclose the character in quotes. The tr command

```
tr : '\11'
```

translates all colons to tabs, just as in the preceding example. Table 4.3 lists characters that you'll often want to specify in octal format.

TABLE 4.3   Octal Values of Some ASCII Characters

Character	Octal Value
Bell	7
Backspace	10
Tab	11
Newline	12
Linefeed	12
Formfeed	14
Carriage Return	15
Escape	33

In the following example, tr takes the output from date and translates all spaces into newline characters. The net result is that each field of output from date appears on a different line.

```
$ date | tr ' ' '\12'        Translate spaces to newlines
Sun
Jul
28
19:13:46
EDT
2002
$
```

tr can also take ranges of characters to translate. For example, the following shows how to translate all lowercase letters in intro to their uppercase equivalents:

```
$ tr '[a-z]' '[A-Z]' < intro
THE UNIX OPERATING SYSTEM WAS PIONEERED BY KEN
THOMPSON AND DENNIS RITCHIE AT BELL LABORATORIES
IN THE LATE 1960S. ONE OF THE PRIMARY GOALS IN
THE DESIGN OF THE UNIX SYSTEM WAS TO CREATE AN
ENVIRONMENT THAT PROMOTED EFFICIENT PROGRAM
DEVELOPMENT.
$
```

The character ranges [a-z] and [A-Z] are enclosed in quotes to keep the shell from replacing the first range with all the files in your directory named a through z, and the second range with all the files in your directory named A through Z. (What do you think happens if no such files exist?)

By reversing the two arguments to tr, you can use it to translate all uppercase letters to lowercase:

```
$ tr '[A-Z]' '[a-z]' < intro
the unix operating system was pioneered by ken
thompson and dennis ritchie at bell laboratories
in the late 1960s. one of the primary goals in
the design of the unix system was to create an
environment that promoted efficient program
development.
$
```

The -s Option

You can use the -s option to tr to "squeeze" out multiple occurrences of characters in *to-chars*. In other words, if more than one consecutive occurrence of a character specified in *to-chars* occurs after the translation is made, the characters will be replaced by a single character.

For example, the following command translates all colons into tab characters, replacing multiple tabs with single tabs:

```
tr -s ':' '\11'
```

So one colon or several consecutive colons on the input will be replaced by a *single* tab character on the output.

Suppose that you have a file called lotsaspaces that has the contents as shown:

```
$ cat lotsaspaces
This      is   an example  of a
file    that contains       a  lot
of    blank spaces.
$
```

You can use tr to squeeze out the multiple spaces by using the -s option and by specifying a single space character as the first and second argument:

```
$ tr -s ' ' ' ' < lotsaspaces
This is an example of a
file that contains a lot
```

```
of blank spaces.
$
```

The options to tr in effect say "translate space characters to space characters, replacing multiple spaces in the output by a single space."

The -d Option

tr can also be used to delete single characters from a stream of input. The general format of tr in this case is

tr -d *from-chars*

where any single character listed in *from-chars* will be deleted from standard input. In the following example, tr is used to delete all spaces from the file intro:

```
$ tr -d ' ' < intro
TheUNIXoperatingSystemwaspioneeredbyKen
ThompsonandDennisRitchieatBellLaboratories
inthelate1960s.Oneoftheprimarygoalsin
thedesignoftheUNIXSystemwastocreatean
environmentthatpromotedefficientprogram
development.
$
```

Of course, you probably realize that you could have also used sed to achieve the same results:

```
$ sed 's/ //g' intro
TheUNIXoperatingsystemwaspioneeredbyKen
ThompsonandDennisRitchieatBellLaboratories
inthelate1960s.Oneoftheprimarygoalsin
thedesignoftheUNIXsystemwastocreatean
environmentthatpromotedefficientprogram
development.
$
```

This is not atypical for the Unix system; there's almost always more than one approach to solving a particular problem. In the case we just saw, either approach is satisfactory (that is, tr or sed); however, tr is probably a better choice in this case because it is a much smaller program and likely to execute a bit faster.

Table 4.4 summarizes how to use tr for translating and deleting characters. Bear in mind that tr works only on *single* characters. So if you need to translate anything longer than a single character (say all occurrences of unix to UNIX), you have to use a different program such as sed instead.

TABLE 4.4 tr Examples

tr Command	Description
tr 'X' 'x'	Translate all capital X's to small x's
tr '()' '{}'	Translate all open parens to open braces, all closed parens to closed braces
tr '[a-z]' '[A-Z]'	Translate all lowercase letters to uppercase
tr '[A-Z]' '[N-ZA-M]'	Translate uppercase letters A–M to N–Z, and N–Z to A–M, respectively
tr ' ' ' '	Translate all tabs (character in first pair of quotes) to spaces
tr -s ' ' ' '	Translate multiple spaces to single spaces
tr -d '\14'	Delete all formfeed (octal 14) characters
tr -d '[0-9]'	Delete all digits

grep

grep allows you to search one or more files for particular character patterns. The general format of this command is

grep *pattern files*

Every line of each file that contains *pattern* is displayed at the terminal. If more than one file is specified to grep, each line is also immediately preceded by the name of the file, thus enabling you to identify the particular file that the pattern was found in.

Let's say that you want to find every occurrence of the word shell in the file ed.cmd:

```
$ grep shell ed.cmd
files, and is independent of the shell.
to the shell, just type in a q.
$
```

This output indicates that two lines in the file ed.cmd contain the word shell.

If the pattern does not exist in the specified file(s), the grep command simply displays nothing:

```
$ grep cracker ed.cmd
$
```

You saw in the section on sed how you could print all lines containing the string UNIX from the file intro with the command

```
sed -n '/UNIX/p' intro
```

But you could also use the following grep command to achieve the same result:

```
grep UNIX intro
```

Recall the phonebook file from before:

```
$ cat phone_book
Alice Chebba     973-555-2015
Barbara Swingle 201-555-9257
Jeff Goldberg    201-555-3378
Liz Stachiw      212-555-2298
Susan Goldberg  201-555-7776
Tony Iannino     973-555-1295
$
```

When you need to look up a particular phone number, the grep command comes in handy:

```
$ grep Susan phone_book
Susan Goldberg  201-555-7776
$
```

The grep command is useful when you have a lot of files and you want to find out which ones contain certain words or phrases. The following example shows how the grep command can be used to search for the word shell in *all* files in the current directory:

```
$ grep shell *
cmdfiles:shell that enables sophisticated
ed.cmd:files, and is independent of the shell.
ed.cmd:to the shell, just type in a q.
grep.cmd:occurrence of the word shell:
grep.cmd:$ grep shell *
grep.cmd:every use of the word shell.
$
```

As noted, when more than one file is specified to grep, each output line is preceded by the name of the file containing that line.

It's generally a good idea to enclose your grep pattern inside a pair of *single* quotes to "protect" it from the shell. For instance, if you want to find all the lines containing asterisks inside the file stars, typing

```
grep * stars
```

does not work as expected because the shell sees the asterisk and automatically substitutes the names of all the files in your current directory!

```
$ ls
circles
polka.dots
squares
stars
stripes
$ grep * stars
$
```

In this case, the shell took the asterisk and substituted the list of files in your current directory. Then it started execution of grep, which took the first argument (circles) and tried to find it in the files specified by the remaining arguments, as shown in Figure 4.1.

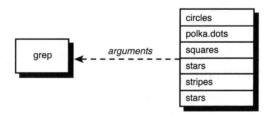

FIGURE 4.1   grep * stars.

Enclosing the asterisk in quotes, however, removes its special meaning from the shell:

```
$ grep '*' stars
The asterisk (*) is a special character that
**********
5 * 4 = 20
$
```

The quotes told the shell to leave the enclosed characters alone. It then started execution of grep, passing it the two arguments * (*without* the surrounding quotes; the shell removes them in the process) and stars (see Figure 4.2).

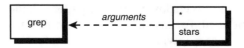

FIGURE 4.2   `grep '*' stars.`

There are characters other than * that otherwise have a special meaning and must be quoted when used in a pattern. The whole topic of how quotes are handled by the shell is fascinating; an entire chapter—Chapter 6, "Can I Quote You on That?"—is devoted to it.

grep takes its input from standard input if no filename is specified. So you can use grep on the other side of a pipe to scan through the output of a command for something. For example, suppose that you want to find out whether the user jim is logged in. You can use grep to search through who's output:

```
$ who | grep jim
jim         tty16              Feb 20 10:25
$
```

Note that by not specifying a file to search, grep automatically scans its standard input. Naturally, if the user jim were not logged in, you simply would get back a new prompt because grep would not find jim in who's output:

```
$ who | grep jim
$
```

Regular Expressions and grep

Let's take another look at the intro file:

```
$ cat intro
The UNIX operating system was pioneered by Ken
Thompson and Dennis Ritchie at Bell Laboratories
in the late 1960s. One of the primary goals in
the design of the UNIX system was to create an
environment that promoted efficient program
development.
$
```

grep allows you to specify your pattern using regular expressions as in ed. Given this information, it means that you can specify the pattern

```
[tT]he
```

to have grep search for either a lower- or uppercase T followed by the characters he.

So here's how to grep out all the lines containing the characters the or The:

```
$ grep '[tT]he' intro
The UNIX operating system was pioneered by Ken
in the late 1960s.  One of the primary goals in
the design of the UNIX system was to create an
$
```

The -i option to grep indicates that upper- and lowercase letters are not to be distinguished in the matching process. That is, the command

```
grep -i 'the' intro
```

tells grep to ignore case when matching the pattern against the lines in intro. Therefore, lines containing the or The will be printed, as will lines containing THE, THe, tHE, and so on.

Table 4.5 shows other types of regular expressions that you can specify to grep and the types of patterns they'll match.

TABLE 4.5   Some grep Examples

Command	Prints
grep '[A-Z]' list	Lines from list containing a capital letter
grep '[0-9]' data	Lines from data containing a number
grep '[A-Z]...[0-9]' list	Lines from list containing five-character patterns that start with a capital letter and end with a digit
grep '\.pic$' filelist	Lines from filelist that end in .pic

The -v Option

Sometimes you're interested not in finding the lines that contain a specified pattern, but those that *don't*. To do this with grep is simple: You use the -v option. In the next example, grep is used to find all the lines in intro that don't contain the characters UNIX.

```
$ grep -v 'UNIX' intro          Print all lines that don't contain UNIX
Thompson and Dennis Ritchie at Bell Laboratories
in the late 1960s.  One of the primary goals in
environment that promoted efficient program
development.
$
```

The -l Option

At times, you may not want to see the actual lines that match a pattern but may be interested in knowing only the names of the files that contain the pattern. For example, suppose that you have a set of C programs in your current directory (these filenames end with the characters .c), and you want to know which files use a variable called Move_history. The following example shows one way of finding the answer:

```
$ grep 'Move_history' *.c              Find Move_history in all C source files
exec.c:MOVE    Move_history[200] = {0};
exec.c:      cpymove(&Move_history[Number_half_moves -1],
exec.c: undo_move(&Move_history[Number_half_moves-1],;
exec.c: cpymove(&last_move,&Move_history[Number_half_moves-1]);
exec.c: convert_move(&Move_history[Number_half_moves-1]),
exec.c:      convert_move(&Move_history[i-1]),
exec.c: convert_move(&Move_history[Number_half_moves-1]),
makemove.c:IMPORT MOVE Move_history[];
makemove.c:      if ( Move_history[j].from != BOOK (i,j,from) OR
makemove.c:             Move_history[j] .to != BOOK (i,j,to) )
testch.c:GLOBAL MOVE Move_history[100] = {0};
testch.c:    Move_history[Number_half_moves-1].from = move.from;
testch.c:    Move_history[Number_half_moves-1].to = move.to;
$
```

Sifting through the preceding output, you discover that three files—exec.c, makemove.c, and testch.c—use the variable.

The -l option to grep gives you just a list of files that contain the specified pattern, not the matching lines from the files:

```
$ grep -l 'Move_history' *.c           List the files that contain Move_history
exec.c
makemove.c
testch.c
$
```

Because grep conveniently lists the files one per line, you can pipe the output from grep -l into wc to count the *number* of *files* that contain a particular pattern:

```
$ grep -l 'Move_history' *.c | wc -l
     3
$
```

So the preceding says that precisely three C program files reference the variable Move_history. (What are you counting if you use grep *without* the -l option?)

The -n Option

If the -n option is used with grep, each line from the file that matches the specified pattern is preceded by its relative line number in the file. From previous examples, you saw that the file testch.c was one of the three files that referenced the variable Move_history; the following shows how you can pinpoint the precise lines in the file that reference the variable:

```
$ grep -n 'Move_history' testch.c        Precede matches with line numbers
13:GLOBAL MOVE Move_history[100] = {0};
197:    Move_history[Number_half_moves-1].from = move.from;
198:    Move_history[Number_half_moves-1].to = move.to;
$
```

As you can see, Move_history is used on lines 13, 197, and 198 in testch.c.

sort

You're familiar with the basic operation of sort:

```
$ sort names
Charlie
Emanuel
Fred
Lucy
Ralph
Tony
Tony
$
```

By default, sort takes each line of the specified input file and sorts it into ascending order. Special characters are sorted according to the internal encoding of the characters. For example, on a machine that encodes characters in ASCII, the space character is represented internally as the number 32, and the double quote as the number 34. This means that the former would be sorted before the latter. Note that the sorting order is implementation dependent, so although you are generally assured that sort will perform as expected on alphabetic input, the ordering of numbers, punctuation, and special characters is not always guaranteed. We will assume we're working with the ASCII character set in all our examples here.

sort has many options that provide more flexibility in performing your sort. We'll just describe a few of the options here.

The -u Option

The -u option tells sort to eliminate duplicate lines from the output.

```
$ sort -u names
Charlie
Emanuel
Fred
Lucy
Ralph
Tony
$
```

Here you see that the duplicate line that contained Tony was eliminated from the output.

The -r Option

Use the -r option to *reverse* the order of the sort:

```
$ sort -r names        Reverse sort
Tony
Tony
Ralph
Lucy
Fred
Emanuel
Charlie
$
```

The -o Option

By default, sort writes the sorted data to standard output. To have it go into a file, you can use output redirection:

```
$ sort names > sorted_names
$
```

Alternatively, you can use the -o option to specify the output file. Simply list the name of the output file right after the -o:

```
$ sort names -o sorted_names
$
```

This sorts names and writes the results to sorted_names.

Frequently, you want to sort the lines in a file and have the sorted data replace the original. Typing

```
$ sort names > names
$
```

won't work—it ends up wiping out the names file. However, with the -o option, it is okay to specify the same name for the output file as the input file:

```
$ sort names -o names
$ cat names
Charlie
Emanuel
Fred
Lucy
Ralph
Tony
Tony
$
```

The -n Option

Suppose that you have a file containing pairs of (x, y) data points as shown:

```
$ cat data
5       27
2       12
3       33
23      2
-5      11
15      6
14      -9
$
```

Suppose that you want to feed this data into a plotting program called plotdata, but that the program requires that the incoming data pairs be sorted in increasing value of x (the first value on each line).

The -n option to sort specifies that the first field on the line is to be considered a *number*, and the data is to be sorted arithmetically. Compare the output of sort used first without the -n option and then with it:

```
$ sort data
-5      11
14      -9
15      6
2       12
23      2
3       33
5       27
$ sort -n data            Sort arithmetically
-5      11
2       12
3       33
5       27
14      -9
15      6
23      2
$
```

Skipping Fields

If you had to sort your data file by the *y* value—that is, the second number in each line—you could tell sort to skip past the first number on the line by using the option

+1n

instead of -n. The +1 says to skip the first field. Similarly, +5n would mean to skip the first five fields on each line and then sort the data numerically. Fields are delimited by space or tab characters by default. If a different delimiter is to be used, the -t option must be used.

```
$ sort +1n data            Skip the first field in the sort
14      -9
23      2
15      6
-5      11
2       12
5       27
3       33
$
```

The -t Option

As mentioned, if you skip over fields, sort assumes that the fields being skipped are delimited by space or tab characters. The -t option says otherwise. In this case, the character that follows the -t is taken as the delimiter character.

Look at our sample password file again:

```
$ cat /etc/passwd
root:*:0:0:The super User:/:/usr/bin/ksh
steve:*:203:100::/users/steve:/usr/bin/ksh
bin:*:3:3:The owner of system files:/:
cron:*:1:1:Cron Daemon for periodic tasks:/:
george:*:75:75::/users/george:/usr/lib/rsh
pat:*:300:300::/users/pat:/usr/bin/ksh
uucp:*:5:5::/usr/spool/uucppublic:/usr/lib/uucp/uucico
asg:*:6:6:The Owner of Assignable Devices:/:
sysinfo:*:10:10:Access to System Information:/:/usr/bin/sh
mail:*:301:301::/usr/mail:
$
```

If you wanted to sort this file by username (the first field on each line), you could just issue the command

```
sort /etc/passwd
```

To sort the file instead by the third colon-delimited field (which contains what is known as your *user id*), you would want an arithmetic sort, skipping the first two fields (+2n), specifying the colon character as the field delimiter (-t:):

```
$ sort +2n -t: /etc/passwd          Sort by user id
root:*:0:0:The Super User:/:/usr/bin/ksh
cron:*:1:1:Cron Daemon for periodic tasks:/:
bin:*:3:3:The owner of system files:/:
uucp:*:5:5::/usr/spool/uucppublic:/usr/lib/uucp/uucico
asg:*:6:6:The Owner of Assignable Devices:/:
sysinfo:*:10:10:Access to System Information:/:/usr/bin/sh
george:*:75:75::/users/george:/usr/lib/rsh
steve:*:203:100::/users/steve:/usr/bin/ksh
pat:*:300:300::/users/pat:/usr/bin/ksh
mail:*:301:301::/usr/mail:
$
```

Here we've emboldened the third field of each line so that you can easily verify that the file was sorted correctly by user id.

Other Options

Other options to sort enable you to skip characters within a field, specify the field to *end* the sort on, merge sorted input files, and sort in "dictionary order" (only letters, numbers, and spaces are used for the comparison). For more details on these options, look under `sort` in your *Unix User's Manual*.

uniq

The `uniq` command is useful when you need to find duplicate lines in a file. The basic format of the command is

uniq *in_file out_file*

In this format, `uniq` copies *in_file* to *out_file*, removing any duplicate lines in the process. uniq's definition of duplicated lines are *consecutive-occurring* lines that match exactly.

If *out_file* is not specified, the results will be written to standard output. If *in_file* is also not specified, `uniq` acts as a filter and reads its input from standard input.

Here are some examples to see how `uniq` works. Suppose that you have a file called names with contents as shown:

```
$ cat names
Charlie
Tony
Emanuel
Lucy
Ralph
Fred
Tony
$
```

You can see that the name Tony appears twice in the file. You can use `uniq` to "remove" such duplicate entries:

```
$ uniq names          Print unique lines
Charlie
Tony
Emanuel
Lucy
Ralph
Fred
Tony
$
```

Tony still appears twice in the preceding output because the multiple occurrences are not consecutive in the file, and thus uniq's definition of duplicate is not satisfied. To remedy this situation, sort is often used to get the duplicate lines adjacent to each other. The result of the sort is then run through uniq:

```
$ sort names | uniq
Charlie
Emanuel
Fred
Lucy
Ralph
Tony
$
```

So the sort moves the two Tony lines together, and then uniq filters out the duplicate line (recall that sort with the -u option performs precisely this function).

The -d Option

Frequently, you'll be interested in finding the duplicate entries in a file. The -d option to uniq should be used for such purposes: It tells uniq to write only the duplicated lines to *out_file* (or standard output). Such lines are written just once, no matter how many consecutive occurrences there are.

```
$ sort names | uniq -d          List duplicate lines
Tony
$
```

As a more practical example, let's return to our /etc/passwd file. This file contains information about each user on the system. It's conceivable that over the course of adding and removing users from this file that perhaps the same username has been inadvertently entered more than once. You can easily find such duplicate entries by first sorting /etc/passwd and piping the results into uniq -d as done previously:

```
$ sort /etc/passwd | uniq -d          Find duplicate entries in /etc/passwd
$
```

So there are no duplicate entries. But we think that you really want to find duplicate entries for the same username. This means that you want to just look at the first field from each line of /etc/passwd (recall that the leading characters of each line of /etc/passwd up to the colon are the username). This can't be done directly through an option to uniq, but can be accomplished indirectly by using cut to extract the username from each line of the password file before sending it to uniq.

```
$ sort /etc/passwd | cut -f1 -d: | uniq -d     Find duplicates
cem
harry
$
```

So there are multiple entries in /etc/passwd for cem and harry. If you wanted more information on the particular entries, you could grep them from /etc/passwd:

```
$ grep -n 'cem' /etc/passwd
20:cem:*:91:91::/users/cem:
166:cem:*:91:91::/users/cem:
$ grep -n 'harry' /etc/passwd
29:harry:*:103:103:Harry Johnson:/users/harry:
79:harry:*:90:90:Harry Johnson:/users/harry:
$
```

The -n option was used to find out where the duplicate entries occur. In the case of cem, there are two entries on lines 20 and 166; in harry's case, the two entries are on lines 29 and 79.

If you now want to remove the second cem entry, you could use sed:

```
$ sed '166d' /etc/passwd > /tmp/passwd          Remove duplicate
$ mv /tmp/passwd /etc/passwd
mv: /etc/passwd: 444 mode y
mv: cannot unlink /etc/passwd
$
```

Naturally, /etc/passwd is one of the most important files on a Unix system. As such, only the *superuser* is allowed to write to the file. That's why the mv command failed.

Other Options

The -c option to uniq behaves like uniq with no options (that is, duplicate lines are removed), except that each output line gets preceded by a count of the number of times the line occurred in the input.

```
$ sort names | uniq -c                          Count line occurrences
      1 Charlie
      1 Emanuel
      1 Fred
      1 Lucy
      1 Ralph
      2 Tony
$
```

Two other options that won't be described enable you to tell uniq to ignore leading characters/fields on a line. For more information, consult your *Unix User's Manual*.

We would be remiss if we neglected to mention the programs awk and perl that can be useful when writing shell programs. However, to do justice to these programs requires more space than we can provide in this text. We'll refer you to the document *Awk—A Pattern Scanning and Processing Language*, by Aho, et al., in the *Unix Programmer's Manual, Volume II* for a description of awk. Kernighan and Pike's *The Unix Programming Environment* (Prentice Hall, 1984) contains a detailed discussion of awk. *Learning Perl* and *Programming Perl*, both from O'Reilly and Associates, present a good tutorial and reference on the language, respectively.

Exercises

1. What will be matched by the following regular expressions?

x*	[0-9]\{3\}
xx*	[0-9]\{3,5\}
x\{1,5\}	[0-9]\{1,3\},[0-9]\{3\}
x\{5,\}	^\...
x\{10\}	[A-Za-z_][A-Za-z_0-9]*
[0-9]	\([A-Za-z0-9]\{1,\}\)\1
[0-9]*	^Begin$
[0-9][0-9][0-9]	^\(.\).*\1$

2. What will be the effect of the following commands?

```
who | grep 'mary'
who | grep '^mary'
grep '[Uu]nix' ch?/*
ls -l | sort +4n
sed '/^$/d' text > text.out
sed 's/\([Uu]nix\)/\1(TM)/g' text > text.out
date | cut -c12-16
date | cut -c5-11,25- | sed 's/\([0-9]\{1,2\}\)/\1,/'
```

3. Write the commands to

   a. Find all logged-in users with usernames of at least four characters.

   b. Find all users on your system whose user ids are greater than 99.

   c. Find the number of users on your system whose user ids are greater than 99.

   d. List all the files in your directory in decreasing order of file size.

5

And Away We Go

Based on the discussions in Chapter 3, "What Is the Shell?," you should realize that whenever you type something like

```
who | wc -l
```

that you are actually programming in the shell! That's because the shell is interpreting the command line, recognizing the pipe symbol, connecting the output of the first command to the input of the second, and initiating execution of both commands.

In this chapter, you'll learn how to write your own commands and how to use shell *variables*.

Command Files

A shell program can be typed directly at the terminal, as in

```
$ who | wc -l
```

or it can be first typed into a file and then the file can be executed by the shell. For example, suppose that you need to find out the number of logged-in users several times throughout the day. It's not unreasonable to type in the preceding pipeline each time you want the information, but for the sake of example, let's type this pipeline into a file. We'll call the file nu (for *n*umber of *u*sers), and its contents will be just the pipeline shown previously:

```
$ cat nu
who | wc -l
$
```

To execute the commands contained inside the file nu, all you now have to do is type nu as the command name to the shell:[1]

```
$ nu
sh: nu: cannot execute
$
```

Oops! We forgot to mention one thing. Before you can execute a program this way, you must change the file's permissions and make it *executable*. This is done with the change mode command chmod. To add execute permission to the file nu, you simply type

chmod +x *file(s)*

The +x says make the *file(s)* that follow executable. The shell requires that a file be *both* readable and executable by you before you can execute it.

```
$ ls -l nu
-rw-rw-r--   1 steve    steve      12 Jul 10 11:42 nu
$ chmod +x nu                              Make it executable
$ ls -l nu
-rwxrwxr-x   1 steve    steve      12 Jul 10 11:42 nu
$
```

Now that you've made it executable, try it again:

```
$ nu
      8
$
```

This time it worked.

You can put any commands at all inside a file, make the file executable, and then execute its contents simply by typing its name to the shell. It's that simple and that powerful.

The standard shell mechanisms such as I/O redirection and pipes can be used on your own programs as well:

```
$ nu > tally
$ cat tally
      8
$
```

---

[1]*Note that the error produced here varies between different shells.*

Suppose that you're working on a proposal called `sys.caps` and that the following command sequence is needed every time you want to print a new copy of the proposal:

```
tbl sys.caps | nroff -mm -Tlp | lp
```

Once again, you can save yourself some typing by simply placing this command sequence into a file—let's call it `run`—making it executable, and then just typing the name `run` whenever you want to get a new copy of the proposal:

```
$ cat run
tbl sys.caps | nroff -mm -Tlp | lp
$ chmod +x run
$ run
request id is laser1-15 (standard input)
$
```

(The `request id` message is issued by the `lp` command.) For the next example, suppose that you want to write a shell program called `stats` that prints the date and time, the number of users logged in, and your current working directory. You know that the three command sequences you need to use to get this information are `date`, `who | wc -l`, and `pwd`:

```
$ cat stats
date
who | wc -l
pwd
$ chmod +x stats
$ stats                          Try it out
Wed Jul 10 11:55:50 EDT 2002
      13
/users/steve/documents/proposals
$
```

You can add some `echo` commands to `stats` to make the output a bit more informative:

```
$ cat stats
echo The current date and time is:
date
echo
echo The number of users on the system is:
who | wc -l
echo
```

```
echo Your current working directory is:
pwd
```
$ stats   *Execute it*
```
The current date and time is:
Wed Jul 10 12:00:27 EDT 2002

The number of users on the system is:
    13

Your current working directory is:
/users/steve/documents/proposals
$
```

Recall that echo without any arguments simply skips a line in the display. Shortly, you'll see how to have the message and the data displayed on the same line, like this:

```
The current date and time is: Wed Jul 10 12:00:27 EDT 2002
```

Comments

The shell programming language would not be complete without a *comment* statement. A comment is a way for you to insert remarks or comments inside the program that otherwise have no effect on its execution.

Whenever the shell encounters the special character # at the start of a word, it takes whatever characters follow the # to the end of the line as comments and simply ignores them.[2] If the # starts the line, the entire line is treated as a comment by the shell. Here are examples of valid comments:

```
# Here is an entire commentary line
who | wc -l        # count the number of users
```

```
#
#  Test to see if the correct arguments were supplied
#
```

Comments are useful for documenting commands or sequences of commands whose purposes may not be obvious or are sufficiently complex so that if you were to look

[2]*Note that the # may be your default erase character. If so, to enter the character into an editor such as* ed *or* vi, *you'll have to "escape" it by preceding it with a* \. *Alternatively, you can change your erase character to something else with the* stty *command.*

at the program again in a week you might forget why they're there or what they do. Judicious use of comments can help make shell programs easier to debug and to maintain—both by you and by someone else who may have to support your programs.

Let's go back to the stats program and insert some comments:

```
$ cat stats
#
# stats -- prints: date, number of users logged on,
#          and current working directory
#

echo The current date and time is:
date

echo
echo The number of users on the system is:
who | wc -l

echo
echo Your current working directory is:
pwd
$
```

The extra blank lines cost little in terms of program space yet add much in terms of program readability. They're simply ignored by the shell.

Variables

Like virtually all programming languages, the shell allows you to store values into *variables*. A shell variable begins with an alphabetic or underscore (_) character and is followed by zero or more alphanumeric or underscore characters.

To store a value inside a shell variable, you simply write the name of the variable, followed immediately by the equals sign =, followed immediately by the value you want to store in the variable:

variable=value

For example, to assign the value 1 to the shell variable count, you simply write

```
count=1
```

and to assign the value /users/steve/bin to the shell variable my_bin, you simply write

```
my_bin=/users/steve/bin
```

A few important points here. First, spaces are not permitted on either side of the equals sign. Keep that in mind, especially if you're in the good programming habit of inserting spaces around operators. In the shell language, you can't put those spaces in.

Second, unlike most other programming languages, the shell has no concept whatsoever of *data types*. Whenever you assign a value to a shell variable, no matter what it is, the shell simply interprets that value as a string of characters. So when you assigned 1 to the variable count previously, the shell simply stored the *character 1* inside the variable count, making no observation whatsoever that an integer value was being stored in the variable.

If you're used to programming in a language such as C or Pascal, where all variables must be *declared*, you're in for another readjustment. Because the shell has no concept of data types, variables are not declared before they're used; they're simply assigned values when you want to use them.

As you'll see later in this chapter, the shell does support integer operations on shell variables that contain strings that are also valid numbers through special built-in operations.

Because the shell is an interpretive language, you can assign values to variables directly at your terminal:

```
$ count=1                    Assign character 1 to count
$ my_bin=/users/steve/bin    Assign /users/steve/bin to my_bin
$
```

So now that you know how to assign values to variables, what good is it? Glad you asked.

Displaying the Values of Variables

The echo command is used to display the value stored inside a shell variable. To do this, you simply write

```
echo $variable
```

The $ character is a special character to the shell. If a valid variable name follows the $, the shell takes this as an indication that the value stored inside that variable is to be substituted at that point. So, when you type

```
echo $count
```

the shell replaces $count with the value stored there; then it executes the echo command:

```
$ echo $count
1
$
```

Remember, the shell performs variable substitution *before* it executes the command (see Figure 5.1).

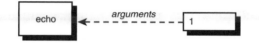

FIGURE 5.1   echo $count.

You can have the value of more than one variable substituted at a time:

```
$ echo $my_bin
/users/steve/bin
$ echo $my_bin $count
/users/steve/bin 1
$
```

In the second example, the shell substitutes the value of my_bin and count and then executes the echo command (see Figure 5.2).

FIGURE 5.2—echo $my_bin $count.

The values of variables can be used anywhere on the command line, as the next examples illustrate:

```
$ ls $my_bin
mon
nu
testx
$ pwd                          Where are we?
/users/steve/documents/memos
$ cd $my_bin                   Change to my bin directory
$ pwd
/users/steve/bin
$ number=99
```

```
$ echo There are $number bottles of beer on the wall
There are 99 bottles of beer on the wall
$
```

Here are some more examples:

```
$ command=sort
$ $command names
Charlie
Emanuel
Fred
Lucy
Ralph
Tony
Tony
$ command=wc
$ option=-l
$ file=names
$ $command $option $file
      7 names
$
```

So you see, even the name of a command can be stored inside a variable. Because the shell performs its substitution before determining the name of the program to execute and its arguments, it scans the line

```
$command $option $file
```

and turns it into

```
wc -l names
```

Then it executes wc, passing the two arguments -l and names.

Variables can even be assigned to other variables, as shown in the next example:

```
$ value1=10
$ value2=value1
$ echo $value2
value1                          Didn't do that right
$ value2=$value1
$ echo $value2
10                              That's better
$
```

Remember that a dollar sign must always be placed before the variable name whenever you want to use the value stored in that variable.

The Null Value

What do you think happens when you try to display the value of a variable that has no value assigned to it? Try it and see:

```
$ echo $nosuch                          Never assigned it a value

$
```

You don't get an error message. Did the echo command display anything at all? Let's see whether we can more precisely determine that:

```
$ echo :$nosuch:                        Surround its value with colons
::
$
```

So you see *no* characters were substituted by the shell for the value of nosuch.

A variable that contains no value is said to contain the *null* value. It is the default case for variables that you never store values in. When the shell performs its variable substitution, any values that are null are *completely* removed from the command line, without a trace:

```
$ wc   $nosuch -l $nosuch $nosuch names
      7 names
$
```

The shell scans the command line substituting the null value for the variable nosuch. After the scan is completed, the line effectively looks like this:

```
wc -l names
```

which explains why it works.

Sometimes you may want to explicitly set a variable null in a program. This can be done by simply assigning no value to the variable, as in

```
dataflag=
```

Alternatively, you can list two adjacent pairs of quotes after the =. So

```
dataflag=""
```

and

```
dataflag=''
```

both have the same effect of assigning the null value to `dataflag`. Be advised that the assignment

```
dataflag=" "
```

is *not* equivalent to the three previous ones because it assigns a single space character to `dataflag`; that's different from assigning *no* characters to it.

Filename Substitution and Variables

Here's a puzzle for you: If you type

```
x=*
```

will the shell store the character * into the variable x, or will it store the names of all the files in your current directory into the variable x? Let's try it out and see:

```
$ ls                            What files do we have?
addresses
intro
lotsaspaces
names
nu
numbers
phonebook
stat
$ x=*
$ echo $x
addresses intro lotsaspaces names nu numbers phonebook stat
$
```

There's a lot to be learned from this small example. Was the list of files stored into the variable x when

```
x=*
```

was executed, or did the shell do the substitution when

```
echo $x
```

was executed?

The answer is that the shell does not perform filename substitution when assigning values to variables. Therefore,

```
x=*
```

assigns the single character * to x. This means that the shell did the filename substitution when executing the echo command. In fact, the precise sequence of steps that occurred when

```
echo $x
```

was executed is as follows:

1. The shell scanned the line, substituting * as the value of x.

2. The shell rescanned the line, encountered the *, and then substituted the names of all files in the current directory.

3. The shell initiated execution of echo, passing it the file list as arguments (see Figure 5.3).

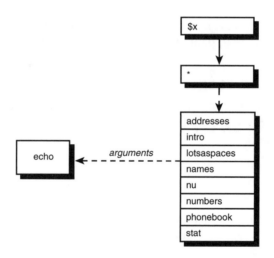

FIGURE 5.3   echo $x.

This order of evaluation is important. Remember, first the shell does variable substitution, then does filename substitution, and then parses the line into arguments.

The ${variable} Construct

Suppose that you have the name of a file stored in the variable filename. If you wanted to rename that file so that the new name was the same as the old, except with an X added to the end, your first impulse would be to type

```
mv $filename $filenameX
```

When the shell scans this command line, it substitutes the value of the variable filename *and also the value of the variable* filenameX. The shell thinks filenameX is the full name of the variable because it's composed entirely of valid variable name characters. To avoid this problem, you can delimit the end of the variable name by enclosing the entire name (but not the leading dollar sign) in a pair of curly braces, as in

```
${filename}X
```

This removes the ambiguity, and the mv command then works as desired:

```
mv $filename ${filename}X
```

Remember that the braces are necessary only if the last character of the variable name is followed by an alphanumeric character or an underscore.

Built-in Integer Arithmetic

The POSIX standard shell provides a mechanism for performing integer arithmetic on shell variables called *arithmetic expansion*. Note that some older shells do not support this feature.

The format for arithmetic expansion is

$((*expression*))

where *expression* is an arithmetic expression using shell variables and operators. Valid shell variables are those that contain numeric values (leading and trailing whitespace is allowed). Valid operators are taken from the C programming language and are listed in Appendix A, "Shell Summary."

The result of computing *expression* is substituted on the command line. For example,

```
echo $((i+1))
```

adds one to the value in the shell variable i and prints the result. Notice that the variable i doesn't have to be preceded by a dollar sign. That's because the shell knows that the only valid items that can appear in arithmetic expansions are operators, numbers, and variables. If the variable is not defined or contains a NULL string, its value is assumed to be zero. So if we have not assigned any value yet to the variable a, we can still use it in an integer expression:

```
$ echo $a                       Variable a not set
$
$ echo $((a = a + 1))           Equivalent to a = 0 + 1
1
$ echo $a
1                               Now a contains 1
$
```

Note that assignment is a valid operator, and the value of the assignment is substituted in the second echo command in the preceding example.

Parentheses may be used freely inside expressions to force grouping, as in

```
echo $((i = (i + 10) * j))
```

If you want to perform an assignment without echo or some other command, you can move the assignment *before* the arithmetic expansion.

So to multiply the variable i by 5 and assign the result back to i you can write

```
i=$(( i * 5 ))
```

Note that spaces are optional inside the double parentheses, but are not allowed when the assignment is outside them.

Finally, to test to see whether i is greater than or equal to 0 and less than or equal to 100, you can write

```
result=$(( i >= 0  &&  i <= 100 ))
```

which assigns result 1 if the expression is true and 0 if it's false:

```
$ i=$(( 100 * 200 / 10 ))
$ j=$(( i < 1000 ))             If i is < 1000, set j = 0; otherwise 1
$ echo $i $j
2000 0                          i is 2000, so j was set to 0
$
```

That concludes our introduction to writing commands and using variables. The next chapter goes into detail on the quoting mechanisms in the shell.

Exercises

1. Which of the following are valid variable names?

XxXxXx	_
12345	HOMEDIR
file.name	_date
file_name	x0-9
file1	5limit

2. Suppose that your HOME directory is /users/steve and that you have subdirectories as shown in the following figure:

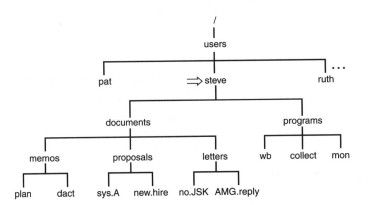

   Assuming that you just logged in to the system and executed the following commands:

   ```
   $ docs=/users/steve/documents
   $ let=$docs/letters
   $ prop=$docs/proposals
   $
   ```

   write the commands in terms of these variables to

   a. List the contents of the documents directory.

   b. Copy all files from the letters directory to the proposals directory.

   c. Move all files whose names contain a capital letter from the letters directory to the current directory.

   d. Count the number of files in the memos directory.

What would be the effect of the following commands?

    a. `ls $let/..`

    b. `cat $prop/sys.A >> $let/no.JSK`

    c. `echo $let/*`

    d. `cp $let/no.JSK $progs`

    e. `cd $prop`

3. Write a program called `nf` to display the number of files in your current directory. Type in the program and test it out.

4. Write a program called `whos` to display a sorted list of the logged-in users. Just display the usernames and no other information. Type in the program and test it out.

6

Can I Quote You on That?

This chapter teaches you about a unique feature of the shell programming language: the way it interprets quote characters. Basically, the shell recognizes four different types of quote characters:

- The single quote character '
- The double quote character "
- The backslash character \
- The back quote character `

The first two and the last characters in the preceding list must occur in pairs, whereas the backslash character is unary in nature. Each of these quotes has a distinct meaning to the shell. We'll cover them in separate sections of this chapter.

The Single Quote

There are several reasons that you might need to use quotes in the shell. One of these is to keep characters otherwise separated by whitespace characters together. Let's look at an example. Here's a file called phonebook that contains names and phone numbers:

```
$ cat phonebook
Alice Chebba      973-555-2015
Barbara Swingle   201-555-9257
Liz Stachiw       212-555-2298
Susan Goldberg    201-555-7776
Susan Topple      212-555-4932
Tony Iannino      973-555-1295
$
```

To look up someone in our phonebook file—which has been kept small here for the sake of example—you use grep:

```
$ grep Alice phonebook
Alice Chebba    973-555-2015
$
```

Look what happens when you look up Susan:

```
$ grep Susan phonebook
Susan Goldberg  201-555-7776
Susan Topple    212-555-4932
$
```

There are two lines that contain Susan, thus explaining the two lines of output. One way to overcome this problem would be to further qualify the name. For example, you could specify the last name as well:

```
$ grep Susan Goldberg phonebook
grep: can't open Goldberg
Susan Goldberg  201-555-7776
Susan Topple    212-555-4932
$
```

Recalling that the shell uses one or more whitespace characters to separate the arguments on the line, the preceding command line results in grep being passed three arguments: Susan, Goldberg, and phonebook (see Figure 6.1).

FIGURE 6.1   grep Susan Goldberg phonebook.

When grep is executed, it takes the first argument as the pattern and the remaining arguments as the names of the files to search for the pattern. In this case, grep thinks it's supposed to look for Susan in the files Goldberg and phonebook. So it tries to open the file Goldberg, can't find it, and issues the error message:

```
grep: can't open Goldberg
```

Then it goes to the next file, phonebook, opens it, searches for the pattern Susan, and prints the two matching lines. The problem boils down to trying to pass whitespace characters as arguments to programs. This can be done by enclosing the entire argument inside a pair of single quotes, as in

```
grep 'Susan Goldberg' phonebook
```

When the shell sees the first single quote, *it ignores any otherwise special characters that follow until it sees the closing quote.*

```
$ grep 'Susan Goldberg' phonebook
Susan Goldberg   201-555-7776
$
```

In this case, the shell encountered the first ', and ignored any special characters until it found the closing '. So the space between Susan and Goldberg, which would have normally delimited the two arguments, was ignored by the shell. The shell therefore divided the command line into *two* arguments, the first Susan Goldberg (which includes the space character) and the second phonebook. It then executed grep, passing it these two arguments (see Figure 6.2).

FIGURE 6.2   grep 'Susan Goldberg' phonebook.

grep then took the first argument, Susan Goldberg, and looked for it in the file specified by the second argument, phonebook. Note that the shell *removes* the quotes from the command line and does not pass them to the program.

No matter how many space characters are enclosed between quotes, they are preserved by the shell.

```
$ echo  one        two      three    four
one two three four
$ echo 'one         two      three    four'
one          two      three    four
$
```

In the first case, the shell removes the extra whitespace characters from the line and passes echo the four arguments one, two, three, and four (see Figure 6.3).

In the second case, the space characters are preserved, and the shell treats the entire string of characters enclosed between the quotes as a single argument when executing echo (see Figure 6.4).

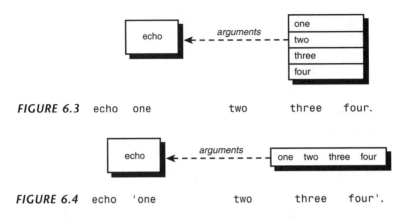

FIGURE 6.3   echo   one   two   three   four.

FIGURE 6.4   echo   'one   two   three   four'.

As we mentioned, all special characters are ignored by the shell if they appear inside single quotes. That explains the output from the following:

```
$ file=/users/steve/bin/prog1
$ echo $file
/users/steve/bin/progl
$ echo '$file'                    $ not interpreted
$file
$ echo *
addresses intro lotsaspaces names nu numbers phonebook stat
$ echo '*'
*
$ echo '< > | ; ( ) { } >> " ` &'
< > | ; ( ) { } >> " ` &
$
```

Even the Enter key will be ignored by the shell if it's enclosed in quotes:

```
$ echo 'How are you today,
> John'
How are you today,
John
$
```

After typing the first line, the shell sees that the quote isn't matched, so it waits for you to type in the closing quote. As an indication that the shell is waiting for you to finish typing in a command, it changes your prompt character from $ to >. This is known as your *secondary* prompt character and is displayed by the shell whenever it's waiting for you to finish typing a command.

Quotes are also needed when assigning values containing whitespace or special characters to shell variables:

```
$ message='I must say, this sure is fun'
$ echo $message
I must say, this sure is fun
$ text='* means all files in the directory'
$ echo $text
names nu numbers phonebook stat means all files in the directory
$
```

The quotes are needed in the assignments made to the variables message and text because of the embedded spaces. In the preceding example, you are reminded that the shell still does filename substitution after variable name substitution, meaning that the * is replaced by the names of all the files in the current directory before the echo is executed. There is a way to overcome this annoyance, and it's through the use of double quotes.

The Double Quote

Double quotes work similarly to single quotes, except that they're not as restrictive. Whereas the single quotes tell the shell to ignore *all* enclosed characters, double quotes say to ignore *most*. In particular, the following three characters are not ignored inside double quotes:

- Dollar signs
- Back quotes
- Backslashes

The fact that dollar signs are not ignored means that variable name substitution is done by the shell inside double quotes.

```
$ x=*
$ echo $x
addresses intro lotsaspaces names nu numbers phonebook stat
$ echo '$x'
$x
$ echo "$x"
*
$
```

Here you see the major differences between no quotes, single quotes, and double quotes. In the first case, the shell sees the asterisk and substitutes all the filenames from the current directory. In the second case, the shell leaves the characters enclosed within the single quotes alone, which results in the display of $x. In the final case, the double quotes indicate to the shell that variable name substitution is still to be performed inside the quotes. So the shell substitutes * for $x. Because file-name substitution is *not* done inside double quotes, * is then passed to echo as the value to be displayed.

So if you want to have the value of a variable substituted, but don't want the shell to treat the substituted characters specially, you must enclose the variable inside double quotes.

Here's another example illustrating the difference between double quotes and no quotes:

```
$ address="39 East 12th Street
> New York, N. Y. 10003"
$ echo $address
39 East 12th Street New York, N. Y. 10003
$ echo "$address"
39 East 12th Street
New York, N. Y. 10003
$
```

It makes no difference whether the value assigned to address is enclosed in single quotes or double quotes. The shell displays the secondary command prompt in either case to tell you it's waiting for the corresponding closed quote.

After assigning the two-line address to address, the value of the variable is displayed by echo. Notice that the address is displayed on a single line. The reason is the same as what caused

```
echo one       two     three   four
```

to be displayed as

```
one two three four
```

Recalling that the shell removes spaces, tabs, and newlines (that is, whitespace characters) from the command line and then cuts it up into arguments, in the case of

```
echo $address
```

the shell simply removes the embedded newline character, treating it as it would a space or tab: as an argument delimiter. Then it passes the *nine* arguments to echo to be displayed. echo never gets a chance to see that newline; the shell gets to it first (see Figure 6.5).

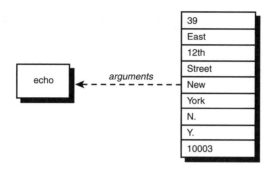

FIGURE 6.5 `echo $address`.

When the command

```
echo "$address"
```

is used instead, the shell substitutes the value of `address` as before, except that the double quotes tell it to leave any embedded whitespace characters alone. So in this case, the shell passes a single argument to `echo`—an argument that contains an embedded newline. `echo` simply displays its single argument at the terminal; Figure 6.6 illustrates this. The newline character is depicted by the characters \n.

FIGURE 6.6 `echo "$address"`.

Double quotes can be used to hide single quotes from the shell, and vice versa:

```
$ x="' Hello,' he said"
$ echo $x
'Hello,' he said
$ article=' "Keeping the Logins from Lagging," Bell Labs Record'
$ echo $article
"Keeping the Logins from Lagging," Bell Labs Record
$
```

The Backslash

Basically, the backslash is equivalent to placing single quotes around a single character, with a few minor exceptions. The backslash quotes the single character that immediately follows it. The general format is

\c

where *c* is the character you want to quote. Any special meaning normally attached to that character is removed. Here is an example:

```
$ echo >
syntax error: 'newline or ;' unexpected
$ echo \>
>
$
```

In the first case, the shell sees the > and thinks that you want to redirect echo's output to a file. So it expects a filename to follow. Because it doesn't, the shell issues the error message. In the next case, the backslash removes the special meaning of the >, so it is passed along to echo to be displayed.

```
$ x=*
$ echo \$x
$x
$
```

In this case, the shell ignores the $ that follows the backslash, and as a result, variable substitution is not performed.

Because a backslash removes the special meaning of the character that follows, can you guess what happens if that character is another backslash? Right, it removes the special meaning of the backslash:

```
$ echo \\
\
$
```

Naturally, you could have also written

```
$ echo '\'
\
$
```

Using the Backslash for Continuing Lines

As mentioned at the start of this section, \c is basically equivalent to 'c'. One exception to this rule is when the backslash is used as the very last character on the line:

```
$ lines=one'
> 'two                    Single quotes tell shell to ignore newline
$ echo "$lines"
one
two
```

```
$ lines=one\                        Try it with a \ instead
> two
$ echo "$lines"
onetwo
$
```

The shell treats a backslash at the end of the line as a line continuation. It *removes* the newline character that follows and also does not treat the newline as an argument delimiter (it's as if it wasn't even typed). This construct is most often used for typing long commands over multiple lines.

The Backslash Inside Double Quotes

We noted earlier that the backslash is one of the three characters interpreted by the shell inside double quotes. This means that you can use the backslash inside these quotes to remove the meaning of characters that otherwise *would* be interpreted inside double quotes (that is, other backslashes, dollar signs, back quotes, newlines, and other double quotes). If the backslash precedes any other character inside double quotes, the backslash is ignored by the shell and passed on to the program:

```
$ echo "\$x"
$x
$ echo "\ is the backslash character"
\ is the backslash character
$ x=5
$ echo "The value of x is \"$x\""
The value of x is "5"
$
```

In the first example, the backslash precedes the dollar sign, interpreted by the shell inside double quotes. So the shell ignores the dollar sign, removes the backslash, and executes echo. In the second example, the backslash precedes a space, *not* interpreted by the shell inside double quotes. So the shell ignores the backslash and passes it on to the echo command. The last example shows the backslash used to enclose double quotes inside a double-quoted string.

As an exercise in the use of quotes, let's say that you want to display the following line at the terminal:

```
<<< echo $x >>> displays the value of x, which is $x
```

The intention here is to substitute the value of x in the second instance of $x, but not in the first. Let's first assign a value to x:

```
$ x=1
$
```

Now try displaying the line without using any quotes:

```
$ echo <<< echo $x >>> displays the value of x, which is $x
syntax error: '<' unexpected
$
```

The < signals input redirection to the shell; this is the reason for the error message.

If you put the entire message inside single quotes, the value of x won't be substituted at the end. If you enclose the entire string in double quotes, both occurrences of $x will be substituted. Here are two different ways to do the quoting properly (realize that there are usually several different ways to quote a string of characters to get the results you want):

```
$ echo "<<< echo \$x >>> displays the value of x, which is $x"
<<< echo $x >>> displays the value of x, which is 1
$ echo '<<< echo $x >>> displays the value of x, which is' $x
<<< echo $x >>> displays the value of x, which is 1
$
```

In the first case, everything is enclosed in double quotes, and the backslash is used to prevent the shell from performing variable substitution in the first instance of $x. In the second case, everything up to the last $x is enclosed in single quotes. If the variable x might have contained some filename substitution or whitespace characters, a safer way of writing the echo would have been

```
echo '<<< echo $x >>> displays the value of x, which is' "$x"
```

Command Substitution

Command substitution refers to the shell's capability to insert the standard output of a command at any point in a command line. There are two ways in the shell to perform command substitution: by enclosing a shell command with back quotes and with the $(...) construct.

The Back Quote

The back quote is unlike any of the previously encountered types of quotes. Its purpose is not to protect characters from the shell but to tell the shell to execute the enclosed command and to insert the standard output from the command at that point on the command line. The general format for using back quotes is

`` `command` ``

where *command* is the name of the command to be executed and whose output is to be inserted at that point.[1]

Here is an example:

```
$ echo The date and time is: `date`
The date and time is: Wed Aug 28 14:28:43 EDT 2002
$
```

When the shell does its initial scan of the command line, it notices the back quote and expects the name of a command to follow. In this case, the shell finds that the date command is to be executed. So it executes date and replaces the `date` on the command line with the output from the date. After that, it divides the command line into arguments in the normal manner and then initiates execution of the echo command.

```
$ echo Your current working directory is `pwd`
Your current working directory is /users/steve/shell/ch6
$
```

Here the shell executes pwd, inserts its output on the command line, and then executes the echo. Note that in the following section, back quotes can be used in all the places where the $(...) construct is used.

The $(...) Construct

The POSIX standard shell supports the newer $(...) construct for command substitution. The general format is

$(*command*)

where, as in the back quoting method, *command* is the name of the command whose standard output is to be substituted on the command line. For example:

```
$ echo The date and time is: $(date)
The date and time is: Wed Aug 28 14:28:43 EDT 2002
$
```

This construct is better than back quotes for a couple of reasons. First, complex commands that use combinations of forward and back quotes can be difficult to

---

[1]*Note that using the back quote for command substitution is no longer the preferred method; however, we cover it here because of the large number of older, canned shell programs that still use this construct. Also, you should know about back quotes in case you ever need to write shell programs that are portable to older Unix systems with shells that don't support the newer $(...) construct.*

read, particularly if the typeface you're using doesn't have visually different single quotes and back quotes; second, $(...) constructs can be easily nested, allowing command substitution *within* command substitution. Although nesting can also be performed with back quotes, it's a little trickier. You'll see an example of nested command substitution later in this section.

You are not restricted to executing a single command between the parentheses: Several commands can be executed if separated by semicolons. Also, pipelines can be used. Here's a modified version of the nu program that displays the number of logged-in users:

```
$ cat nu
echo There are $(who | wc -l) users logged in
$ nu                                        Execute it
There are 13 users logged in
$
```

Because single quotes protect everything, the following output should be clear:

```
$ echo '$(who | wc -l) tells how many users are logged in'
$(who | wc -l) tells how many users are logged in
$
```

But command substitution *is* interpreted inside double quotes:

```
$ echo "You have $(ls | wc -l) files in your directory"
You have       7 files in your directory
$
```

(What causes those leading spaces before the 7?) Remember that the shell is responsible for executing the command enclosed between the parentheses. The only thing the echo command sees is the output that has been inserted by the shell.

Suppose that you're writing a shell program and want to assign the current date and time to a variable called now, perhaps to display it later at the top of a report, or log it into a file. The problem here is that you somehow want to take the output from date and assign it to the variable. Command substitution can be used for this:

```
$ now=$(date)                   Execute date and store the output in now
$ echo $now                     See what got assigned
Wed Aug 28 14:47:26 EDT 2002
$
```

When you write

```
now=$(date)
```

the shell realizes that the entire output from date is to be assigned to now. Therefore, you don't need to enclose $(date) inside double quotes.

Even commands that produce more than a single line of output can be stored inside a variable:

```
$ filelist=$(ls)
$ echo $filelist
addresses intro lotsaspaces names nu numbers phonebook stat
$
```

What happened here? You end up with a horizontal listing of the files even though the newlines from ls were stored inside the filelist variable (take our word for it). The newlines got eaten up when the value of filelist was substituted by the shell in processing the echo command line. Double quotes around the variable will preserve the newlines:

```
$ echo "$filelist"
addresses
intro
lotsaspaces
names
nu
numbers
phonebook
stat
$
```

To store the contents of a file into a variable, you can use cat:

```
$ namelist=$(cat names)
$ echo "$names"
Charlie
Emanuel
Fred
Lucy
Ralph
Tony
Tony
$
```

If you want to mail the contents of the file memo to all the people listed in the names file (who we'll assume here are users on your system), you can do the following:

```
$ mail $(cat names) < memo
$
```

Here the shell executes the `cat` and inserts the output on the command line so it looks like this:

```
mail Charlie Emanuel Fred Lucy Ralph Tony Tony < memo
```

Then it executes `mail`, redirecting its standard input from the file `memo` and passing it the names of seven users who are to receive the mail.

Notice that `Tony` receives the same mail twice because he's listed twice in the `names` file. You can remove any duplicate entries from the file by using `sort` with the `-u` option (remove duplicate lines) rather than `cat` to ensure that each person only receives mail once:

```
$ mail $(sort -u names) < memo
$
```

It's worth noting that the shell does filename substitution *after* it substitutes the output from commands. Enclosing the commands inside double quotes prevents the shell from doing the filename substitution on this output if desired.

Command substitution is often used to change the value stored in a shell variable. For example, if the shell variable `name` contains someone's name, and you want to convert every character in that variable to uppercase, you could use `echo` to get the variable to `tr`'s input, perform the translation, and then assign the result back to the variable:

```
$ name="Ralph Kramden"
$ name=$(echo $name | tr '[a-z]' '[A-Z]')        Translate to uppercase
$ echo $name
RALPH KRAMDEN
$
```

The technique of using `echo` in a pipeline to write data to the standard input of the following command is a simple yet powerful technique; it's used often in shell programs.

The next example shows how `cut` is used to extract the first character from the value stored in a variable called `filename`:

```
$ filename=/users/steve/memos
$ firstchar=$(echo $filename | cut -c1)
$ echo $firstchar
/
$
```

sed is also often used to "edit" the value stored in a variable. Here it is used to extract the last character from the variable file:

```
$ file=exec.o
$ lastchar=$(echo $file | sed 's/.*\(.\)$/\1/')
$ echo $lastchar
o
$
```

The sed command says to replace all the characters on the line with the last one. The result of the sed is stored in the variable lastchar. The single quotes around the sed command are important because they prevent the shell from messing around with the backslashes (would double quotes also have worked?).

Finally, command substitutions can be nested. Suppose that you want to change every occurrence of the first character in a variable to something else. In a previous example, firstchar=$(echo $filename | cut -c1) gets the first character from filename, but how do we use this character to change every occurrence in filename? A two-step process is one way:

```
$ filename=/users/steve/memos
$ firstchar=$(echo $filename | cut -c1)
$ filename=$(echo $filename | tr "$firstchar" "^")     translate / to ^
$ echo $filename
^users^steve^memos
$
```

Or a single, nested command substitution can perform the same operation:

```
$ filename=/users/steve/memos
$ filename=$(echo $filename | tr "$(echo $filename | cut -c1)" "^")
$ echo $filename
^users^steve^memos
$
```

If you have trouble understanding this example, compare it to the previous one: Note how the firstchar variable in the earlier example is replaced by the nested command substitution; otherwise, the two examples are the same.

The expr Command

Although the POSIX standard shell supports built-in integer arithmetic operations, older shells don't. It's likely that you may see command substitution with a Unix program called expr, which evaluates an expression given to it on the command line:

```
$ expr 1 + 2
3
$
```

Each operator and operand given to expr must be a separate argument, thus explaining the output from the following:

```
$ expr 1+2
1+2
$
```

The usual arithmetic operators are recognized by expr: + for addition, - for subtraction, / for division, * for multiplication, and % for modulus (remainder).

```
$ expr 10 + 20 / 2
20
$
```

Multiplication, division, and modulus have higher precedence than addition and subtraction. Thus, in the preceding example the division was performed before the addition.

```
$ expr 17 * 6
expr: syntax error
$
```

What happened here? The answer: The shell saw the * and substituted the names of all the files in your directory! It has to be quoted to keep it from the shell:

```
$ expr "17 * 6"
17 * 6
$
```

That's not the way to do it. Remember that expr must see each operator and operand as a separate argument; the preceding example sends the whole expression in as a single argument.

```
$ expr 17 \* 6
102
$
```

Naturally, one or more of the arguments to expr can be the value stored inside a shell variable because the shell takes care of the substitution first anyway:

```
$ i=1
$ expr $i + 1
```

```
2
$
```

This is the older method for performing arithmetic on shell variables. Do the same type of thing as shown previously only use the command substitution mechanism to assign the output from expr back to the variable:

```
$ i=1
$ i=$(expr $i + 1)          Add 1 to i
$ echo $i
2
$
```

In legacy shell programs, you're more likely to see expr used with back quotes:

```
$ i=`expr $i + 1`          Add 1 to i
$ echo $i
3
$
```

Note that like the shell's built-in integer arithmetic, expr only evaluates integer arithmetic expressions. You can use awk or bc if you need to do floating point calculations. Also note that expr has other operators. One of the most frequently used ones is the : operator, which is used to match characters in the first operand against a regular expression given as the second operand. By default, it returns the number of characters matched.

The expr command

```
expr "$file" : ".*"
```

returns the number of characters stored in the variable file, because the regular expression .* matches all the characters in the string. For more details on expr, consult your *Unix User's Manual*.

Table A.5 in Appendix A summarizes the way quotes are handled by the shell.

Exercises

1. Given the following assignments:

```
$ x=*
$ y=?
$ z='one
> two
```

```
> three'
$ now=$(date)
$ symbol='>'
$
```

and these files in your current directory:

```
$ echo *
names test1 u vv zebra
$
```

What will the output be from the following commands?

```
echo *** error ***          echo 'Is 5 * 4 > 18 ?'

echo $x                     echo What is your name?

echo $y                     echo Would you like to play a game?

echo "$y"                   echo \*\*\*

echo $z | wc -l             echo \$$symbol

echo "$z" | wc -l           echo $\$symbol

echo '$z' I wc -l           echo "\"

echo _$now_                 echo "\\"

echo hello $symbol out      echo \\

echo "\""                   echo I don't understand
```

2. Write the commands to remove all the space characters stored in the shell variable text. Be sure to assign the result back to text. First use tr to do it and then do the same thing with sed.

3. Write the commands to count the number of characters stored in the shell variable text. Then write the commands to count all the alphabetic characters. (Hint: Use sed and wc.) What happens to special character sequences such as \n if they're stored inside text?

4. Write the commands to assign the unique lines in the file names to the shell variable namelist.

7

Passing Arguments

Shell programs become far more useful after you learn how to process arguments passed to them. In this chapter, you'll learn how to write shell programs that take arguments typed on the command line. Recall the program run that you wrote in Chapter 5, "And Away We Go," to run the file sys.caps through tbl, nroff, and lp:

```
$ cat run
tbl sys.caps | nroff -mm -Tlp | lp
$
```

Suppose that you need to run other files besides sys.caps through this same command sequence. You could make a separate version of run for each such file; or, you could modify the run program so that you could specify the name of the file to be run on the command line. That is, you could change run so that you could type

```
run new.hire
```

for example, to specify that the file new.hire is to be run through this command sequence, or

```
run sys.caps
```

to specify the file sys.caps.

Whenever you execute a shell program, the shell automatically stores the first argument in the special shell variable 1, the second argument in the variable 2, and so on. These special variables—more formally known as *positional parameters*—are assigned after the shell has done its normal command-line processing (that is, I/O redirection, variable substitution, filename substitution, and so on).

To modify the run program to accept the name of the file as an argument, all you do to the program is change the reference to the file sys.caps so that it instead references the first argument typed on the command line:

```
$ cat run
tbl $1 | nroff -mm -Tlp | lp
$ run new.hire                    Execute it with new.hire as the argument
request id is laser1-24 (standard input)
$
```

Each time you execute the run program, whatever word follows on the command line will be stored inside the first positional parameter by the shell. In the example, new.hire will be stored in this parameter. Substitution of positional parameters is identical to substitution of other types of variables, so when the shell sees

```
tbl $1
```

it replaces the $1 with the first argument supplied to the program: new.hire.

As another example, the following program, called ison, lets you know if a specified user is logged on:

```
$ cat ison
who | grep $1
$ who                             See who's on
root     console Jul 7 08:37
barney   tty03   Jul 8 12:28
fred     tty04   Jul 8 13:40
joanne   tty07   Jul 8 09:35
tony     tty19   Jul 8 08:30
lulu     tty23   Jul 8 09:55
$ ison tony
tony     tty19   Jul 8 08:30
$ ison pat
$                                 Not logged on
```

The $# Variable

Whenever you execute a shell program, the special shell variable $# gets set to the number of arguments that were typed on the command line. As you'll see in the next chapter, this variable can be tested by the program to determine whether the correct number of arguments was typed by the user.

The next program called args was written just to get you more familiar with the way arguments are passed to shell programs. Study the output from each example and make sure that you understand it:

```
$ cat args                              Look at the program
echo $# arguments passed
echo arg 1 = :$1: arg 2 = :$2: arg 3 = :$3:
$ args a b c                            Execute it
3 arguments passed
arg 1 = :a: arg 2 = :b: arg 3 = :c:
$ args a b                              Try it with two arguments
2 arguments passed
arg 1 = :a: arg 2 = :b: arg 3 = ::     Unassigned args are null
$ args                                  Try it with no arguments
0 arguments passed
arg 1 =:: arg 2 =:: arg 3 = ::
$ args "a b c"                          Try quotes
1 arguments passed
arg 1 = :a b c: arg 2 = :: arg 3 = ::
$ ls x*                                 See what files start with x
xact
xtra
$ args x*                               Try file name substitution
2 arguments passed
arg 1 = :xact: arg 2 = :xtra: arg 3 = ::
$ my_bin=/users/steve/bin
$ args $my_bin                          And variable substitution
1 arguments passed
arg 1 = :/users/steve/bin: arg 2 = :: arg 3 = ::
$ args $(cat names)                     Pass the contents of names
7 arguments passed
arg 1 = :Charlie: arg 2 = :Emanuel: arg3 = :Fred:
$
```

As you can see, the shell does its normal command-line processing even when it's executing your shell programs. This means that you can take advantage of the normal niceties such as filename substitution and variable substitution when specifying arguments to your programs.

The $* Variable

The special variable $* references *all* the arguments passed to the program. This is often useful in programs that take an indeterminate or *variable* number of arguments. You'll see some more practical examples later. Here's a program that illustrates its use:

```
$ cat args2
echo $# arguments passed
echo they are :$*:
$ args2 a b c
3 arguments passed
they are :a b c:
$ args2 one              two
2 arguments passed
they are :one two:
$ args2
0 arguments passed
they are ::
$ args2 *
8 arguments passed
they are :args args2 names nu phonebook stat xact xtra:
$
```

A Program to Look Up Someone in the Phone Book

Here's the phonebook file from previous examples:

```
$ cat phonebook
Alice Chebba     973-555-2015
Barbara Swingle 201-555-9257
Liz Stachiw      212-555-2298
Susan Goldberg  201-555-7776
Susan Topple     212-555-4932
Tony Iannino     973-555-1295
$
```

You know how to look up someone in the file by using grep:

```
$ grep Cheb phonebook
Alice Chebba     973-555-2015
$
```

And you know that if you want to look up someone by the full name, you'd better put quotes around it to keep the argument together:

```
$ grep "Susan T" phonebook
Susan Topple     212-555-4932
$
```

It would be nice to write a shell program that you could use to look up someone. Let's call the program `lu` and have it take as its argument the name of the person to look up:

```
$ cat lu
#
# Look someone up in the phone book
#

grep $1 phonebook
$
```

Here's a sample use of `lu`:

```
$ lu Alice
Alice Chebba      973-555-2015
$ lu Susan
Susan Goldberg   201-555-7776
Susan Topple     212-555-4932
$ lu "Susan T"
grep: can't open T
phonebook:Susan Goldberg   201-555-7776
phonebook:Susan Topple     212-555-4932
$
```

In the preceding example, you were careful to enclose Susan T in double quotes; so what happened? Look again at the grep executed in the lu program:

```
grep $1 phonebook
```

Even though enclosing Susan T inside double quotes results in its getting passed to lu as a single argument, when the shell substitutes this value for $1 on grep's command line, it then passes it as *two* arguments to grep. (Remember we had this same sort of discussion when we talked about variable substitution—first the shell substitutes the value of the variable; then it divides the line into arguments.)

You can alleviate this problem by enclosing $1 inside double quotes (why not single?) in the lu program:

```
$ cat lu
#
# Look someone up in the phone book -- version 2
#

grep "$1" phonebook
$
```

Now let's try it again:

```
$ lu Tony
Tony Iannino    973-555-1295        This still works
$ lu "Susan T"                      Now try this again
Susan Topple    212-555-4932
$
```

A Program to Add Someone to the Phone Book

Let's continue with the development of programs that work with the phonebook file. You'll probably want to add someone to the file, particularly because our phonebook file is so small. You can write a program called add that takes two arguments: the name of the person to be added and the number. Then you can simply write the name and number, separated from each other by a tab character, onto the end of the phonebook file:

```
$ cat add
#
# Add someone to the phone book
#

echo "$1        $2" >> phonebook
$
```

Although you can't tell, there's a tab character that separates the $1 from the $2 in the preceding echo command. This tab must be quoted to make it to echo without getting gobbled up by the shell.

Let's try out the program:

```
$ add 'Stromboli Pizza' 973-555-9478
$ lu Pizza                          See if we can find the new entry
Stromboli Pizza 973-555-9478        So far, so good
$ cat phonebook                     See what happened
Alice Chebba     973-555-2015
Barbara Swingle  201-555-9257
Liz Stachiw      212-555-2298
Susan Goldberg   201-555-7776
Susan Topple     212-555-4932
Tony Iannino     973-555-1295
Stromboli Pizza 973-555-9478
$
```

`Stromboli Pizza` was quoted so that the shell passed it along to `add` as a single argument (what would have happened if it wasn't quoted?). After `add` finished executing, `lu` was run to see whether it could find the new entry, and it did. The `cat` command was executed to see what the modified `phonebook` file looked like. The new entry was added to the end, as intended. Unfortunately, the new file is no longer sorted. This won't affect the operation of the `lu` program, but you can add a `sort` to the `add` program to keep the file sorted after new entries are added:

```
$ cat add
#
# Add someone to the phonebook file -- version 2
#

echo "$1          $2" >> phonebook
sort -o phonebook phonebook
$
```

Recall that the `-o` option to sort specifies where the sorted output is to be written, and that this can be the same as the input file:

```
$ add 'Billy Bach' 201-555-7618
$ cat phonebook
Alice Chebba     973-555-2015
Barbara Swingle 201-555-9257
Billy Bach       201-555-7618
Liz Stachiw      212-555-2298
Stromboli Pizza 973-555-9478
Susan Goldberg  201-555-7776
Susan Topple     212-555-4932
Tony Iannino     973-555-1295
$
```

So each time a new entry is added, the `phonebook` file will get re-sorted.

A Program to Remove Someone from the Phone Book

No set of programs that enable you to look up or add someone to the phone book would be complete without a program to remove someone from the phone book. We'll call the program `rem` and have it take as its argument the name of the person to be removed. What should the strategy be for developing the program? Essentially, you want to remove the line from the file that contains the specified name. The `-v` option to `grep` can be used here because it prints lines from a file that *don't* match a pattern:

```
$ cat rem
#
# Remove someone from the phone book
#

grep -v "$1" phonebook > /tmp/phonebook
mv /tmp/phonebook phonebook
$
```

The grep writes all lines that don't match into the file /tmp/phonebook.[1] After the grep is done, the old phonebook file is replaced by the new one from /tmp.

```
$ rem 'Stromboli Pizza'            Remove this entry
$ cat phonebook
Alice Chebba     973-555-2015
Barbara Swingle  201-555-9257
Billy Bach       201-555-7618
Liz Stachiw      212-555-2298
Susan Goldberg   201-555-7776
Susan Topple     212-555-4932
Tony Iannino     973-555-1295
$ rem Susan
$ cat phonebook
Alice Chebba     973-555-2015
Barbara Swingle  201-555-9257
Billy Bach       201-555-7618
Liz Stachiw      212-555-2298
Tony Iannino     973-555-1295
$
```

The first case, where Stromboli Pizza was removed, worked fine. In the second case, however, both Susan entries were removed because they both matched the pattern. You can use the add program to add them back to the phone book:

```
$ add 'Susan Goldberg' 201-555-7776
$ add 'Susan Topple' 212-555-4932
$
```

In Chapter 8, "Decisions, Decisions," you'll learn how to determine whether more than one matching entry is found and take some other action if that's the case. For

---

[1] /tmp *is a directory on all Unix systems that anyone can write to. It's used by programs to create "temporary" files. Each time the system gets rebooted, all the files in* /tmp *are usually removed.*

example, you might want to alert the user that more than one match has been found and further qualification of the name is required. (This can be very helpful, because most implementations of grep will match *everything* if an empty string is passed as the pattern.)

Incidentally, before leaving this program, note that sed could have also been used to delete the matching entry. In such a case, the grep could be replaced with

```
sed "/$1/d" phonebook > /tmp/phonebook
```

to achieve the same result. The double quotes are needed around the sed command to ensure that the value of $1 is substituted, while at the same time ensuring that the shell doesn't see a command line like

```
sed /Stromboli Pizza/d phonebook > /tmp/phonebook
```

and pass three arguments to sed rather than two.

${*n*}

If you supply more than nine arguments to a program, you cannot access the tenth and greater arguments with $10, $11, and so on. If you try to access the tenth argument by writing

```
$10
```

the shell actually substitutes the value of $1 followed by a 0. Instead, the format

```
${n}
```

must be used. So to directly access argument 10, you must write

```
${10}
```

in your program.

The shift Command

The shift command allows you to effectively *left shift* your positional parameters. If you execute the command

```
shift
```

whatever was previously stored inside $2 will be assigned to $1, whatever was previously stored in $3 will be assigned to $2, and so on. The old value of $1 will be irretrievably lost.

When this command is executed, $# (the number of arguments variable) is also automatically decremented by one:

```
$ cat tshift              Program to test the shift
echo $# $*
shift
echo $# $*
shift
echo $# $*
shift
echo $# $*
shift
echo $# $*
shift
echo $# $*
$ tshift a b c d e
5 a b c d e
4 b c d e
3 c d e
2 d e
1 e
0
$
```

If you try to shift when there are no variables to shift (that is, when $# already equals zero), you'll get an error message from the shell (the error will vary from one shell to the next):

prog: shift: bad number

where *prog* is the name of the program that executed the offending shift.

You can shift more than one "place" at once by writing a *count* immediately after shift, as in

```
shift 3
```

This command has the same effect as performing three separate shifts:

```
shift
shift
shift
```

The shift command is useful when processing a variable number of arguments. You'll see it put to use when you learn about loops in Chapter 9, "'Round and 'Round She Goes."

Exercises

1. Modify `lu` so that it ignores case when doing the lookup.

2. What happens if you forget to supply an argument to the `lu` program? What happens if the argument is null (as in, `lu ""`)?

3. The program `ison` from this chapter has a shortcoming as shown in the following example:

```
$ ison ed
fred      tty03     Sep  4 14:53
$
```

The output indicates that `fred` is logged on, while we were checking to see whether `ed` was logged on.

Modify `ison` to correct this problem.

4. Write a program called `twice` that takes a single integer argument and doubles its value:

```
$ twice 15
30
$ twice 0
0
$
```

What happens if a noninteger value is typed? What if the argument is omitted?

5. Write a program called `home` that takes the name of a user as its single argument and prints that user's home directory. So

```
home steve
```

would print

```
/users/steve
```

if `/users/steve` is `steve`'s home directory. (Hint: Recall that the home directory is the sixth field stored in the file `/etc/passwd`.)

6. Write a program called `suffix` that renames a file by adding the characters given as the second argument to the end of the name of the file given as the first argument. So

```
suffix memo1 .sv
```

should rename `memo1` to `memo1.sv`.

7. Write a program called `unsuffix` that removes the characters given as the second argument from the end of the name of the file given as the first argument. So

```
unsuffix memo1.sv .sv
```

should rename `memo1.sv` to `memo1`. Be sure that the characters are removed from the end, so

```
unsuffix test1test test
```

should result in `test1test` being renamed to `test1`. (Hint: Use `sed` and command substitution.)

8

Decisions, Decisions

This chapter introduces a statement that is present in almost all programming languages: if. It enables you to test a condition and then change the flow of program execution based on the result of the test.

The general format of the if command is

```
if command_t
then
        command
        command
        ...
fi
```

where *command*_t is executed and its *exit status* is tested. If the exit status is zero, the commands that follow between the then and the fi are executed; otherwise, they are skipped.

Exit Status

Whenever any program completes execution under the Unix system, it returns an exit status back to the system. This status is a number that usually indicates whether the program successfully ran. By convention, an exit status of zero indicates that a program succeeded, and nonzero indicates that it failed. Failures can be caused by invalid arguments passed to the program, or by an error condition detected by the program. For example, the cp command returns a nonzero exit status if the copy fails for some reason (for example, if it can't create the destination file), or if the arguments aren't correctly specified (for example, wrong number of arguments, or more than two arguments and the last one isn't a directory). In the case of grep, an exit status of zero (success) is returned if it finds the specified pattern in at least one of the files; a nonzero value is returned if it can't find the pattern or if an error occurs (the arguments aren't correctly specified, or it can't open one of the files).

In a pipeline, the exit status is that of the last command in the pipe. So in

```
who | grep fred
```

the exit status of the grep is used by the shell as the exit status for the pipeline. In this case, an exit status of zero means that fred was found in who's output (that is, fred was logged on at the time that this command was executed).

The $? Variable

The shell variable $? is automatically set by the shell to the exit status of the last command executed. Naturally, you can use echo to display its value at the terminal.

```
$ cp phonebook phone2
$ echo $?
0                       Copy "succeeded"
$ cp nosuch backup
cp: cannot access nosuch
$ echo $?
2                       Copy "failed"
$ who                   See who's logged on
root    console Jul 8 10:06
wilma   tty03   Jul 8 12:36
barney  tty04   Jul 8 14:57
betty   tty15   Jul 8 15:03
$ who | grep barney
barney  tty04   Jul 8 14:57
$ echo $?               Print exit status of last command (grep)
0                       grep "succeeded"
$ who | grep fred
$ echo $?
1                       grep "failed"
$ echo $?
0                       Exit status of last echo
$
```

Note that the numeric result of a "failure" for some commands can vary from one Unix version to the next, but success is always signified by a zero exit status.

Let's now write a shell program called on that tells us whether a specified user is logged on to the system. The name of the user to check will be passed to the program on the command line. If the user is logged on, we'll print a message to that effect; otherwise we'll say nothing. Here is the program:

```
$ cat on
#
# determine if someone is logged on
#

user="$1"

if who | grep "$user"
then
    echo "$user is logged on"
fi
$
```

This first argument typed on the command line is stored in the shell variable user. Then the if command executes the pipeline

```
who | grep "$user"
```

and tests the exit status returned by grep. If the exit status is zero, grep found user in who's output. In that case, the echo command that follows is executed. If the exit status is nonzero, the specified user is not logged on, and the echo command is skipped. The echo command is indented from the left margin for aesthetic reasons only (tab characters are usually used for such purposes because it's easier to type a tab character than an equivalent number of spaces). In this case, just a single command is enclosed between the then and fi. When more commands are included, and when the nesting gets deeper, indentation can have a dramatic effect on the program's readability. Later examples will help illustrate this point.

Here are some sample uses of on:

```
$ who
root       console Jul 8 10:37
barney     tty03   Jul 8 12:38
fred       tty04   Jul 8 13:40
joanne     tty07   Jul 8 09:35
tony       tty19   Jul 8 08:30
lulu       tty23   Jul 8 09:55
$ on tony                    We know he's on
tony       tty19   Jul 8 08:30    Where did this come from?
tony is logged on
$ on steve                   We know he's not on
```

```
$ on ann                        Try this one
joanne   tty07   Jul 8 09:35
ann is logged on
$
```

We seem to have uncovered a couple of problems with the program. When the specified user is logged on, the corresponding line from who's output is also displayed.
This may not be such a bad thing, but the program requirements called for only a
message to be displayed and nothing else.

This line is displayed because not only does grep return an exit status in the pipeline

```
who | grep "$user"
```

but it also goes about its normal function of writing any matching lines to standard
output, even though we're really not interested in that. We can dispose of grep's
output by redirecting it to the system's "garbage can," /dev/null. This is a special
file on the system that anyone can read from (and get an immediate end of file) or
write to. When you write to it, the bits go to that great bit bucket in the sky!

```
who | grep "$user" > /dev/null
```

The second problem with on appears when the program is executed with the argument ann. Even though ann is not logged on, grep matches the characters ann for the
user joanne. What you need here is a more restrictive pattern specification, which
you learned how to do in Chapter 4, "Tools of the Trade," where we talked about
regular expressions. Because who lists each username in column one of each output
line, we can anchor the pattern to match the beginning of the line by preceding the
pattern with the character ^:

```
who | grep "^$user" > /dev/null
```

But that's not enough. grep still matches a line like

```
bobby    tty07   Jul 8 09:35
```

if you ask it to search for the pattern bob. What you need to do is also anchor the
pattern on the right. Realizing that who ends each username with one or more
spaces, the pattern

```
"^$user "
```

now only matches lines for the specified user.

Let's try the new and improved version of on:

```
$ cat on
#
# determine if someone is logged on -- version 2
#
user="$1"

if who | grep "^$user " > /dev/null
then
        echo "$user is logged on"
fi
$ who                          Who's on now?
root      console Jul 8 10:37
barney    tty03   Jul 8 12:38
fred      tty04   Jul 8 13:40
joanne    tty07   Jul 8 09:35
tony      tty19   Jul 8 08:30
lulu      tty23   Jul 8 09:55
$ on lulu
lulu is logged on
$ on ann                       Try this again
$ on                           What happens if we don't give any arguments?
$
```

If no arguments are specified, user will be null. grep will then look through who's output for lines that start with a blank (why?). It won't find any, and so just a command prompt will be returned. In the next section, you'll see how to test whether the correct number of arguments has been supplied to a program and, if not, take some action.

The test Command

A built-in shell command called test is most often used for testing one or more conditions in an if command. Its general format is

test *expression*

where *expression* represents the condition you're testing. test evaluates *expression*, and if the result is *true*, it returns an exit status of zero; otherwise, the result is *false*, and it returns a nonzero exit status.

String Operators

As an example of the use of `test`, the following command returns a zero exit status if the shell variable `name` contains the characters `julio`:

```
test "$name" = julio
```

The = operator is used to test whether two values are identical. In this case, we're testing to see whether the *contents* of the shell variable `name` are identical to the characters `julio`. If it is, `test` returns an exit status of zero; nonzero otherwise.

Note that `test` must see all operands (`$name` and `julio`) and operators (=) as separate arguments, meaning that they must be delimited by one or more whitespace characters.

Getting back to the `if` command, to `echo` the message "Would you like to play a game?" if `name` contains the characters `julio`, you would write your `if` command like this:

```
if test "$name" = julio
then
        echo "Would you like to play a game?"
fi
```

(Why is it better to play it safe and enclose the message that is displayed by `echo` inside quotes?) When the `if` command gets executed, the command that follows the `if` is executed, and its exit status is tested. The `test` command is passed the three arguments $name (with its value substituted, of course), =, and `julio`. `test` then tests to see whether the first argument is identical to the third argument and returns a zero exit status if it is and a nonzero exit status if it is not.

The exit status returned by `test` is then tested. If it's zero, the commands between `then` and `fi` are executed; in this case, the single `echo` command is executed. If the exit status is nonzero, the `echo` command is skipped.

It's good programming practice to enclose shell variables that are arguments to `test` inside a pair of *double* quotes (to allow variable substitution). This ensures that `test` sees the argument in the case where its value is null. For example, consider the following example:

```
$ name=                          Set name null
$ test $name = julio
sh: test: argument expected
$
```

Because `name` was null, only two arguments were passed to `test`: = and `julio` because the shell substituted the value of `name` *before* parsing the command line into arguments. In fact, after $name was substituted by the shell, it was as if you typed the following:

```
test = julio
```

When test executed, it saw only two arguments (see Figure 8.1) and therefore issued the error message.

FIGURE 8.1   test $name = julio with name null.

By placing double quotes around the variable, you ensure that test sees the argument because quotes act as a "placeholder" when the argument is null.

```
$ test "$name" = julio
$ echo $?                       Print the exit status
1
$
```

Even if name is null, the shell still passes three arguments to test, the first one null (see Figure 8.2).

FIGURE 8.2   test "$name" = julio with name null.

Other operators can be used to test character strings. These operators are summarized in Table 8.1.

TABLE 8.1   test String Operators

Operator	Returns TRUE (exit status of 0) if
$string_1$ = $string_2$	$string_1$ is identical to $string_2$.
$string_1$!= $string_2$	$string_1$ is *not* identical to $string_2$.
string	*string* is not null.
-n *string*	*string* is not null (and *string* must be seen by test).
-z *string*	*string* is null (and *string* must be seen by test).

You've seen how the = operator is used. The != operator is similar, only it tests two strings for inequality. That is, the exit status from test is zero if the two strings are not equal, and nonzero if they are.

Let's look at three similar examples.

```
$ day="monday"
$ test "$day" = monday
$ echo $?
0                              True
$
```

The test command returns an exit status of 0 because the value of day is equal to the characters monday. Now look at the following:

```
$ day="monday "
$ test "$day" = monday
$ echo $?
1                              False
$
```

Here we assigned the characters monday—*including the space character that immediately followed*—to day. Therefore, when the previous test was made, test returned false because the characters "monday " were not identical to the characters "monday".

If you wanted these two values to be considered equal, omitting the double quotes would have caused the shell to "eat up" the trailing space character, and test would have never seen it:

```
$ day="monday "
$ test $day = monday
$ echo $?
0
$                              True
```

Although this seems to violate our rule about always quoting shell variables that are arguments to test, it's okay to omit the quotes if you're sure that the variable is not null (and not composed entirely of whitespace characters).

You can test to see whether a shell variable has a null value with the third operator listed in Table 8.1:

```
test "$day"
```

This returns true if day is not null and false if it is. Quotes are not necessary here because test doesn't care whether it sees an argument in this case. Nevertheless, you are better off using them here as well because if the variable consists entirely of whitespace characters, the shell will get rid of the argument if not enclosed in quotes.

```
$ blanks="    "
$ test $blanks          Is it not null?
$ echo $?
1                       False—it's null
$ test "$blanks"        And now?
$ echo $?
0                       True—it's not null
$
```

In the first case, test was not passed *any* arguments because the shell ate up the four spaces in blanks. In the second case, test got one argument consisting of four space characters; obviously not null.

In case we seem to be belaboring the point about blanks and quotes, realize that this is a sticky area that is a frequent source of shell programming errors. It's good to really understand the principles here to save yourself a lot of programming headaches in the future.

There is another way to test whether a string is null, and that's with either of the last two operators listed previously in Table 8.1. The -n operator returns an exit status of zero if the argument that follows is not null. Think of this operator as testing for nonzero length.

The -z operator tests the argument that follows to see whether it is null and returns an exit status of zero if it is. Think of this operator as testing to see whether the following argument has zero length.

So the command

```
test -n "$day"
```

returns an exit status of 0 if day contains at least one character. The command

```
test -z "$dataflag"
```

returns an exit status of 0 if dataflag doesn't contain any characters.

Be forewarned that both of the preceding operators expect an argument to follow; therefore, get into the habit of enclosing that argument inside double quotes.

```
$ nullvar=
$ nonnullvar=abc
$ test -n "$nullvar"        Does nullvar have nonzero length?
$ echo $?
1                           No
$ test -n "$nonnullvar"     And what about nonnullvar?
$ echo $?
0                           Yes
$ test -z "$nullvar"        Does nullvar have zero length?
$ echo $?
0                           Yes
$ test -z "$nonnullvar"     And nonnullvar?
$ echo $?
1                           No
$
```

Note that test can be picky about its arguments. For example, if the shell variable symbol contains an equals sign, look at what happens if you try to test it for zero length:

```
$ echo $symbol
=
$ test -z "$symbol"
sh: test: argument expected
$
```

The = operator has higher precedence than the -z operator, so test expects an argument to follow. To avoid this sort of problem, you can write your command as

```
test X"$symbol" = X
```

which will be true if symbol is null, and false if it's not. The X in front of symbol prevents test from interpreting the characters stored in symbol as an operator.

An Alternative Format for test

The test command is used so often by shell programmers that an alternative format of the command is recognized. This format improves the readability of the command, especially when used in if commands.

You'll recall that the general format of the test command is

test *expression*

This can also be expressed in the alternative format as

[*expression*]

The [is actually the name of the command (who said anything about command names having to be alphanumeric characters?). It still initiates execution of the same test command, only in this format, test expects to see a closing] at the end of the expression. Naturally, spaces must appear after the [and before the].

You can rewrite the test command shown in a previous example with this alternative format as shown:

```
$ [ -z "$nonnullvar" ]
$ echo $?
1
$
```

When used in an if command, this alternative format looks like this:

```
if [ "$name" = julio ]
then
        echo "Would you like to play a game?"
fi
```

Which format of the if command you use is up to you; we prefer the [...] format, so that's what we'll use throughout the remainder of the book.

Integer Operators

test has an assortment of operators for performing integer comparisons. Table 8.2 summarizes these operators.

TABLE 8.2 test Integer Operators

Operator	Returns TRUE (exit status of 0) if
int_1 -eq int_2	int_1 is equal to int_2.
int_1 -ge int_2	int_1 is greater than or equal to int_2.
int_1 -gt int_2	int_1 is greater than int_2.
int_1 -le int_2	int_1 is less than or equal to int_2.
int_1 -lt int_2	int_1 is less than int_2.
int_1 -ne int_2	int_1 is not equal to int_2.

For example, the operator -eq tests to see whether two integers are equal. So if you had a shell variable called count and you wanted to see whether its value was equal to zero, you would write

```
[ "$count" -eq 0 ]
```

Other integer operators behave similarly, so

```
[ "$choice" -lt 5 ]
```

tests to see whether the variable choice is less than 5; the command

```
[ "$index" -ne "$max" ]
```

tests to see whether the value of index is not equal to the value of max; and, finally

```
[ "$#" -ne 0 ]
```

tests to see whether the number of arguments passed to the command is not equal to zero.

The test command interprets the value as an integer when an integer operator is used, and not the shell, so these comparisons work regardless of the shell variable's type.

Let's reinforce the difference between test's string and integer operators by taking a look at a few examples.

```
$ x1="005"
$ x2="  10"
$ [ "$x1" = 5 ]        String comparison
$ echo $?
1                      False
$ [ "$x1" -eq 5 ]      Integer comparison
$ echo $?
0                      True
$ [ "$x2" = 10 ]       String comparison
$ echo $?
1                      False
$ [ "$x2" -eq 10 ]     Integer comparison
$ echo $?
0                      True
$
```

The first test

```
[ "$x1" = 5 ]
```

uses the string comparison operator = to test whether the two strings are identical. They're not, because the first string is composed of the three characters 005, and the second the single character 5.

In the second test, the integer comparison operator -eq is used. Treating the two values as integers, 005 is equal to 5, as verified by the exit status returned by test.

The third and fourth tests are similar, only in this case you can see how even a leading space stored in the variable x2 can influence a test made with a string operator versus one made with an integer operator.

File Operators

Virtually every shell program deals with one or more files. For this reason, a wide assortment of operators is provided by test to enable you to ask various questions about files. Each of these operators is *unary* in nature, meaning that they expect a single argument to follow. In all cases, this argument is the name of a file (and that includes a directory file, of course).

Table 8.3 lists the commonly used file operators.

TABLE 8.3   Commonly Used test File Operators

Operator	Returns TRUE (exit status of 0) if
-d *file*	*file* is a directory.
-e *file*	*file* exists.
-f *file*	*file* is an ordinary file.
-r *file*	*file* is readable by the process.
-s *file*	*file* has nonzero length.
-w *file*	*file* is writable by the process.
-x *file*	*file* is executable.
-L *file*	*file* is a symbolic link.

The command

```
[ -f /users/steve/phonebook ]
```

tests whether the file /users/steve/phonebook exists and is an ordinary file (that is, not a directory and not a special file).

The command

```
[ -r /users/steve/phonebook ]
```

tests whether the indicated file exists and is also readable by you.

The command

```
[ -s /users/steve/phonebook ]
```

tests whether the indicated file contains at least one byte of information in it. This is useful, for example, if you create an error log file in your program and you want to see whether anything was written to it:

```
if [ -s $ERRFILE ]
then
        echo "Errors found:"
        cat $ERRFILE
fi
```

A few more test operators, when combined with the previously described operators, enable you to make more complex types of tests.

The Logical Negation Operator !

The unary logical negation operator ! can be placed in front of any other test expression to *negate* the result of the evaluation of that expression. For example,

```
[ ! -r /users/steve/phonebook ]
```

returns a zero exit status (true) if /users/steve/phonebook is *not* readable; and

```
[ ! -f "$mailfile" ]
```

returns true if the file specified by $mailfile does *not* exist or is not an ordinary file. Finally,

```
[ ! "$x1" = "$x2" ]
```

returns true if $x1 is not identical to $x2 and is obviously equivalent to

```
[ "$x1" != "$x2" ]
```

The Logical AND Operator -a

The operator -a performs a logical *AND* of two expressions and returns true only if the two joined expressions are both true. So

```
[ -f "$mailfile"   -a   -r "$mailfile" ]
```

returns true if the file specified by $mailfile is an ordinary file and is readable by you. An extra space was placed around the -a operator to aid in the expression's readability and obviously has no effect on its execution.

The command

```
[ "$count" -ge 0   -a   "$count" -lt 10 ]
```

will be true if the variable count contains an integer value greater than or equal to zero but less than 10. The -a operator has lower *precedence* than the integer comparison operators (and the string and file operators, for that matter), meaning that the preceding expression gets evaluated as

```
("$count" -ge 0) -a ("$count" -lt 10)
```

as you would expect.

Parentheses

Incidentally, you *can* use parentheses in a test expression to alter the order of evaluation; just make sure that the parentheses are quoted because they have a special meaning to the shell. So to translate the preceding example into a test command, you would write

```
[ \( "$count" -ge 0 \) -a \( "$count" -lt 10 \) ]
```

As is typical, spaces must surround the parentheses because test expects to see them as separate arguments.

The Logical OR Operator -o

The -o operator is similar to the -a operator, only it forms a logical *OR* of two expressions. That is, evaluation of the expression will be true if *either* the first expression is true or the second expression is true.

```
[ -n "$mailopt" -o -r $HOME/mailfile ]
```

This command will be true if the variable mailopt is not null *or* if the file $HOME/mailfile is readable by you.

The -o operator has lower precedence than the -a operator, meaning that the expression

```
"$a" -eq 0   -o   "$b" -eq 2   -a   "$c" -eq 10
```

gets evaluated by test as

```
"$a" -eq 0   -o   ("$b" -eq 2   -a   "$c" -eq 10)
```

Naturally, you can use parentheses to change this order if necessary:

```
\( "$a" -eq 0   -o   "$b" -eq 2 \) -a "$c" -eq 10
```

You will see many uses of the `test` command throughout the book. Table A.11 in Appendix A, "Shell Summary," summarizes all available `test` operators.

The `else` Construct

A construct known as the `else` can be added to the `if` command, with the general format as shown:

```
if command,
then
        command
        command
        ...
else
        command
        command
        ...
fi
```

Execution of this form of the command starts as before; *command*$_t$ is executed and its exit status tested. If it's zero, the commands that follow between the `then` and the `else` are executed, and the commands between the `else` and `fi` are skipped. Otherwise, the exit status is nonzero and the commands between the `then` and `else` are skipped and the commands between the `else` and `fi` are executed. In either case, only one set of commands gets executed: the first set if the exit status is zero, and the second set if it's nonzero.

Let's now write a modified version of on. Instead of printing nothing if the requested user is not logged on, we'll have the program print a message to that effect. Here is version 3 of the program:

```
$ cat on
#
# determine if someone is logged on -- version 3
#

user="$1"

if who | grep "^$user " > /dev/null
then
        echo "$user is logged on"
else
```

```
        echo "$user is not logged on"
fi
$
```

If the user specified as the first argument to on is logged on, the grep will succeed and the message $user is logged on will be displayed; otherwise, the message $user is not logged on will be displayed.

```
$ who                               Who's on?
root      console Jul 8 10:37
barney    tty03   Jul 8 12:38
fred      tty04   Jul 8 13:40
joanne    tty07   Jul 8 09:35
tony      tty19   Jul 8 08:30
lulu      tty23   Jul 8 09:55
$ on pat
pat is not logged on
$ on tony
tony is logged on
$
```

Another nice touch when writing shell programs is to make sure that the correct number of arguments is passed to the program. If an incorrect number is supplied, an error message to that effect can be displayed, together with information on the proper usage of the program.

```
$ cat on
#
# determine if someone is logged on -- version 4
#

#
# see if the correct number of arguments were supplied
#
if [ "$#" -ne 1 ]
then
        echo "Incorrect number of arguments"
        echo "Usage: on user"
else
        user="$1"

        if who | grep "^$user " > /dev/null
        then
```

```
                    echo "$user is logged on"
        else
                    echo "$user is not logged on"
        fi
fi
$
```

Compare this program with the previous version and note the changes that were made. An additional `if` command was added to test whether the correct number of arguments was supplied. If `$#` is not equal to 1, the program prints two messages; otherwise, the commands after the `else` clause are executed. These commands are the same as appeared in the last version of on: They assign `$1` to `user` and then see whether `user` is logged on, printing a message in either case. Note that two `fi`s are required because two `if` commands are used.

The indentation used goes a long way toward aiding the program's readability. Make sure that you get into the habit of setting and following indentation rules in your programs.

```
$ on                              No arguments
Incorrect number of arguments
Usage:  on user
$ on priscilla                    One argument
priscilla is not logged on
$ on jo anne                      Two arguments
Incorrect number of arguments
Usage:  on user
$
```

The `exit` Command

A built-in shell command called `exit` enables you to immediately terminate execution of your shell program. The general format of this command is

```
exit n
```

where *n* is the exit status that you want returned. If none is specified, the exit status used is that of the last command executed before the `exit`.

Be advised that executing the `exit` command directly from your terminal will log you off the system because it will have the effect of terminating execution of your login shell.

A Second Look at the rem Program

exit is frequently used as a convenient way to terminate execution of a shell program. For example, let's take another look at the rem program, which removes an entry from the phonebook file:

```
$ cat rem
#
# Remove someone from the phone book
#

grep -v "$1" phonebook > /tmp/phonebook
mv /tmp/phonebook phonebook
$
```

This program has the potential to do unintended things to the phonebook file. For example, suppose that you type

```
rem Susan Topple
```

Here the shell will pass two arguments to rem. The rem program will end up removing all Susan entries, as specified by $1.

It's always best to take precautions with a potentially destructive program like rem and to be certain as possible that the action intended by the user is consistent with the action that the program is taking.

One of the first checks that can be made in rem is for the correct number of arguments, as was done before with the on program. This time, we'll use the exit command to terminate the program if the correct number of arguments isn't supplied:

```
$ cat rem
#
# Remove someone from the phone book -- version 2
#

if [ "$#" -ne 1 ]
then
        echo "Incorrect number of arguments."
        echo "Usage: rem name"
        exit 1
fi

grep -v "$1" phonebook > /tmp/phonebook
```

```
mv /tmp/phonebook phonebook
$ rem Susan Goldberg                          Try it out
Incorrect number of arguments.
Usage: rem name
$
```

The exit command returns an exit status of 1, to signal "failure," in case some other program wants to check it. How could you have written the preceding program with an if-else instead of using the exit (hint: look at the last version of on)?

Whether you use the exit or an if-else is up to you. Sometimes the exit is a more convenient way to get out of the program quickly, particularly if it's done early in the program.

The elif Construct

As your programs become more complex, you may find yourself needing to write nested if statements of the following form:

```
if command₁
then
        command
        command
        ...
else
        if command₂
        then
                command
                command
                ...
        else
                ...
                if commandₙ
                then
                        command
                        command
                        ...
                else
                        command
                        command
                        ...
                fi
                ...
        fi
fi
```

This type of command sequence is useful when you need to make more than just a two-way decision as afforded by the if-else construct. In this case, a multiway decision is made, with the last else clause executed if none of the preceding conditions is satisfied.

As an example, suppose that you wanted to write a program called greetings that would print a friendly "Good morning," "Good afternoon," or "Good evening" whenever you logged on to the system. For purposes of the example, consider any time from midnight to noon to be the morning, noon to 6:00 p.m. the afternoon, and 6:00 p.m. to midnight the evening.

To write this program, you have to find out what time it is. date serves just fine for this purpose. Take another look at the output from this command:

```
$ date
Wed Aug 29 10:42:01 EDT 2002
$
```

The format of date's output is fixed, a fact that you can use to your advantage when writing greetings because this means that the time will always appear in character positions 12 through 19. Actually, for this program, you really only need the hour displayed in positions 12 and 13. So to get the hour from date, you can write

```
$ date | cut -c12-13
10
$
```

Now the task of writing the greetings program is straightforward:

```
$ cat greetings
#
# Program to print a greeting
#

hour=$(date | cut -c12-13)

if [ "$hour" -ge 0 -a "$hour" -le 11 ]
then
        echo "Good morning"
else
        if [ "$hour" -ge 12 -a "$hour" -le 17 ]
        then
```

```
                echo "Good afternoon"
        else
                echo "Good evening"
        fi
fi
$
```

If hour is greater than or equal to 0 (midnight) and less than or equal to 11 (up to 11:59:59), "Good morning" is displayed. If hour is greater than or equal to 12 (noon) and less than or equal to 17 (up to 5:59:59 p.m.), "Good afternoon" is displayed. If neither of the preceding two conditions is satisfied, "Good evening" is displayed.

```
$ greetings
Good morning
$
```

As noted, the nested if command sequence used in greetings is so common that a special elif construct is available to more easily express this sequence. The general format of this construct is

if *command_1*
then
        command
        command
        . . .
elif *command_2*
then
        command
        command
        . . .
elif *command_n*
then
        command
        command
        . . .
else
        command
        command
        . . .
fi

command_1, *command_2*, ..., *command_n* are executed in turn and their exit statuses tested. As soon as one returns an exit status of zero, the commands listed after the then that follows are executed up to another elif, else, or fi. If none of the commands returns a zero exit status, the commands listed after the optional else are executed.

You could rewrite the greetings program using this new format as shown:

```
$ cat greetings
#
# Program to print a greeting -- version 2
#

hour=$(date | cut -c12-13)

if [ "$hour" -ge 0 -a "$hour" -le 11 ]
then
        echo "Good morning"
elif [ "$hour" -ge 12 -a "$hour" -le 17 ]
then
        echo "Good afternoon"
else
        echo "Good evening"
fi
$
```

This version is easier to read, and it doesn't have the tendency to disappear off the right margin due to excessive indentation. Incidentally, you should note that date provides a wide assortment of options. One of these, %H, can be used to get the hour directly from date:

```
$ date +%H
10
$
```

As an exercise, you should change greetings to make use of this fact.

Yet Another Version of rem

Another way to add some robustness to the rem program would be to check the *number* of entries that matched before doing the removal. If there's more than one match, you could issue a message to the effect and then terminate execution of the program. But how do you determine the number of matching entries? One approach is to do a normal grep on the phonebook file and then count the number of matches that come out with wc. If the number of matches is greater than one, the appropriate message can be issued.

```
$ cat rem
#
# Remove someone from the phone book -- version 3
#

if [ "$#" -ne 1 ]
then
        echo "Incorrect number of arguments."
        echo "Usage: rem name"
        exit 1
fi

name=$1

#
# Find number of matching entries
#

matches=$(grep "$name" phonebook | wc -l)

#
# If more than one match, issue message, else remove it
#

if [ "$matches" -gt 1 ]
then
        echo "More than one match; please qualify further"
elif [ "$matches" -eq 1 ]
then
        grep -v "$name" phonebook > /tmp/phonebook
        mv /tmp/phonebook phonebook
else
        echo "I couldn't find $name in the phone book"
fi
$
```

The positional parameter $1 is assigned to the variable name after the number of arguments check is performed to add readability to the program. Subsequently using $name is a lot clearer than using $1.

The if...elif...else command first checks to see whether the number of matches is greater than one. If it is, the "More than one match" message is printed. If it's not, a test is made to see whether the number of matches is equal to one. If it is, the entry is removed from the phone book. If it's not, the number of matches must be zero, in which case a message is displayed to alert the user of this fact.

Note that the grep command is used twice in this program: first to determine the number of matches and then with the -v option to remove the single matching entry.

Here are some sample runs of the third version of rem:

```
$ rem
Incorrect number of arguments.
Usage: rem name
$ rem Susan
More than one match; please qualify further
$ rem 'Susan Topple'
$ rem 'Susan Topple'
I couldn't find Susan Topple in the phone book     She's history
$
```

Now you have a fairly robust rem program: It checks for the correct number of arguments, printing the proper usage if the correct number isn't supplied; it also checks to make sure that precisely one entry is removed from the phonebook file.

The case Command

The case command allows you to compare a single value against other values and to execute one or more commands when a match is found. The general format of this command is

```
case value in
pat₁)    command
         command
         . . .
         command;;
pat₂)    command
         command
         . . .
         command;;
. . .
patₙ)    command
         command
         . . .
         command;;
esac
```

The word *value* is successively compared against the values pat_1, pat_2, ..., pat_n, until a match is found. When a match is found, the commands listed after the matching value, up to the double semicolons, are executed. After the double semicolons are reached, execution of the case is terminated. If a match is not found, none of the commands listed in the case is executed.

As an example of the use of the case, the following program called number takes a single digit and translates it to its English equivalent:

```
$ cat number
#
# Translate a digit to English
#

if [ "$#" -ne 1 ]
then
        echo "Usage: number digit"
        exit 1
fi

case "$1"
in
        0) echo zero;;
        1) echo one;;
        2) echo two;;
        3) echo three;;
        4) echo four;;
        5) echo five;;
        6) echo six;;
        7) echo seven;;
        8) echo eight;;
        9) echo nine;;
esac
$
```

Now to test it:

```
$ number 0
zero
$ number 3
three
$ number                    Try no arguments
Usage: number digit
```

```
$ number 17               Try a two-digit number
$
```

The last case shows what happens when you type in more than one digit: $1 doesn't match any of the values listed in the case, so none of the echo commands is executed.

Special Pattern Matching Characters

The shell lets you use the same special characters for specifying the patterns in a case as you can with filename substitution. That is, ? can be used to specify any single character; * can be used to specify zero or more occurrences of any character; and [...] can be used to specify any single character enclosed between the brackets.

Because the pattern * matches *anything* (just as when it's used for filename substitution it matches all the files in your directory), it's frequently used at the end of the case as the "catchall" value. That is, if none of the previous values in the case match, this one is guaranteed to match. Here's a second version of the number program that has such a catchall case.

```
$ cat number
#
# Translate a digit to English -- version 2
#

if [ "$#" -ne 1 ]
then
        echo "Usage: number digit"
        exit 1
fi

case "$1"
in
        0) echo zero;;
        1) echo one;;
        2) echo two;;
        3) echo three;;
        4) echo four;;
        5) echo five;;
        6) echo six;;
        7) echo seven;;
        8) echo eight;;
        9) echo nine;;
        *) echo "Bad argument; please specify a single digit";;
esac
```

```
$ number 9
nine
$ number 99
Bad argument; please specify a single digit
$
```

Here's another program called ctype that prints the type of the single character given as an argument. Character types recognized are digits, uppercase letters, lowercase letters, and special characters (anything not in the first three categories). As an added check, the program makes sure that just a single character is given as the argument.

```
$ cat ctype
#
# Classify character given as argument
#

if [ $# -ne 1 ]
then
        echo Usage: ctype char
        exit 1
fi


#
# Ensure that only one character was typed
#

char="$1"
numchars=$(echo "$char" | wc -c)

if [ "$numchars" -ne 1 ]
then
        echo Please type a single character
        exit 1
fi

#
# Now classify it
#

case "$char"
in
```

```
        [0-9] ) echo digit;;
        [a-z] ) echo lowercase letter;;
        [A-Z] ) echo uppercase letter;;
        *     ) echo special character;;
esac
$
```

Some sample runs:

```
$ ctype a
Please type a single character
$ ctype 7
Please type a single character
$
```

The -x Option for Debugging Programs

Something seems to be amiss. The counting portion of our program doesn't seem to be working properly. This seems like a good point to introduce the shell's -x option. You can trace the execution of any program by typing sh -x followed by the name of the program and its arguments. This starts up a new shell to execute the indicated program with the -x option enabled. In this mode, commands are printed at the terminal as they are executed, preceded by a plus sign. Let's try it out.

```
$ sh -x ctype a                 Trace execution
+ [ 1 -ne 1 ]                   $# equals 1
+ char=a                        Assignment of $1 to char
+ echo a
+ wc -c
+ numchars=      2              wc returned 2???
+ [       2 -ne 1 ]             That's why this test succeeded
+ echo please type a single character
please type a single character
+ exit 1
$
```

The trace output indicates that wc returned 2 when

```
echo "$char" | wc -c
```

was executed. But why? There seemed to be only one character in wc's input. The truth of the matter is that two characters were actually given to wc: the single character a and the "invisible" newline character that echo automatically prints at the end of each line. So the program really should be testing for the number of characters equal to two: the character typed plus the newline added by echo.

Go back to the ctype program and replace the if command that reads

```
if [ "$numchars" -ne 1 ]
then
        echo Please type a single character
        exit 1
fi
```

with

```
if [ "$numchars" -ne 2 ]
then
        echo Please type a single character
        exit 1
fi
```

and try it again.

```
$ ctype a
lowercase letter
$ ctype abc
Please type a single character
$ ctype 9
digit
$ ctype K
uppercase letter
$ ctype :
special character
$ ctype
Usage: ctype char
$
```

Now it seems to work just fine. (What do you think happens if you use ctype *
without enclosing the * in quotes?)

In Chapter 12, "More on Parameters," you'll learn how you can turn this trace
feature on and off at will from *inside* your program.

Before leaving the ctype program, here's a version that avoids the use of wc and
handles everything with the case:

```
$ cat ctype
#
# Classify character given as argument -- version 2
#
```

```
if [ $# -ne 1 ]
then
        echo Usage: ctype char
        exit 1
fi

#
# Now classify char, making sure only one was typed
#

char=$1

case "$char"
in
        [0-9] ) echo digit;;
        [a-z] ) echo lowercase letter;;
        [A-Z] ) echo uppercase letter;;
        ?     ) echo special character;;
        *     ) echo Please type a single character;;
esac
$
```

The ? matches any single character. If this pattern is matched, the character is a special character. If this pattern isn't matched, more than one character was typed, so the catchall case is executed to print the message.

```
$ ctype u
lowercase letter
$ ctype '>'
special character
$ ctype xx
Please type a single character
$
```

Back to the case

The symbol | has the effect of a logical OR when used between two patterns. That is, the pattern

pat_1 | pat_2

specifies that either pat_1 or pat_2 is to be matched. For example,

```
-l | -list
```

matches either the value -l or -list, and

```
dmd | 5620 | tty5620
```

matches either dmd or 5620 or tty5620.

The greetings program that you saw earlier in this chapter can be rewritten to use a case statement rather than the if-elif. Here is such a version of the program. This time, we took advantage of the fact that date with the +%H option writes a two-digit hour to standard output.

```
$ cat greetings
#
# Program to print a greeting -- case version
#

hour=$(date +%H)


case "$hour"
in
        0? | 1[01] ) echo "Good morning";;
        1[2-7]     ) echo "Good afternoon";;
        *          ) echo "Good evening";;
esac
$
```

The two-digit hour obtained from date is assigned to the shell variable hour. Then the case statement is executed. The value of hour is compared against the first pattern:

```
0? | 1[01]
```

which matches any value that starts with a zero followed by any character (midnight through 9:00 a.m.), or any value that starts with a one and is followed by a zero or one (10:00 or 11:00 a.m.).

The second pattern

```
1[2-7]
```

matches a value that starts with a one and is followed by any one of the digits two through seven (noon through 5:00 p.m.).

The last case, the catchall, matches anything else (6:00 p.m. through 11:00 p.m.).

```
$ date
Wed Aug 28 15:45:12 EDT 2002
```

```
$ greetings
Good afternoon
$
```

The Null Command :

This seems about as good a time as any to talk about the shell's built-in *null* command. The format of this command is simply

```
:
```

and the purpose of it is—you guessed it—to do nothing. So what good is it? Well, in most cases it's used to satisfy the requirement that a command appear, particularly in if commands. Suppose that you want to make sure that the value stored in the variable system exists in the file /users/steve/mail/systems, and if it doesn't, you want to issue an error message and exit from the program. So you start by writing something like

```
if grep "^$system" /users/steve/mail/systems > /dev/null
then
```

but you don't know what to write after the then because you want to test for the nonexistence of the system in the file and don't want to do anything special if the grep succeeds. Unfortunately, the shell requires that you write a command after the then. Here's where the null command comes to the rescue:

```
if grep "^$system" /users/steve/mail/systems > /dev/null
then
        :
else
        echo "$system is not a valid system"
        exit 1
fi
```

So if the system is valid, nothing is done. If it's not valid, the error message is issued and the program exited.

Remember this simple command when these types of situations arise.

The && and || Constructs

The shell has two special constructs that enable you to execute a command based on whether the preceding command succeeds or fails. In case you think this sounds similar to the if command, well it is. It's sort of a shorthand form of the if.

If you write

command₁ && *command₂*

anywhere where the shell expects to see a command, *command₁* will be executed, and if it returns an exit status of zero, *command₂* will be executed. If *command₁* returns an exit status of nonzero, *command₂* gets skipped.

For example, if you write

```
sort bigdata > /tmp/sortout && mv /tmp/sortout bigdata
```

then the mv command will be executed only if the sort is successful. Note that this is equivalent to writing

```
if sort bigdata > /tmp/sortout
then
        mv /tmp/sortout bigdata
fi
```

The command

```
[ -z "$EDITOR" ] && EDITOR=/bin/ed
```

tests the value of the variable EDITOR. If it's null, /bin/ed is assigned to it.

The || construct works similarly, except that the second command gets executed only if the exit status of the first is nonzero. So if you write

```
grep "$name" phonebook || echo "Couldn't find $name"
```

the echo command will get executed only if the grep fails (that is, if it can't find $name in phonebook, or if it can't open the file phonebook). In this case, the equivalent if command would look like

```
if grep "$name" phonebook
then
        :
else
        echo "Couldn't find $name"
fi
```

You can write a pipeline on either the left- or right-hand sides of these constructs. On the left, the exit status tested is that of the last command in the pipeline; thus

```
who | grep "^$name " > /dev/null || echo "$name's not logged on"
```

causes execution of the echo if the grep fails.

The && and || can also be combined on the same command line:

```
who | grep "^$name " > /dev/null && echo "$name's not logged on" \
    || echo "$name is logged on"
```

(Recall that when \ is used at the end of the line, it signals line continuation to the shell.) The first echo gets executed if the grep succeeds; the second if it fails.

These constructs are also often used in if commands:

```
if validsys "$sys" && timeok
then
        sendmail "$user@$sys" < $message
fi
```

If validsys returns an exit status of zero, timeok is executed. The exit status from this program is then tested for the if. If it's zero, then the sendmail program is executed. If validsys returns a nonzero exit status, timeok is not executed, and this is used as the exit status that is tested by the if. In that case, sendmail won't be executed.

The use of the && operator in the preceding case is like a "logical AND"; both programs must return an exit status of zero for the sendmail program to be executed. In fact, you could have even written the preceding if as

```
validsys "$sys" && timeok && sendmail "$user@$sys" < $message
```

When the || is used in an if, the effect is like a "logical OR":

```
if endofmonth || specialrequest
then
        sendreports
fi
```

If endofmonth returns a zero exit status, sendreports is executed; otherwise, specialrequest is executed and if its exit status is zero, sendreports is executed. The net effect is that sendreports is executed if endofmonth or specialrequest return an exit status of zero.

In Chapter 9, "'Round and 'Round She Goes," you'll learn about how to write loops in your programs. However, before proceeding to that chapter, try the exercises that follow.

Exercises

1. Write a program called `valid` that prints "yes" if its argument is a valid shell variable name and "no" otherwise:

```
$ valid foo_bar
yes
$ valid 123
no
$
```

(Hint: Define a regular expression for a valid variable name and then enlist the aid of `grep` or `sed`.)

2. Write a program called `t` that displays the time of day in a.m. or p.m. notation rather than in 24-hour clock time. Here's an example showing `t` run at night:

```
$ date
Wed Aug 28 19:34:01 EDT 2002
$ t
7:34 pm
$
```

Use the shell's built-in integer arithmetic to convert from 24-hour clock time. Then rewrite the program to use a `case` command instead. Rewrite it again to perform arithmetic with the `expr` command.

3. Write a program called `mysed` that applies the sed script given as the first argument against the file given as the second. If the `sed` succeeds (that is, exit status of zero), replace the original file with the modified one. So

```
mysed '1,10d' text
```

will use sed to delete the first 10 lines from `text`, and, if successful, will replace text with the modified file.

4. Write a program called `isyes` that returns an exit status of 0 if its argument is "yes," and 1 otherwise. For purposes of this exercise, consider y, yes, Yes, YES, and Y all to be valid "yes" arguments:

```
$ isyes yes
$ echo $?
0
$ isyes no
$ echo $?
1
$
```

Write the program using an `if` command and then rewrite it using a `case` command. This program can be useful when reading yes/no responses from the terminal (which you'll learn about in Chapter 10, "Reading and Printing Data").

5. Use the `date` and `who` commands to write a program called `conntime` that prints the number of hours and minutes that a user has been logged on to the system (assume that this is less than 24 hours).

9

'Round and 'Round She Goes

In this chapter you'll learn how to set up program loops. These loops will enable you to execute repeatedly a set of commands either a specified number of times or until some condition is met. The three built-in looping commands are

- for
- while
- until

You'll learn about each one of these loops in separate sections of this chapter.

The for Command

The for command is used to execute a set of commands a specified number of times. Its basic format is as shown:

for *var* in *word₁ word₂ ... wordₙ*
do
        command
        command
        . . .
done

The commands enclosed between the do and the done form what's known as the *body* of the loop. These commands are executed for as many words as you have listed after the in. When the loop is executed, the first word, *word₁*, is assigned to the variable *var*, and the body of the loop is then executed. Next, the second word in the list, *word₂*, is assigned to *var*, and the body of the loop is executed. This process continues with successive words in the list being assigned to *var* and the commands in the loop body being executed until the last word in the list, *wordₙ*, is assigned to *var* and the body of the loop executed. At that point, no words are left in the list, and execution of the for command is then finished. Execution then continues with the command that immediately follows the done. So if there are *n* words listed after the in, the body of the loop will have been executed a total of *n* times after the loop has finished.

Here's a loop that will be executed a total of three times:

```
for i in 1 2 3
do
        echo $i
done
```

To try it out, you can type this in directly at the terminal, just like any other shell command:

```
$ for i in 1 2 3
> do
>           echo $i
> done
1
2
3
$
```

While the shell is waiting for the done to be typed to close off the for command, it displays your secondary command prompt. When it gets the done, the shell then proceeds to execute the loop. Because three words are listed after the in (1, 2, and 3), the body of the loop—in this case a single echo command—will be executed a total of three times.

The first time through the loop, the first word in the list, 1, is assigned to the variable i. Then the body of the loop is executed. This displays the value of i at the terminal. Then the next word in the list, 2, is assigned to i and the echo command re-executed, resulting in the display of 2 at the terminal. The third word in the list, 3, is assigned to i the third time through the loop and the echo command executed. This results in 3 being displayed at the terminal. At that point, no more words are left in the list, so execution of the for command is then complete, and the shell displays your command prompt to let you know it's done.

Recall the run program from Chapter 7, "Passing Arguments," that enabled you to run a file through tbl, nroff, and lp:

```
$ cat run
tbl $1 | nroff -mm -Tlp | lp
$
```

If you wanted to run the files memo1 through memo4 through this program, you could type the following at the terminal:

```
$ for file in memo1 memo2 memo3 memo4
> do
>          run $file
> done
request id is laser1-33 (standard input)
request id is laser1-34 (standard input)
request id is laser1-35 (standard input)
request id is laser1-36 (standard input)
$
```

The four words memo1, memo2, memo3, and memo4 will be assigned to the variable file in order, and the run program will be executed with the value of this variable as the argument. Execution will be just as if you typed in the four commands:

```
$ run memo1
request id is laser1-33 (standard input)
$ run memo2
request id is laser1-34 (standard input)
$ run memo3
request id is laser1-35 (standard input)
$ run memo4
request id is laser1-36 (standard input)
$
```

Incidentally, the shell permits filename substitution in the list of words in the for, meaning that the previous loop could have also been written this way:

```
for file in memo[1-4]
do
        run $file
done
```

And if you wanted to run all the files in your current directory through run, you could type

```
for file in *
do
```

```
        run $file
done
```

If the file `filelist` contains a list of the files that you want to run through `run`, you can type

```
files=$(cat filelist)

for file in $files
do
        run $file
done
```

to run each of the files, or, more succinctly,

```
for file in $(cat filelist)
do
        run $file
done
```

If you found that you were using the `run` program often to process several files at once, you could go inside the `run` program and modify it to allow any number of files to be passed as arguments to the program.

```
$ cat run
#
# process files through nroff -- version 2
#
for file in $*
do
        tbl $file | nroff -rom -Tlp | lp
done
$
```

Recall that the special shell variable $* stands for *all* the arguments typed on the command line. So if you executed the new version of run by typing

run memo1 memo2 memo3 memo4

the $* in the for's list would be replaced by the four arguments memo1, memo2, memo3, and memo4. Of course, you could also type

run memo[1-4]

to achieve the same results.

The $@ Variable

While we're on the subject of $*, let's look at it in a bit more detail. We'll write a program called args that displays all the arguments typed on the command line, one per line.

```
$ cat args
echo Number of arguments passed is $#

for arg in $*
do
        echo $arg
done
$
```

Now to try it:

```
$ args a b c
Number of arguments passed is 3
a
b
c
$ args 'a b' c
Number of arguments passed is 2
a
b
c
$
```

In the second case, even though a b was passed as a single argument to args, the $* in the for command was replaced by the shell with a b c, which is three words. Thus the loop was executed three times.

Whereas the shell replaces the value of $* with $1, $2, . . ., if you instead use the special shell variable "$@" it will be replaced with "$1", "$2", ... The double quotes are necessary around $@ because without them this variable behaves just like $*.

Go back to the args program and replace the $* with "$@":

```
$ cat args
echo Number of arguments passed is $#

for arg in "$@"
do
        echo $arg
```

```
done
$
```

Now try it:

```
$ args a b c
Number of arguments passed is 3
a
b
c
$ args 'a b' c
Number of arguments passed is 2
a b
c
$ args                           Try it with no arguments
Number of arguments passed is 0
$
```

In the last case, no arguments were passed to the program. So the variable "$@" was replaced by *nothing*. The net result is that the body of the loop was not executed at all.

The for Without the List

A special notation is recognized by the shell when writing for commands. If you write

```
for var
do
        command
        command
        . . .
done
```

(note the absence of the in), the shell automatically sequences through all the arguments typed on the command line, just as if you had written

```
for var in "$@"
do
        command
        command
        . . .
done
```

Here's the third and last version of the args program:

```
$ cat args
echo Number of arguments passed is $#

for arg
do
        echo $arg
done
$ args a b c
Number of arguments passed is 3
a
b
c
$ args 'a b' c
Number of arguments passed is 2
a b
c
$
```

The while **Command**

The second type of looping command to be described in this chapter is the while. The format of this command is

```
while command_t
do
        command
        command
        ...
done
```

$command_t$ is executed and its exit status tested. If it's zero, the commands enclosed between the do and done are executed. Then $command_t$ is executed again and its exit status tested. If it's zero, the commands enclosed between the do and done are once again executed. This process continues until $command_t$ returns a nonzero exit status. At that point, execution of the loop is terminated. Execution then proceeds with the command that follows the done.

Note that the commands between the do and done might never be executed if $command_t$ returns a nonzero exit status the first time it's executed.

Here's a program called twhile that simply counts to 5:

```
$ cat twhile
i=1

while [ "$i" -le 5 ]
do
        echo $i
        i=$((i + 1))
done
$ twhile                    Run it
1
2
3
4
5
$
```

The variable i is used as the counting variable and is initially set equal to 1. Then the while loop is entered. It continues execution as long as i is less than or equal to 5. Inside the loop, the value of i is displayed at the terminal. Then it is incremented by one.

The while loop is often used in conjunction with the shift command to process a variable number of arguments typed on the command line. The next program, called prargs, prints each of the command-line arguments one per line.

```
$ cat prargs
#
# Print command line arguments one per line
#

while [ "$#" -ne 0 ]
do
        echo "$1"
        shift
done
$ prargs a b c
a
b
c
$ prargs 'a b' c
a b
c
$ prargs *
```

```
addresses
intro
lotsaspaces
names
nu
numbers
phonebook
stat
$ prargs          No arguments
$
```

While the number of arguments is not equal to zero, the value of $1 is displayed and then a shift executed. Recall that this shifts down the variables (that is, $2 to $1, $3 to $2, and so on) and also decrements $#. When the last argument has been displayed and shifted out, $# will equal zero, at which point execution of the while will be terminated. Note that if no arguments are given to prargs (as was done in the last case), the echo and shift are never executed because $# is equal to zero as soon as the loop is entered.

The until Command

The while command continues execution as long as the command listed after the while returns a zero exit status. The until command is similar to the while, only it continues execution as long as the command that follows the until returns a *nonzero* exit status. As soon as a zero exit status is returned, the loop is terminated. Here is the general format of the until:

```
until command_t
do
        command
        command
        . . .
done
```

Like the while, the commands between the do and done might never be executed if *command_t* returns a zero exit status the first time it's executed.

The until command is useful for writing programs that wait for a particular event to occur. For example, suppose that you want to see whether sandy is logged on because you have to give her something important. You could send her electronic mail, but you know that she usually doesn't get around to reading her mail until late in the day. One approach is to use the on program from Chapter 8, "Decisions, Decisions," to see whether sandy's logged on:

```
$ on sandy
sandy is not logged on
$
```

You could execute this program periodically throughout the day, until sandy eventu-
ally logs on, or you could write your own program to continually check until she
does. Let's call the program mon and have it take a single argument: the name of the
user you want to monitor. Instead of having the program continually check for that
user logging on, we'll have it check only once every minute. To do this, you have to
know about a command called sleep that suspends execution of a program for a
specified number of seconds. So the Unix command (this isn't a shell built-in)

```
sleep n
```

suspends execution of the program for *n* seconds. At the end of that interval, the
program resumes execution where it left off—with the command that immediately
follows the sleep.

```
$ cat mon
#
# Wait until a specified user logs on
#

if [ "$#" -ne 1 ]
then
        echo "Usage: mon user"
        exit 1
fi

user="$1"

#
# Check every minute for user logging on
#

until who | grep "^$user " > /dev/null
do
        sleep 60
done

#
# When we reach this point, the user has logged on
#
```

```
echo "$user has logged on"
$
```

After checking that one argument was provided, the program assigns $1 to user. Then an until loop is entered. This loop will be executed until the exit status returned by grep is zero; that is, until the specified user logs on. As long as the user isn't logged on, the body of the loop—the sleep command—is executed. This command suspends execution of the program for one minute (60 seconds). At the end of the minute, the pipeline listed after the until is re-executed and the process repeated.

When the until loop is exited—signaling that the monitored user has logged on—a message is displayed at the terminal to that effect.

```
$ mon sandy                 Time passes
sandy has logged on
$
```

Using the program as shown here is not very practical because it ties up your terminal until sandy logs on. A better idea is to run mon in the background so that you can use your terminal for other work:

```
$ mon sandy &               Run it in the background
[1] 4392                    Job number and process id
$ nroff newmemo             Do other work
   ...
sandy has logged on         Happens sometime later
```

So now you can do other work and the mon program continues executing in the background until sandy logs on, or until you log off the system.[1]

Because mon only checks once per minute for the user's logging on, it won't hog the system's resources while it's running (an important consideration when submitting programs to the background for execution).

Unfortunately, after the specified user logs on, there's a chance you might miss that one-line message (you may be cating a file and might not even notice it come and go right off your screen). Also if you're editing a file with a screen editor such as vi when the message comes, it may turn your screen into a mess, and you still might miss the message. A better alternative to writing the message to the terminal might be to mail it instead. Actually, you can let the user select his or her preference by adding an option to the program that, if selected, indicates that the message is to be mailed. If the option is not selected, the message can be displayed at the terminal.

---

[1]*All your processes are automatically terminated when you log off the system. If you want a program to continue executing after you've logged off, you can run it with the* nohup *command, or schedule it to run with* at *or from the* cron. *Consult your* Unix User's Manual *for more details.*

In the version of mon that follows, a -m option has been added for this purpose:

```
$ cat mon
#
# Wait until a specified user logs on -- version 2
#

if [ "$1" = -m ]
then
        mailopt=TRUE
        shift
else
        mailopt=FALSE
fi

if [ "$#" -eq 0  -o  "$#" -gt 1 ]
then
        echo "Usage: mon [-m] user"
        echo"    -m means to be informed by mail"
        exit 1
fi

user="$1"

#
# Check every minute for user logging on
#

until who | grep "^$user " > /dev/null
do
        sleep 60
done

#
# When we reach this point, the user has logged on
#

if [ "$mailopt" = FALSE ]
then
        echo "$user has logged on"
else
        echo "$user has logged on" | mail steve
fi
$
```

The first test checks to see whether the -m option was supplied. If it was, the characters TRUE are assigned to the variable mailopt, and shift is executed to "shift out" the first argument (moving the name of the user to be monitored to $1 and decrementing $#). If the -m option wasn't specified as the first argument, the characters FALSE are assigned to mailopt.

Execution then proceeds as in the previous version. However, this time when the loop is exited a test is made to see whether the -m option was selected. If it wasn't, the message is written to standard output; otherwise, it's mailed to steve.

```
$ mon sandy -m
Usage: mon [-m] user
        -m means to be informed by mail
$ mon -m sandy &
[1] 5435
$ vi newmemo                    Work continues
   ...
you have mail
$ mail
From steve Wed Aug 28 17:44:46 EDT 2002
sandy has logged on

?d
$
```

Of course, we could have written mon to accept the -m option as either the first or second argument, but that goes against the recommended command syntax standard, which specifies that all options should precede any other types of arguments on the command line.[2]

Also note that the old version of mon could have been executed as follows:

```
$ mon sandy | mail steve &
[1] 5522
$
```

to achieve the same net result as adding the -m option.

Two last points before leaving the discussion of mon: First, you'll probably always want to run this program in the background. It would be nice if mon itself could take care of that. Later you'll see how to do it.

---

[2]*The command syntax standard consists of a set of rules as outlined in the Utility Argument Syntax section of the POSIX standard.*

Second, the program always sends mail to steve; not very nice if someone else wants to run it. A better way is to determine the user running the program and then send him or her the mail if the -m option is selected. But how do you do that? One way is to execute the who command with the am i options and get the user name that comes back. This tells you who's logged on to the terminal that the program was run from. You can then use cut to extract the username from who's output and use that name as the recipient of the mail. All this can be done in the last if command of mon if it's changed to read as shown:

```
if [ "$#" -eq 1 ]
then
        echo "$user has logged on"
else
        runner=$(who am i | cut -c1-8)
        echo "$user has logged on" | mail $runner
fi
```

Now the program can be run by anyone, and the mail will be properly sent.

More on Loops

Breaking Out of a Loop

Sometimes you may want to make an immediate exit from a loop. To just exit from the loop (and not from the program), you can use the break command, whose format is simply

```
break
```

When the break is executed, control is sent immediately out of the loop, where execution then continues as normal with the command that follows the done.

The Unix command true serves no purpose but to return an exit status of zero. The command false also does nothing but return a nonzero exit status. If you write

```
while true
do
      ...
done
```

the while loop will theoretically be executed forever because true always returns a zero exit status. By the way, the : command also does nothing but return a zero exit status, so an "infinite" loop can also be set up with

```
while :
do
        ...
done
```

Because `false` always returns a nonzero exit status, the loop

```
until false
do
        ...
done
```

will theoretically execute forever.

The `break` command is often used to exit from these sorts of infinite loops, usually when some error condition or the end of processing is detected:

```
while true
do
        cmd=$(getcmd)

        if [ "$cmd" = quit ]
        then
                break
        else
                processcmd "$cmd"
        fi
done
```

Here the `while` loop will continue to execute the `getcmd` and `processcmd` programs until `cmd` is equal to `quit`. At that point, the `break` command will be executed, thus causing the loop to be exited.

If the `break` command is used in the form

```
break n
```

the *n* innermost loops are immediately exited, so in

```
for file
do
        ...
        while [ "$count" -lt 10 ]
        do
                ...
```

```
                if [  -n "$error" ]
                then
                        break 2
                fi
                ...
        done
        ...
done
```

both the while *and* the for loops will be exited if error is nonnull.

Skipping the Remaining Commands in a Loop

The continue command is similar to break, only it doesn't cause the loop to be exited, merely the remaining commands in the loop to be skipped. Execution of the loop then continues as normal. Like the break, an optional number can follow the continue, so

continue *n*

causes the commands in the innermost *n* loops to be skipped; but execution of the loops then continues as normal.

```
for file
do
        if [ ! -e "$file" ]
        then
                echo "$file not found!"
                continue
        fi

        #
        # Process the file
        #

        ...
done
```

Each value of file is checked to make sure that the file exists. If it doesn't, a message is printed, and further processing of the file is skipped. Execution of the loop then continues with the next value in the list. Note that the preceding example is equivalent to writing

```
for file
do
        if [ ! -e "$file" ]
```

```
        then
                echo "$file not found!"
        else
                #
                # Process the file
                #

                ...
        fi
done
```

Executing a Loop in the Background

An entire loop can be sent to the background for execution simply by placing an ampersand after the done:

```
$ for file in memo[1-4]
> do
>         run $file
> done &                      Send it to the background
[1] 9932
$
request id is laser1-85 (standard input)
request id is laser1-87 (standard input)
request id is laser1-88 (standard input)
request id is laser1-92 (standard input)
```

I/O Redirection on a Loop

You can also perform I/O redirection on the entire loop. Input redirected into the loop applies to all commands in the loop that read their data from standard input. Output redirected from the loop to a file applies to all commands in the loop that write to standard output:

```
$ for i in 1 2 3 4
> do
>         echo $i
> done > loopout            Redirect loop's output to loopout
$ cat loopout
1
2
3
4
$
```

You can override redirection of the entire loop's input or output by explicitly redirecting the input and/or output of commands inside the loop. To force input or output of a command to come from or go to the terminal, use the fact that /dev/tty always refers to your terminal. In the following loop, the echo command's output is explicitly redirected to the terminal to override the global output redirection applied to the loop:

```
for file
do
        echo "Processing file $file" > /dev/tty
        ...
done > output
```

echo's output is redirected to the terminal while the rest goes to the file output.

Naturally, you can also redirect the standard error output from a loop, simply by tacking on a 2> *file* after the done:

```
while [ "$endofdata" -ne TRUE ]
do
        ...
done 2> errors
```

Here output from all commands in the loop writing to standard error will be redirected to the file errors.

Piping Data Into and Out of a Loop

A command's output can be piped into a loop, and the entire output from a loop can be piped into another command in the expected manner. Here's a highly manufactured example of the output from a for command piped into wc:

```
$ for i in 1 2 3 4
> do
>          echo $i
> done | wc -l
      4
$
```

Typing a Loop on One Line

If you find yourself frequently executing loops directly at the terminal, you'll want to use the following shorthand notation to type the entire loop on a single line: Put a semicolon after the last item in the list and one after each command in the loop. Don't put a semicolon after the do.

Following these rules, the loop

```
for i in 1 2 3 4
do
        echo $i
done
```

becomes

```
for i in 1 2 3 4; do echo $i; done
```

And you can type it in directly this way:

```
$ for i in 1 2 3 4; do echo $i; done
1
2
3
4
$
```

The same rules apply to `while` and `until` loops.

`if` commands can also be typed on the same line using a similar format:

```
$ if [ 1 = 1 ]; then echo yes; fi
yes
$ if [ 1 = 2 ]; then echo yes; else echo no; fi
no
$
```

Note that no semicolons appear after the `then` and the `else`.

The getopts Command

Let's extend our mon program further. We'll add a `-t` option to it that specifies the time interval, in seconds, to perform the check. Now our mon program takes both `-m` and `-t` options. We'll allow it to take these options in any order on the command line, provided that if they are used, they appear before the name of the user that we're monitoring. So valid mon command lines look like this:

```
mon ann
mon -m ann
mon -t 600 ann
mon -m -t 600 ann
mon -t 600 -m ann
```

and invalid ones look like this:

mon	*Missing user name*
mon -t600 ann	*Need a space after* -t
mon ann -m	*Options must appear first*
mon -t ann	*Missing argument after* -t

If you start writing the code to allow this sort of flexibility on the command line, you will soon discover that it can start to get a bit complex. Luckily, the shell provides a built-in command called getopts that exists for the express purpose of processing command-line arguments. The general format of the command is

getopts *options variable*

The getopts command is designed to be executed inside a loop. Each time through the loop, getopts examines the next command line argument and determines whether it is a valid option. This determination is made by checking to see whether the argument begins with a minus sign and is followed by any single letter contained inside *options*. If it does, getopts stores the matching option letter inside the specified *variable* and returns a zero exit status.

If the letter that follows the minus sign is not listed in *options*, getopts stores a question mark inside *variable* before returning with a zero exit status. It also writes an error message to standard error.

If no more arguments are left on the command line or if the next argument doesn't begin with a minus sign, getopts returns a nonzero exit status.

Suppose that you want getopts to recognize the options -a, -i, and -r for a command called foo. Your getopts call might look like this:

getopts air option

Here the first argument—air—specifies the three acceptable options to the command, and option specifies the variable that getopts will use as previously described.

The getopts command permits options to be "stacked" together on the command line. This is done by following a single minus sign with one or more consecutive options letters. For example, our foo command can be executed like this:

foo -a -r -i

or like this:

foo -ari

using this stacking feature.

The getopts command also handles the case where an option must be followed by an argument. For example, the new -t option to be added to the mon command requires a following argument. To handle options that take arguments, getopts requires that at least one whitespace character separate the option from the argument. Furthermore, such options cannot be stacked.

To indicate to getopts that an option takes a following argument, you write a colon character after the option letter on the getopts command line. So our mon program, which takes -m and -t options, should call getopts like this:

```
getopts mt: option
```

If getopts doesn't find an argument after an option that requires one, it stores a question mark inside the specified variable and writes an error message to standard error. Otherwise, it stores the actual argument inside a special variable called OPTARG.

One final note about getopts: Another special variable called OPTIND is used by the command. This variable is initially set to one and is updated each time getopts returns to reflect the number of the *next* command-line argument to be processed.

Here is the third version of mon that uses the getopts command to process the command-line arguments. It also incorporates the previously noted change to send mail to the user running the program.

```
$ cat mon
#
# Wait until a specified user logs on -- version 3
#

# Set up default values

mailopt=FALSE
interval=60

# process command options

while getopts mt: option
do
        case "$option"
        in
                m) mailopt=TRUE;;
                t) interval=$OPTARG;;
                \?) echo "Usage: mon [-m] [-t n] user"
                    echo "    -m means to be informed by mail"
                    echo "    -t means check every n secs."
```

```
                exit 1;;
        esac
done

# Make sure a user name was specified

if [ "$OPTIND" -gt "$#" ]
then
        echo "Missing user name!"
        exit 2
fi

shiftcount=$((OPTIND - 1))
shift $shiftcount
user=$1

#
# Check for user logging on
#

until who | grep "^$user " > /dev/null
do
        sleep $interval
done

#
# When we reach this point, the user has logged on
#

if [ "$mailopt" = FALSE ]
then
        echo "$user has logged on"
else
        runner=$(who am i | cut -c1-8)
        echo "$user has logged on" | mail $runner
fi
```

```
$ mon -m
Missing user name!
$ mon -x fred                    Illegal option
mon: illegal option -- x
```

```
Usage: mon [-m] [-t n] user
    -m means to be informed by mail
    -t means check every n secs.
$ mon -m -t 600 ann &                    Check every 10 min. for ann
[1] 5792
$
```

When the line

```
mon -m -t 600 ann &
```

is executed, the following occurs inside the `while` loop in mon: getopts is executed, and it stores the character m inside the variable option, sets OPTIND to two, and returns a zero exit status. The case command is then executed to determine what was stored inside option. A match on the character m indicates that the "send mail" option was selected, so mailopt is set to TRUE. (Note that the ? inside the case is quoted. This is to remove its special meaning as a pattern-matching character from the shell.)

The second time getopts is executed, getopts stores the character t inside option, stores the next command-line argument (600) inside OPTARG, sets OPTIND to three, and returns a zero exit status. The case command then matches the character t stored inside option. The code associated with that case copies the value of 600 that was stored in OPTARG into the variable interval.

The third time getopts is executed, getopts returns a nonzero exit status, indicating the end of options. The program then checks the value of OPTIND against $# to make sure that the username was typed on the command line. If OPTIND is greater than $#, then no more arguments remain on the command line and the user forgot the username argument. Otherwise, the shift command is executed to move the username argument into $1. The actual number of places to shift is one less than the value of OPTIND.

The rest of the mon program remains as before; the only change is the use of the interval variable to specify the number of seconds to sleep.

Exercises

1. Modify the prargs program to precede each argument by its number. So typing

   ```
   prargs a 'b c' d
   ```

   should give the following output:

   ```
   1: a
   2: b c
   3: d
   ```

2. Modify the `mon` program to also print the `tty` number that the user logs on to. That is, the output should say

```
sandy logged onto tty13
```

if sandy logs on to `tty13`.

3. Add a `-f` option to `mon` to have it periodically check for the existence of a file (ordinary file or directory) instead of for a user logging on. So typing

```
mon -f /usr/spool/uucppublic/steve/newmemo &
```

should cause `mon` to periodically check for the existence of the indicated file and inform you when it does (by displaying a message or by mail if the `-m` option is also selected).

4. Add a `-n` option to `mon` that inverts the monitoring function. So

```
mon -n sandy
```

checks for sandy logging off the system, and

```
mon -n -f /tmp/dataout &
```

periodically checks for the removal of the specified file.

5. Write a program called `collect` that runs in the background and counts the number of users logged in at the end of each interval. Allow the interval to be specified with a `-t` option (see the previous exercise), with the default 10 minutes.

6. Write a shell program called `wgrep` that searches a file for a given pattern, just as `grep` does. For each line in the file that matches, print a "window" around the matching line. That is, print the line preceding the match, the matching line, and the line following the match. Be sure to properly handle the special cases where the pattern matches the first line of the file and where the pattern matches the last line of the file.

7. Modify `wgrep` to take an optional `-w` option that specifies the window size; so

```
wgrep -w 3 UNIX text
```

should print three lines before and after each line from `text` that contains the pattern `UNIX`.

8. Modify `wgrep` to take a variable number of filenames as arguments. Precede each output line with the name of the file in which the match occurs (as `grep` does).

10
Reading and Printing Data

In this chapter you'll learn how to read data from the terminal or from a file using the read command and how to print formatted data to standard output using the printf command.

The read Command

The general format of the read command is

read *variables*

When this command is executed, the shell reads a line from standard input and assigns the first word read to the first variable listed in *variables*, the second word read to the second variable, and so on. If there are more words on the line than there are variables listed, the excess words get assigned to the last variable. So for example, the command

read x y

reads a line from standard input, storing the first word read in the variable x, and the remainder of the line in the variable y. It follows from this that the command

read text

reads and stores an entire line into the shell variable text.

A Program to Copy Files

Let's put the read command to work. We'll write a simplified version of the cp command that will be a bit more user friendly than the standard Unix one. We'll call it mycp, and we'll have it take two arguments: the source file and the destination file. If the destination file already exists, we'll tell the user and then ask him (or her) if he wants to proceed with the copy. If the answer is "yes," we'll go ahead with it; otherwise, we won't.

```
$ cat mycp
#
# Copy a file
#

if [ "$#" -ne 2 ]
then
        echo "Usage: mycp from to"
        exit 1
fi

from="$1"
to="$2"

#
# See if the destination file already exists
#

if [ -e "$to" ]
then
        echo "$to already exists; overwrite (yes/no)?"
        read answer

        if [ "$answer" != yes ]
        then
                echo "Copy not performed"
                exit 0
        fi
fi

#
# Either destination doesn't exist or "yes" was typed
#

cp $from $to        # proceed with the copy
$
```

And now for the test:

```
$ ls                        What files are around?
addresses
intro
lotsaspaces
mycp
names
nu
numbers
phonebook
stat
$ mycp                      No arguments
Usage: mycp from to
$ mycp names names2         Make a copy of names
$ ls -l names*              Did it work?
-rw-r--r--  1 steve    steve      43 Jul  20 11:12 names
-rw-r--r--  1 steve    steve      43 Jul  21 14:16 names2
$ mycp names numbers        Try to overwrite an existing file
numbers already exists; overwrite (yes/no)?
no
Copy not performed
$
```

To complete the test cases, try answering yes and ensuring that the program proceeds with the copy.

There are a few things worthy of mention with the mycp program. First, if the file already exists, the echo command that prompts for the yes/no response is executed. The read command that follows causes the shell to wait for you to type something in. Note that the shell does not prompt you when it's waiting for you to enter data; it's up to you to add your own prompt message to the program.

The data that is typed is stored in the variable answer and is then tested against the characters "yes" to determine whether the copy is to proceed. The quotes around answer in the test

```
[ "$answer" != yes]
```

are necessary in case the user just presses the Enter key without typing any data. In that case, the shell would store a null value in answer, and test would issue an error message if the quotes were omitted.

Special echo **Escape Characters**

A slight annoyance with mycp is that after the echo command is executed to alert the user that the file already exists, the response that is typed by the user appears on the next line. This happens because the echo command always automatically displays a terminating newline character after the last argument.

This can be suppressed if the last two characters given to echo are the special *escape* characters \c. This tells echo to leave the cursor right where it is after displaying the last argument and not to go to the next line. So if you changed the echo command in mycp to read like this:

```
echo "$to already exists; overwrite (yes/no)? \c"
```

the user's input would be typed right after the message on the same line. Bear in mind that the \c is interpreted by echo and not by the shell, meaning that it must be quoted so that the backslash makes it to echo.

echo interprets other special characters. These must each be preceded by a backslash. They're summarized in Table 10.1.

TABLE 10.1   echo Escape Characters

Character	Prints
\b	Backspace
\c	The line without a terminating newline
\f	Formfeed
\n	Newline
\r	Carriage return
\t	Tab character
\\	Backslash character
\0nnn	The character whose ASCII value is *nnn*, where *nnn* is a one- to three-digit octal number

An Improved Version of mycp

Suppose that you have a program called prog1 in your current directory and you want to copy it into your bin directory directly below. Take another look at the mycp program and determine what happens if you type in

```
mycp prog1 bin
```

The -e test on bin will succeed (because –e tests for existence of a file), and mycp will display the "already exists" message and wait for a yes/no answer.

If the second argument is a directory, mycp should check to see whether the from file exists *inside* this directory. The next version of mycp performs this check. It also has the modified echo command that includes the \c to suppress the terminating newline.

```
$ cat mycp
#
# Copy a file -- version 2
#

if [ "$#" -ne 2 ]
then
        echo "Usage: mycp from to"
        exit 1
fi

from="$1"
to="$2"

#
# See if destination file is a directory
#

if [ -d "$to" ]
then
        to="$to/$(basename $from)"
fi

#
# See if the destination file already exists
#

if [ -e "$to" ]
then
        echo "$to already exists; overwrite (yes/no)? \c"
        read answer

        if [ "$answer" != yes ]
        then
                echo "Copy not performed"
                exit 0
        fi
fi
```

```
#
# Either destination doesn't exist or ''yes'' was typed
#

cp $from $to         # proceed with the copy
$
```

If the destination file is a directory, the program changes the variable to to more precisely identify the file inside the directory as $to/$(basename $from). This ensures that the following test on the existence of the ordinary file $to will be done on the file in the directory, not on the directory itself as the previous version of mycp did. The basename command gives the base filename of its argument (for example, basename /usr/bin/troff gives troff; basename troff gives troff). This ensures that the copy is made to the correct place. (For example, if mycp /tmp/data bin is typed, where bin is a directory, you want to copy /tmp/data into bin/data and not into bin/tmp/data.)

Here's some sample output. Note the effect of the \c escape characters.

```
$ ls                Check out current directory
bin
prog1
$ ls bin            Look inside bin
lu
nu
prog1
$ mycp prog1 prog2  Simple case
$ mycp prog1 bin    Copy into directory
bin/prog1 already exists; overwrite (yes/no)? yes
$
```

A Final Version of mycp

The last modification to mycp makes the program virtually equivalent to the standard Unix cp command by allowing a variable number of arguments. Recall that any number of files can precede the name of a directory, as in

```
cp prog1 prog2 greetings bin
```

To modify mycp to accept any number of files, you can use this approach:

1. Get each argument but the last from the command line and store it in the shell variable filelist.

2. Store the last argument in the variable to.

3. If $to is not a directory, there must be exactly two arguments.

4. For each file in $filelist, check whether the file already exists. If it does, ask the user whether the file should be overwritten. If the answer is "yes," or if the file doesn't already exist, add the file to the variable copylist.

5. If copylist is nonnull, copy the files in it to $to.

If this algorithm seems a bit fuzzy, perhaps the program, followed by a detailed explanation, will help clear things up. Note the modified command usage message.

```
$ cat mycp
#
# Copy a file -- final version
#

numargs=$#                      # save this for later use
filelist=
copylist=


#
# Process the arguments, storing all but the last in filelist
#

while [ "$#" -gt 1 ]
do
        filelist="$filelist $1"
        shift
done

to="$1"


#
# If less than two args, or if more than two args and last arg
# is not a directory, then issue an error message
#

if [ "$numargs" -lt 2  -o  "$numargs" -gt 2  -a  ! -d "$to" ]
then
    echo "Usage: mycp file1 file2"
    echo "       mycp file(s) dir"
    exit 1
fi
```

```
#
# Sequence through each file in filelist
#

for from in $filelist
do
    #
    # See if destination file is a directory
    #

    if [ -d "$to" ]
    then
            tofile="$to/$(basename $from)"
    else
            tofile="$to"
    fi

    #
    # Add file to copylist if file doesn't already exist
    # or if user says it's okay to overwrite
    #

    if [ -e "$tofile" ]
    then
            echo "$tofile already exists; overwrite (yes/no)? \c"
            read answer

            if [ "$answer" = yes ]
            then
                    copylist="$copylist $from"
            fi
    else
            copylist="$copylist $from"
    fi
done

#
# Now do the copy -- first make sure there's something to copy
#
if [ -n "$copylist" ]
then
        cp $copylist $to        # proceed with the copy
fi
$
```

```
$ ls                          See what's around
bin
lu
names
prog1
prog2
$ ls bin                      And what's in bin?
lu
nu
prog1
$ mycp                        No arguments
Usage: mycp file1 file2
       mycp file(s) dir
$ mycp names prog1 prog2      Last arg isn't a directory
Usage: mycp file1 file2
       mycp file(s) dir
$ mycp names prog1 prog2 lu bin    Legitimate use
bin/prog1 already exists; overwrite (yes/no)? yes
bin/lu already exists; overwrite (yes/no)? no
$ ls -l bin                   See what happened
total 5
-rw-r--r--   1 steve    steve    543 Jul 19 14:10 lu
-rw-r--r--   1 steve    steve    949 Jul 21 17:11 names
-rw-r--r--   1 steve    steve     38 Jul 19 09:55 nu
-rw-r--r--   1 steve    steve    498 Jul 21 17:11 prog1
-rw-r--r--   1 steve    steve    498 Jul 21 17:11 prog2
$
```

In the last case, prog1 was overwritten and lu wasn't, as per the user's request.

When the program starts execution, it saves the number of arguments in the variable numargs. This is done because it's changed later in the program by the shift command.

Next a loop is entered that is executed as long as the number of arguments is greater than one. The purpose of this loop is to get the last argument on the line. While doing this, the loop stashes away the first argument into the shell variable filelist, which contains a list of all the files to be copied. The statement

```
filelist="$filelist $1"
```

says to take the previous value of filelist, add on a space followed by the value of $1, and then store the result back into filelist. Then the shift command is executed to "move" all the arguments over by one. Eventually, $# will be equal to one, and the loop will be exited. At that point, filelist will contain a space-delimited list of all the files to be copied, and $1 will contain the last argument, which is the destination file (or directory). To see how this works, consider execution of the while loop when the command is executed as

```
mycp names prog1 prog2 lu bin
```

Figure 10.1 depicts the changing values of the variables through each iteration of the loop. The first line shows the state of the variables before the loop is entered.

```
$#  $1     $2     $3    $4   $5    filelist
5   names  prog1  prog2 lu   bin   null
4   prog1  prog2  lu    bin        names
3   prog2  lu     bin              names prog1
2   lu     bin                     names prog1 prog2
1   bin                            names prog1 prog2 lu
```

FIGURE 10.1   Processing command-line arguments.

After the loop is exited, the last argument contained in $1 is stored in the variable to. Next, a test is made to ensure that at least two arguments were typed on the command line and if more than two were typed, that the last argument is a directory. If either condition isn't satisfied, usage information is displayed to the user, and the program exits with a status of 1.

Following this, a for loop is entered for the purpose of individually examining each file in the list to see whether it already exists. If it does, the user is prompted as before. If the user wants to overwrite the file, or if the file doesn't already exist, the file is added to the shell variable copylist. The technique used here is the same used to accumulate the arguments inside filelist.

When the for loop is exited, copylist contains a list of all the files to be copied. This list can be null if each of the destination files exists and the user types "no" for each one. So a test is made to ensure copylist is nonnull, and if it is, the copy is performed.

Take some time to review the logic of the final version of mycp; it does a good job at illustrating many of the features you've learned so far in this book. Some exercises at the end of this chapter will help test your understanding of this program.

A Menu-Driven Phone Program

One nice thing about the read command is that it enables you to write menu-driven shell programs. As an example, we'll return to our phone book programs add, lu, and rem and gather their execution together under one program, which we'll call rolo (for rolodex program). rolo will display a list of choices to the user and then execute the appropriate program depending on the selection. It will also prompt for the proper arguments to the program. Here, then, is the program:

```
$ cat rolo
#
# rolo - rolodex program to look up, add, and
#        remove people from the phone book
#

#
# Display menu
#

echo '
     Would you like to:

          1. Look someone up
          2. Add someone to the phone book
          3. Remove someone from the phone book

     Please select one of the above (1-3): \c'

#
# Read and process selection
#

read choice
echo
case "$choice"
in
     1) echo "Enter name to look up: \c"
        read name
        lu "$name";;
     2) echo "Enter name to be added: \c"
        read name
        echo "Enter number: \c"
        read number
```

```
            add "$name" "$number";;
        3) echo "Enter name to be removed: \c"
           read name
           rem "$name";;
        *) echo "Bad choice";;
esac
$
```

A single echo command is used to display the menu at the terminal, taking advantage of the fact that the quotes preserve the embedded newline characters. Then the read command is executed to get the selection from the user and store it in the variable choice.

A case statement is next entered to determine what choice was made. If choice 1 was selected, the user wants to look up someone in the phone book. In that case, the user is asked to enter the name to be looked up, and the lu program is called, passing it the name typed in by the user as the argument. Note that the double quotes around name in

```
lu "$name"
```

are necessary to ensure that two or more words typed in by the user are handed over to lu as a single argument.

A similar sequence occurs if the user selects menu items 2 or 3.

The programs lu, rem, and add are from earlier chapters (lu is from page 137 rem from page 167, and add from page 138).

Here are some sample runs of rolo:

$ rolo

```
    Would you like to:

        1.  Look someone up
        2.  Add someone to the phone book
        3.  Remove someone from the phone book

Please select one of the above (1-3): 2
Enter name to be added: El Coyote
Enter number: 212-555-3232
$ rolo                        Try it again

    Would you like to:
```

```
        1. Look someone up
        2. Add someone to the phone book
        3. Remove someone from the phone book

     Please select one of the above (1-3): 1

Enter name to look up: Coyote
El Coyote        212-555-3232
$ rolo                          Once again

     Would you like to:

        1. Look someone up
        2. Add someone to the phone book
        3. Remove someone from the phone book

     Please select one of the above (1-3): 4
Bad choice
$
```

When an invalid choice is entered, the program simply displays Bad choice and then terminates. A friendlier approach would be to reprompt the user until a proper choice is made. This can be done by enclosing the entire program inside an until loop that will be executed until a valid selection is made. To determine when a valid choice has been made, we can test a variable in the until that won't be assigned a value in the program until either 1, 2, or 3 is selected by the user.

Another change to make to rolo involves the way it will be used. Because the most common operation performed will be one of lookup, there will probably be a tendency on the part of the user to avoid typing rolo, then making selection 1, and then typing the name to be found when instead he or she can still type in

lu *name*

directly. Given all this, it might be a good idea to allow rolo to take command-line arguments. If any arguments are typed, rolo can assume that a lookup is being requested and just call lu directly. So if the user wants to perform a quick lookup, he or she can type rolo followed by the name. On the other hand, if the user wants to see the menu, typing just rolo causes the program to display its menu and prompt for a choice.

The preceding two changes (looping until a valid choice is selected and doing a quick lookup) were added to version 2 of rolo that is shown next.

```
$ cat rolo
#
# rolo - rolodex program to look up, add, and
#     remove people from the phone book -- version 2
#


#
# If arguments are supplied, then do a lookup
#

if [ "$#" -ne 0 ]
then
        lu "$@"
        exit
fi

validchoice=""          # set it null

#
# Loop until a valid selection is made
#

until [ -n "$validchoice" ]
do
        #
        # Display menu
        #

        echo '

        Would you like to:

            1. Look someone up
            2. Add someone to the phone book
            3. Remove someone from the phone book

        Please select one of the above (1-3): \c'

        #
        # Read and process selection
        #
        read choice
```

```
            echo

            case "$choice"
            in
                1) echo "Enter name to look up: \c"
                        read name
                        lu "$name"
                        validchoice=TRUE;;
                2) echo "Enter name to be added: \c"
                        read name
                        echo "Enter number: \c"
                        read number
                        add "$name" "$number"
                        validchoice=TRUE;;
                3) echo "Enter name to be removed: \c"
                        read name
                        rem "$name"
                        validchoice=TRUE;;
                *) echo "Bad choice";;
            esac
done
$
```

If $# is nonzero, lu is called directly with the arguments typed on the command line. Then the program exits. Otherwise, the until loop is executed until the variable validchoice is nonnull. The only way it can ever become nonnull is if the command

```
validchoice=TRUE
```

is executed inside the case on selection of either 1, 2, or 3. Otherwise, the program continues to loop until one of these three choices is made.

```
$ rolo Bill                         Quick lookup
Billy Bach      201-555-7618
$ rolo                              Let's have the menu this time
        Would you like to:

            1. Look someone up
            2. Add someone to the phone book
            3. Remove someone from the phone book

        Please select one of the above (1-3): 4
Bad choice
```

```
Would you like to:

    1. Look someone up
    2. Add someone to the phone book
    3. Remove someone from the phone book

Please select one of the above (1-3): 0
Bad choice


Would you like to:

    1. Look someone up
    2. Add someone to the phone book
    3. Remove someone from the phone book

Please select one of the above (1-3): 1
```

```
Enter name to look up: Tony
Tony Iannino    973-555-1295
$
```

The $$ Variable and Temporary Files

If two or more people on your system use the rolo program at the same time, a potential problem may occur. Look at the rem program and see whether you can spot it. The problem occurs with the temporary file /tmp/phonebook that is used to create a new version of the phone book file.

```
grep -v "$name" phonebook > /tmp/phonebook
mv /tmp/phonebook phonebook
```

If more than one person uses rolo to remove an entry at the same time, there's a chance that the phone book file can get messed up because the same temporary file will be used by all rolo users.[1] Naturally, the chances of this happening (that is, the preceding two commands being executed at the same time by more than one user) are rather small, but, nevertheless there still is that chance. Anyway, it brings up an important point when dealing with temporary files in general.

---

[1] *Actually, it depends on the users' default file creation mask (known as umask). If one person has created /tmp/phonebook and it's not writable by anyone else, the next person who comes along and tries to create it will get an error message from the shell. The net result is that the first user's file will get properly updated, and the second user's won't; neither file will get corrupted.*

When writing shell programs to be run by more than one person, make your temporary files unique. One way is to create the temporary file in the user's home directory, for example. Another way is to choose a temporary filename that will be unique for that particular process. To do this, you can use the special $$ shell variable, which contains the process id number (PID) of the current process:

```
$ echo $$
4668
$ ps
  PID  TTY TIME COMMAND
  4668 co  0:09 sh
  6470 co  0:03 ps
$
```

As you can see, $$ is equal to the process id number of your login shell. Because each process on the Unix system is given a unique process id number, using the value of $$ in the name of a file minimizes the possibility of another process using the same file. So you can replace the two lines from rem with these

```
grep -v "$name" phonebook > /tmp/phonebook$$
mv /tmp/phonebook$$ phonebook
```

to circumvent any potential problems. Each person running rolo will run it as a different process, so the temporary file used in each case will be different.

The Exit Status from read

read always returns an exit status of zero unless an end of file condition is detected on the input. If the data is coming from the terminal, this means that Ctrl+d has been typed. If the data is coming from a file, it means that there's no more data to read from the file.

Knowing about the exit status returned by read makes it easy to write a loop that will read any number of lines of data from a file or from the terminal. The next program, called addi, reads in lines containing pairs of integers. Each pair of numbers is summed, and the result written to standard output.

```
$ cat addi
#
# add pairs of integers on standard input
#
```

```
while read n1 n2
do
        echo $((n1 + n2))
done
$
```

The while loop is executed as long as the read command returns an exit status of zero; that is, as long as there's still data to be read. Inside the loop, the two values read from the line (presumably integers—no error checking is done here) are summed and the result written to standard output by echo.

```
$ addi
10 25
35
-5 12
7
123 3
126
Ctrl+d
$
```

It goes without saying that standard input for addi can be redirected, as can standard output:

```
$ cat data
1234 7960
593 -595
395 304
3234 999
-394 -493
$ addi < data > sums
$ cat sums
9194
-2
699
4233
-887
$
```

The following program, called number, is a simplified version of the standard Unix nl command: It takes one or more files given as arguments and displays them preceded by line numbers. If no arguments are supplied, it uses standard input instead.

```
$ cat number
#
```

```
# Number lines from files given as argument or from
# standard input if none supplied
#

lineno=1

cat $* |
while read line
do
        echo "$lineno: $line"
        lineno=$((lineno + 1))
done
$
```

The variable lineno—the line number count—is initially set to 1. Then the arguments typed to number are given to cat to be collectively written to standard output. If no arguments are supplied, $* will be null, and cat will be passed no arguments. This will cause it to read from standard input.

The output from cat is piped into the while loop. For each line read by read, the line is echoed at the terminal, preceded by the value of lineno, whose value is then incremented by one.

```
$ number phonebook
1: Alice Chebba      973-555-2015
2: Barbara Swingle   201-555-9257
3: Billy Bach        201-555-7618
4: El Coyote         212-555-3232
5: Liz Stachiw       212-555-2298
6: Susan Goldberg    201-555-7776
7: Teri Zak          201-555-6000
8: Tony Iannino      973-555-1295
$ who | number                      Try from standard input
1: root      console  Jul 25 07:55
2: pat       tty03    Jul 25 09:26
3: steve     tty04    Jul 25 10:58
4: george    tty13    Jul 25 08:05
$
```

Note that number won't work too well for lines that contain backslashes or leading whitespace characters. The following example illustrates this point.

```
$ number
            Here are some backslashes: \ \*
1: Here are some backslashes: *
```

```
$
```

Leading whitespace characters are removed from any line that's read. The backslash characters are also interpreted by the shell when it reads the line. You can use the -r option to read to prevent it from interpreting the backslash character. If we change the

```
while read line
```

in number to

```
while read -r line
```

the output will look better:

```
$ number
        Here are some backslashes: \ \*
1: Here are some backslashes: \ \*
$
```

In Chapter 12, "More on Parameters," you'll learn how to preserve the leading whitespace characters and also how to have some control over the parsing of the input data.

The printf Command

Although echo is adequate for displaying simple messages, sometimes you'll want to print *formatted* output: for example, lining up columns of data. Unix systems provide the printf command. Those of you familiar with the C programming language will notice many similarities.

The general format of the printf command is

```
printf "format" arg1 arg2 ...
```

where *format* is a string that describes how the remaining arguments are to be displayed. (Note that the format string is a single argument, so it's a good idea to get into the habit of enclosing it in quotes because it often contains whitespace.) Characters in the format string that are not preceded by a percent sign (%) are written to standard output. One or more characters preceded by a percent sign are called *conversion specifications* and tell printf how the corresponding argument should be displayed. So, for each percent sign in the format string there should be a corresponding argument, except for the special conversion specification %%, which causes a single percent sign to be displayed.

Here's a simple example of printf:

```
$ printf "This is a number: %d\n" 10
This is a number: 10
$
```

printf doesn't add a newline character to its output like echo; however, printf understands the same escape characters that echo does (refer to Table 10.1 earlier in this chapter), so adding \n to the end of the format string causes the prompt to appear on the next line.

Although this is a simple case that could easily be handled by echo, it helps to illustrate how the conversion specification (%d) is interpreted by printf: When the format string is scanned by printf, it outputs each character in the string without modification until it sees the percent sign; then it reads the d and recognizes that the %d should be replaced by the next argument, which must be an integer number. After that argument (10) is sent to standard output, printf sees the \n and outputs a newline.

Table 10.2 summarizes the different conversion specification characters.

TABLE 10.2   printf Conversion Specification Characters

Character	Use for Printing
d	Integers
u	Unsigned integers
o	Octal integers
x	Hexadecimal integers, using a-f
X	Hexadecimal integers, using A-F
c	Single characters
s	Literal strings
b	Strings containing backslash escape characters
%	Percent signs

The first five conversion specification characters are all used for displaying integers. %d displays signed integers, and %u displays unsigned integers; %u can also be used to display the positive representation of a negative number (note that the result is machine dependent). By default, integers displayed as octal or hexadecimal numbers do not have a leading 0 or 0x, but we'll show you how to enable this later in this section.

Strings are printed using %s or %b. %s is used to print strings literally, without any processing of backslash escape characters; %b is used to force interpretation of the backslash escape characters in the string argument.

Here are a few `printf` examples:

```
$ printf "The octal value for %d is %o\n" 20 20
The octal value for 20 is 24
$ printf "The hexadecimal value for %d is %x\n" 30 30
The hexadecimal value for 30 is 1e
$ printf "The unsigned value for %d is %u\n" -1000 -1000
The unsigned value for -1000 is 4294966296
$ printf "This string contains a backslash escape: %s\n" "test\nstring"
This string contains a backslash escape: test\nstring
$ printf "This string contains an interpreted escape: %b\n" "test\nstring"
This string contains an interpreted escape: test string
$ printf "A string: %s and a character: %c\n" hello A
A string: hello and a character: A
$
```

In the last `printf`, %c is used to display a single character. If the corresponding argument is longer than one character, only the first is displayed:

```
$ printf "Just the first character: %c\n" abc
a
$
```

The general format of a conversion specification is

%[*flags*][*width*][*.precision*]*type*

The *type* is the conversion specification character from Table 10.2. As you can see, only the percent sign and *type* are required; the other parameters are called *modifiers* and are optional. Valid *flags* are -, +, #, and the space character. - left justifies the value being printed; this will make more sense when we discuss the *width* modifier. + causes `printf` to precede integers with a + or - sign (by default, only negative integers are printed with a sign). # causes `printf` to precede octal integers with 0 and hexadecimal integers with 0x or 0X for %#x or %#X, respectively. The space character causes `printf` to precede positive integers with a space and negative integers with a -.

```
$ printf "%+d\n%+d\n%+d\n" 10 -10 20
+10
-10
+20
$ printf "% d\n% d\n% d\n" 10 -10 20
 10
-10
 20
$ printf "%#o %#x\n" 100 200
0144 0xc8
$
```

As you can see, using + or space as the *flag* lines up columns of positive and negative numbers nicely.

The *width* modifier is a positive number that specifies the minimum *field width* for printing an argument. The argument is right justified within this field unless the – flag is used:

```
$ printf "%20s%20s\n" string1 string2
             string1             string2
$ printf "%-20s%-20s\n" string1 string2
string1             string2
$ printf "%5d%5d%5d\n" 1 10 100
    1   10  100
$ printf "%5d%5d%5d\n" -1 -10 -100
   -1  -10 -100
$ printf "%-5d%-5d%-5d\n" 1 10 100
1    10   100
$
```

The *width* modifier can be useful for lining up columns of text or numbers (note that signs for numbers and leading 0, 0x, and 0X characters are counted as part of the argument's width). The *width* specifies a *minimum* size for the field; if the width of an argument exceeds *width*, it is not truncated.

The *.precision* modifier is a positive number that specifies a minimum number of digits to be displayed for %d, %u, %o, %x, and %X. This results in *zero padding* on the left of the value:

```
$ printf "%.5d %.4X\n" 10 27
00010 001B
$
```

For strings, the *.precision* modifier specifies the maximum number of characters to be printed from the string; if the string is longer than *precision* characters, it is truncated on the right:

```
$ printf "%.5s\n" abcdefg
abcde
$
```

A *width* can be combined with *.precision* to specify both a field width and zero padding (for numbers) or truncation (for strings):

```
$ printf ":%#10.5x:%5.4x:%5.4d\n" 1 10 100
:   0x00001: 000a: 0100
$ printf ":%9.5s:\n" abcdefg
:    abcde:
$ printf ":%-9.5s:\n" abcdefg
:abcde    :
$
```

Finally, if a * is used in place of a number for *width* or *precision*, the argument *preceding* the value to be printed must be a number and will be used as the width or precision, respectively. If a * is used in place of both, two integer arguments must precede the value being printed and are used for the width and precision:

```
$ printf "%*s%*.*s\n" 12 "test one" 10 2 "test two"
    test one        te
$ printf "%12s%10.2s\n" "test one" "test two"
    test one        te
$
```

As you can see, the two `printf`s in this example produce the same results. In the first `printf`, 12 is used as the width for the first string, 10 as the width for the second string, and 2 as the precision for the second string. In the second `printf`, these numbers are specified as part of the conversion specification.

Table 10.3 summarizes the various conversion specification modifiers.

TABLE 10.3   `printf` Conversion Specification Modifiers

Modifier	Meaning
flags	
-	Left justify value.
+	Precede integer with + or -.
(space)	Precede positive integer with space character.
#	Precede octal integer with 0, hexadecimal integer with 0x or 0X.

TABLE 10.3   Continued

Modifier	Meaning
width	Minimum width of field; * means use next argument as width.
precision	Minimum number of digits to display for integers; maximum number of characters to display for strings; * means use next argument as precision.

Here's a simple example that uses `printf` to align two columns of numbers from a file:

```
$ cat align
#
# Align two columns of numbers
# (works for numbers up to 12 digits long, including sign)

cat $* |
while read number1 number2
do
        printf "%12d %12d\n" $number1 $number2
done
$ cat data
1234 7960
593 -595
395 304
3234 999
-394 -493
$ align data
        1234         7960
         593         -595
         395          304
        3234          999
        -394         -493
$
```

In Chapters 12, 14, and 15 you'll see more uses for `printf`. But first try your hand at the following exercises.

Exercises

1. What happens to `mycp` if one or more of the files to be copied doesn't exist? Can you make any suggestions to better handle the situation?

2. What happens to `mycp` if one of the filenames contains a character that has a special meaning to the shell such as ; or |?

3. Write a program called `mymv` that does with the `mv` command what `mycp` does with the `cp` command. How many changes did you have to make to `mycp` to produce this new program?

4. Modify `mycp` to prompt for arguments if none are supplied. A typical execution of the modified version should look like this:

```
$ mycp
Source file name? voucher
Destination file name? voucher.sv
$
```

Make sure that the program allows one or both of the files to be specified with filename substitution characters.

5. Add a `-n` option to `mycp` that suppresses the normal check for the existence of the destination files.

6. Modify `mycp` to use `sed` instead of the `while` loop to process the arguments typed on the command line.

7. Modify the `rem` program used by `rolo` so that if multiple entries are found, the program will prompt the user for the entry to be removed.

Here's a sample session:

```
$ rolo
    ...
    Please select one of the above (1-3): 3

Enter name to be removed: Susan

More than one match; please select the one to remove:
Susan Goldberg     Remove (y/n)? n
Susan Topple       Remove (y/n)? y
$
```

8. Modify `rolo` so that the menu is redisplayed after each selection is made and processed. To allow the user to get out of this, add another selection to the menu to exit from the program.

9. What happens to the `rolo` program if just an Enter is given as the name for the add, look up, or remove options?

10. Modify `lu` to use `printf` to print the name and phone number so that they line up in columns for names up to 40 characters in length (Hint: use `cut -f` and the fact that the fields in the `phonebook` are separated by tabs).

11

Your Environment

When you log on to the system, you're effectively given your own copy of the shell program. This shell maintains what's known as your *environment*—an environment that is distinct from other users on the system. This environment is maintained from the moment you log on until the moment you log off. In this chapter you'll learn about this environment in detail, and you'll see how it relates to writing and running programs.

Local Variables

Type the following program called vartest into your computer:

```
$ cat vartest
echo :$x:
$
```

vartest consists of a solitary echo command that displays the value of the variable x, surrounded by colons. Now assign any value you want to the variable x from your terminal:

```
$ x=100
```

Here we chose 100. Question: What do you think will be displayed when vartest is now executed? Answer:

```
$ vartest
::
$
```

vartest doesn't know about the value of x. Therefore, its value is null. The variable x that was assigned the value 100 in the login shell is known as a *local* variable. The reason why it has this name will become clear shortly.

Here's another example. This program is called `vartest2`:

```
$ cat vartest2
x=50
echo :$x:
$ x=100
$ vartest2                    Execute it
:50:
$
```

Now the question is: What's the value of x?

```
$ echo $x
100
$
```

So you see that `vartest2` didn't change the value of x that you set equal to `100` in your login shell.

Subshells

The behavior exhibited by `vartest` and `vartest2` is due to the fact that these two programs are run as *subshells* by your login shell. A subshell is, for all intents and purposes, an entirely new shell executed by your login shell to run the desired program. So when you ask your login shell to execute `vartest`, it starts up a new shell to execute the program. Whenever a new shell runs, it runs in its own environment, with its own set of local variables. *A subshell has no knowledge of local variables that were assigned values by the login shell (the "parent" shell).* Furthermore, a subshell cannot change the value of a variable in the parent shell, as evidenced by `vartest2`.

Let's review the process that goes on here. Before executing `vartest2`, your login shell has a variable called x that has been assigned the value `100` (assume for now that this is the only variable defined in the shell). This is depicted in Figure 11.1.

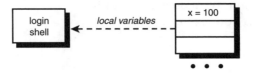

FIGURE 11.1   Login shell with x=100.

When you ask to have `vartest2` executed, your login shell starts up a subshell to run it, giving it an empty list of local variables to start with (see Figure 11.2).

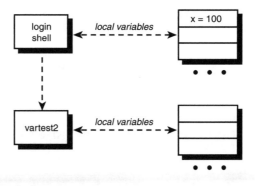

FIGURE 11.2   Login shell executes `vartest2`.

After the first command in `vartest2` is executed (that assigns 50 to x), the local variable x *that exists in the subshell's environment* will have the value 50 (see Figure 11.3). Note that this has no relation whatsoever to the variable x that still maintains its value of 100 in the login shell.

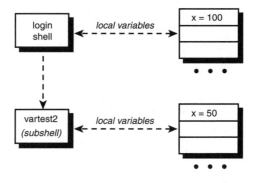

FIGURE 11.3   `vartest2` executes x=50.

When `vartest2` finishes execution, the subshell goes away, *together with any variables assigned values*.

Exported Variables

There *is* a way to make the value of a variable known to a subshell, and that's by *exporting* it with the `export` command. The format of this command is simply

`export` *variables*

where *variables* is the list of variable names that you want exported. For any subshells that get executed from that point on, the value of the exported variables will be passed down to the subshell.

Here's a program called `vartest3` to help illustrate the difference between local and exported variables:

```
$ cat vartest3
echo x = $x
echo y = $y
$
```

Assign values to the variables x and y in the login shell, and then run `vartest3`:

```
$ x=100
$ y=10
$ vartest3
x =
y =
$
```

x and y are both local variables, so their values aren't passed down to the subshell that runs `vartest3`. Now let's export the variable y and try it again:

```
$ export y                    Make y known to subshells
$ vartest3
x =
y = 10
$
```

This time, `vartest3` knew about y because it is an exported variable. Conceptually, whenever a subshell is executed, the list of exported variables gets "copied down" to the subshell, whereas the list of local variables does not (see Figure 11.4).

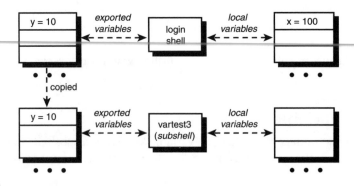

FIGURE 11.4   Execution of `vartest3`.

Now it's time for another question: What do you think happens if a subshell changes the value of an exported variable? Will the parent shell know about it after the subshell has finished? To answer this question, here's a program called vartest4:

```
$ cat vartest4
x=50
y=5
$
```

We'll assume that you haven't changed the values of x and y, and that y is still exported.

```
$ vartest4
$ echo $x $y
100 10
$
```

So the subshell couldn't even change the value of the exported variable y; it merely changed the copy of y that was passed to its environment when it was executed (see Figure 11.5). Just as with local variables, when a subshell goes away, so do the values of the exported variables. *There is no way to change the value of a variable in a parent shell from within a subshell.*

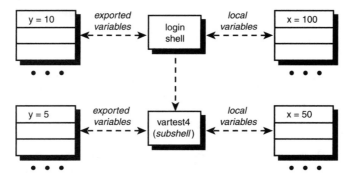

FIGURE 11.5   Execution of vartest4.

In the case of a subshell executing another subshell (for example, the rolo program executing the lu program), the process is repeated: The exported variables from the subshell are copied to the new subshell. These exported variables may have been exported from above, or newly exported from within the subshell.

After a variable is exported, it remains exported to all subshells subsequently executed.

Consider a modified version of `vartest4`:

```
$ cat vartest4
x=50
y=5
z=1
export z
vartest5
$
```

and also consider `vartest5`:

```
$ cat vartest5
echo x = $x
echo y = $y
echo z = $z
$
```

When `vartest4` gets executed, the exported variable y will be copied into the subshell's environment. `vartest4` sets the value of x to 50, changes the value of y to 5, and sets the value of z to 1. Then it exports z. This makes the value of z accessible to any subshell subsequently run by `vartest4`. `vartest5` is such a subshell, and when it is executed, the shell copies into its environment the exported variables from `vartest4`: y and z. This should explain the following output:

```
$ vartest4
x =
y = 5
z = 1
$
```

This entire operation is depicted in Figure 11.6.

To summarize the way local and exported variables work:

1. Any variable that is not exported is a local variable whose existence will not be known to subshells.

2. Exported variables and their values are copied into a subshell's environment, where they may be accessed and changed. However, such changes have no effect on the variables in the parent shell.

3. Exported variables retain this characteristic not only for directly spawned subshells, but also for subshells spawned by those subshells (and so on down the line).

4. A variable can be exported any time before or after it is assigned a value.

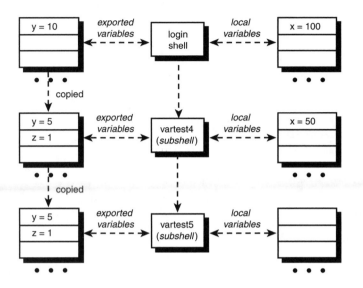

FIGURE 11.6   Subshell execution.

`export -p`

If you simply type `export -p`, you'll get a list of the variables and their values exported by your shell:

```
$ export -p
export LOGNAME=steve
export PATH=/bin:/usr/bin:.
export TIMEOUT=600
export TZ=EST5EDT
export y=10
$
```

As you can see, there are actually more exported variables here than you were initially led to believe. Note that y shows up on the list, together with other variables that were exported when you logged on.

Note that the variables listed include those that have been inherited from a parent shell.

PS1 **and** PS2

The characters that the shell displays as your command prompt are stored in the variable PS1. You can change this variable to be anything you want. As soon as you change it, it'll be used by the shell from that point on.

```
$ echo :$PS1:
:$ :
$ PS1="==> "
==> pwd
/users/steve
==> PS1="I await your next command, master: "
I await your next command, master: date
Wed Sep 18 14:46:28 EDT 2002
I await your next command, master: PS1="$ "
$                                             Back to normal
```

Your secondary command prompt, normally >, is kept in the variable PS2, where you can change it to your heart's content:

```
$ echo :$PS2:
:> :
$ PS2="=======> "
$ for x in 1 2 3
=======> do
=======> echo $x
=======> done
1
2
3
$
```

Like any other shell variables, after you log off the system, the values of those variables go with it. So if you change PS1, the shell will use the new value for the remainder of your login session. Next time you log in, however, you'll get the old value again. You can make the change yourself every time you log in, or you can have the change made automatically by adding it to your .profile file (discussed later in this chapter).

HOME, James

Your home directory is where you're placed whenever you log on to the system. A special shell variable called HOME is also automatically set to this directory when you log on:

```
$ echo $HOME
/users/steve
$
```

This variable can be used by your programs to identify your home directory. It's also used by the cd command whenever you type just cd with no arguments:

```
$ pwd                         Where am I?
/usr/src/lib/libc/port/stdio
$ cd
$ pwd
/users/steve                  There's no place like home
$
```

You can change your HOME variable to anything you want, but be warned that doing so may affect the operation of any programs that rely on it:

```
$ HOME=/users/steve/book      Change it
$ pwd
/users/steve
$ cd
$ pwd                         See what happened
/users/steve/book
$
```

Your PATH

Return for a moment to the rolo program from Chapter 10, "Reading and Printing Data":

```
$ rolo Liz
Liz Stachiw    212-555-2298
$
```

Let's see what directory this program was created in:

```
$ pwd
/users/steve/bin
$
```

Okay, now change directory to anywhere you want:

```
$ cd                          Go home
$
```

And now try to look up Liz in the phone book:

```
$ rolo Liz
sh: rolo: not found
$
```

Unless you already know where this discussion is leading, you are likely to get the preceding results.

Whenever you type in the name of a program to be executed, the shell searches a list of directories until it finds the requested program.[1] When found, it initiates its execution. This list of directories is contained in a special shell variable called PATH. This variable is automatically set for you when you log on to the system. See what it's set to now:

```
$ echo $PATH
/bin:/usr/bin:.
$
```

Chances are that your PATH has a slightly different value. As noted, the PATH specifies the directories that the shell searches to execute a command. These directories are separated from one another by colons (:). In the preceding example, three directories are listed: /bin, /usr/bin, and . (which, you'll recall, stands for the current directory). So whenever you type in the name of a program, say for example rolo, the shell searches the directories listed in PATH from left to right until it finds an executable file called rolo. First it looks in /bin, then in /usr/bin, and finally in the current directory for an executable file called rolo. As soon as it finds rolo, the shell executes it; if the shell doesn't find rolo, the shell issues a "not found" message.

The path

```
/bin:.:/usr/bin
```

specifies to search /bin, followed by the current directory, followed by /usr/bin. To have the current directory searched first, you put the period at the start of the path:

```
.:/bin:/usr/bin
```

For security reasons, it's generally not a good idea to have your current directory searched before the system ones.[2]

The period for specifying the current directory is optional; for example, the path

```
:/bin:/usr/bin
```

---

[1]*Actually, the shell is a bit more intelligent, because it keeps track of where it finds each command you execute. When you re-execute one of these commands, the shell remembers where it was found and doesn't go searching for it again. This feature is known as* hashing.

[2]*This is to avoid the so-called* Trojan horse *problem: Someone stores her own version of a command such as* su *(the command that changes you to another user) in a directory she can write into and waits for another user to change to that directory and run* su. *If the* PATH *specifies that the current directory be searched first, then the horsed version of* su *will be executed. This version will get the password that is typed and then print out* Sorry. *The user will think he just typed the wrong password.*

is equivalent to the previous one; however, throughout this text we'll specify the current directory with a period for clarity.

You can always override the PATH variable by specifying a path to the file to be executed. For example, if you type

```
/bin/date
```

the shell goes directly to /bin to execute date. The PATH in this case is ignored, as it is if you type in

```
../bin/lu
```

or

```
./rolo
```

This last case says to execute the program rolo in the current directory.

So now you understand why you couldn't execute rolo from your HOME directory: /users/steve/bin wasn't included in your PATH, and so the shell couldn't find rolo. This is a simple matter to rectify. You can simply add this directory to your PATH:

```
$ PATH=/bin:/usr/bin:.:/users/steve/bin
$
```

Now *any* program in /users/steve/bin can be executed by you from *anywhere*:

```
$ pwd                        Where am I?
/users/steve
$ rolo Liz
grep: can't open phonebook
$
```

This time the shell finds rolo and executes it, but grep can't find the phonebook file. Look back at the rolo program, and you'll see that the grep error message must be coming from lu. Take another look at lu:

```
$ cat /users/steve/bin/lu
#
# Look someone up in the phone book -- version 3
#

if [ "$#" -ne 1 ]
then
        echo "Incorrect number of arguments"
```

```
        echo "Usage: lu name"
        exit 1
fi

grep "$name" phonebook
$
```

grep is trying to open the phonebook file in the current directory, which is
/users/steve (that's where the program is being executed from—the current directory has no relation to the directory in which the program itself resides).

The PATH only specifies the directories to be searched for programs to be executed,
and not for any other types of files. So phonebook must be precisely located for lu.
There are several ways to fix this problem—a problem which, by the way, exists with
the rem and add programs as well. One approach is to have the lu program change
directory to /users/steve/bin before it does the grep. That way, grep finds
phonebook because it exists in the current directory:

```
    . . .
cd /users/steve/bin
grep "$1" phonebook
```

This approach is a good one to take when you're doing a lot of work with different
files in a particular directory: simply cd to the directory first and then you can
directly reference all the files you need.

A second approach is to simply list a full path to phonebook in the grep command:

```
    . . .
grep "$1" /users/steve/bin/phonebook
```

But suppose that you want to let others use your rolo program (and associated lu,
add, and rem programs). You can give them each their own copy, and then you'll
have several copies of the identical program on the system—programs that you'll
probably have to maintain. And what happens if you make a small change to rolo?
Are you going to update all their copies as well? A better solution might be to keep
just one copy of rolo but to give other users access to it.[3]

If you change all the references of phonebook to explicitly reference *your* phone book,
everyone else who uses your rolo program will be using *your* phone book, and not
his own. One way to solve the problem is to require that everyone have a phonebook

---

[3]*This can be done by giving them execute permission on all the directories leading to rolo, as well as read
and execute permissions on the programs themselves. They can always copy your programs at that point,
but you won't have to maintain them.*

file in his home directory; this way, if the program references the file as
$HOME/phonebookw, it will be relative to the home directory of the person running
the program.

Let's try this approach: Define a variable inside rolo called PHONEBOOK and set it to
$HOME/phonebook. If you then export this variable, lu, rem, and add (which are
executed as subshells by rolo) can use the value of PHONEBOOK to reference the file.
One advantage of this is if in the future you change the location of the phonebook
file, all you'll have to do is change this one variable in rolo; the other three
programs can remain untouched.

Here is the new rolo program, followed by modified lu, add, and rem programs.

```
$ cd /users/steve/bin
$ cat rolo
#
# rolo - rolodex program to look up, add, and
#        remove people from the phone book
#


#
# Set PHONEBOOK to point to the phone book file
# and export it so other progs know about it
#

PHONEBOOK=$HOME/phonebook
export PHONEBOOK

if [ ! -f "$PHONEBOOK" ]
then
        echo "No phone book file in $HOME!"
        exit 1
fi


#
# If arguments are supplied, then do a lookup
#

if [ "$#" -ne 0 ]
then
        lu "$@"
        exit
fi
validchoice=""          # set it null
```

```
#
# Loop until a valid selection is made
#

until [ -n "$validchoice" ]
do
        #
        # Display menu
        #

        echo '
        Would you like to:

        1. Look someone up
        2. Add someone to the phone book
        3. Remove someone from the phone book

Please select one of the above (1-3): \c'

        #
        # Read and process selection
        #

        read choice
        echo

        case "$choice"
        in
                1) echo "Enter name to look up: \c"
                   read name
                   lu "$name"
                   validchoice=TRUE;;
                2) echo "Enter name to be added: \c"
                   read name
                   echo "Enter number: \c"
                   read number
                   add "$name" "$number"
                   validchoice=TRUE;;
                3) echo "Enter name to be removed: \c"
                   read name
                   rem "$name"
                   validchoice=TRUE;;
```

```
             *) echo "Bad choice";;
         esac
done
$ cat add
#
# Program to add someone to the phone book file
#

if [ "$#" -ne 2 ]
then
        echo "Incorrect number of arguments"
        echo "Usage: add name number"
        exit 1
fi

echo "$1        $2" >> $PHONEBOOK
sort -o $PHONEBOOK $PHONEBOOK
$ cat lu
#
# Look someone up in the phone book
#

if [ "$#" -ne 1 ]
then
        echo "Incorrect number of arguments"
        echo "Usage: lu name"
        exit 1
fi

name=$1
grep "$name" $PHONEBOOK

if [ $? -ne 0 ]
then
        echo "I couldn't find $name in the phone book"
fi
$ cat rem
#
# Remove someone from the phone book
#

if [ "$#" -ne 1 ]
```

```
then
        echo "Incorrect number of arguments"
        echo "Usage: rem name"
        exit 1
fi

name=$1

#
# Find number of matching entries
#

matches=$(grep "$name" $PHONEBOOK | wc -l)

#
# If more than one match, issue message, else remove it
#

if [ "$matches" -gt 1 ]
then
        echo "More than one match; please qualify further"
elif [ "$matches" -eq 1 ]
then
        grep -v "$name" $PHONEBOOK > /tmp/phonebook$$
        mv /tmp/phonebook$$ $PHONEBOOK
else
        echo "I couldn't find $name in the phone book"
fi
$
```

(In an effort to be more user-friendly, a test was added to the end of lu to see whether the grep succeeds; if it doesn't, a message is displayed to the user.)

Now to test it:

`$ cd`	*Return home*
`$ rolo Liz`	*Quick lookup*
`No phonebook file in /users/steve!`	*Forgot to move it*
`$ mv /users/steve/bin/phonebook .`	
`$ rolo Liz`	*Try again*
`Liz Stachiw     212-555-2298`	
`$ rolo`	*Try menu selection*
`    Would you like to:`	

```
         1. Look someone up
         2. Add someone to the phone book
         3. Remove someone from the phone book

      Please select one of the above (1-3): 2

Enter name to be added: Teri Zak
Enter number: 201-555-6000
$ rolo Teri
Teri Zak         201-555-6000
$
```

rolo, lu, and add seem to be working fine. rem should also be tested to make sure that it's okay as well.

If you still want to run lu, rem, or add standalone, you can do it provided that you first define PHONEBOOK and export it:

```
$ PHONEBOOK=$HOME/phonebook
$ export PHONEBOOK
$ lu Harmon
I couldn't find Harmon in the phone book
$
```

If you do intend to run these programs standalone, you'd better put checks in the individual programs to ensure that PHONEBOOK is set to some value.

Your Current Directory

Your current directory is also part of your environment. Take a look at this small shell program called cdtest:

```
$ cat cdtest
cd /users/steve/bin
pwd
$
```

The program does a cd to /users/steve/bin and then executes a pwd to verify that the change was made. Let's run it:

```
$ pwd                        Get my bearings
/users/steve
$ cdtest
/users/steve/bin
$
```

Now for the $64,000 question: If you execute a pwd command now, will you be in
/users/steve or /users/steve/bin?

```
$ pwd
/users/steve
$
```

The cd executed in cdtest had no effect on your current directory. Because the
current directory is part of the environment, when a cd is executed from a subshell,
the current directory of that subshell is altered. *There is no way to change the current
directory of a parent shell from a subshell.*

When cd is invoked, it sets the PWD shell variable to the full pathname of the new
current directory, so the command

```
echo $PWD
```

produces the same output as the pwd command:

```
$ pwd
/users/steve
$ echo $PWD
/users/steve
$ cd bin
$ echo $PWD
/users/steve/bin
$
```

cd also sets OLDPWD to the full pathname of the previous current directory.

Incidentally, cd is a shell built-in command.

CDPATH

The CDPATH variable works like the PATH variable: It specifies a list of directories to be
searched by the shell whenever you execute a cd command. This search is done only
if the specified directory is not given by a full pathname and if CDPATH is not null
(obviously). So if you type in

```
cd /users/steve
```

the shell changes your directory directly to /users/steve; but if you type

```
cd memos
```

the shell looks at your CDPATH variable to find the memos directory. And if your CDPATH looks like this:

```
$ echo $CDPATH
.:/users/steve:/users/steve/docs
$
```

the shell first looks in your current directory for a memos directory, and if not found then looks in /users/steve for a memos directory, and if not found there tries /users/steve/docs in a last ditch effort to find the directory. If the directory that it finds is not relative to your current one, the cd command prints the full path to the directory to let you know where it's taking you:

```
$ cd /users/steve
$ cd memos
/users/steve/docs/memos
$ cd bin
/users/steve/bin
$
```

Like the PATH variable, use of the period for specifying the current directory is optional, so

```
:/users/steve:/users/steve/docs
```

is equivalent to

```
.:/users/steve:/users/steve/docs
```

Judicious use of the CDPATH variable can save you a lot of typing, especially if your directory hierarchy is fairly deep and you find yourself frequently moving around in it (or if you're frequently moving around into other directory hierarchies as well).

Unlike the PATH, you'll probably want to put your current directory first in the CDPATH list. This gives you the most natural use of CDPATH (because you're used to doing a cd x to switch to the subdirectory x). If the current directory isn't listed first, you may end up in an unexpected directory.

More on Subshells

It's important for you to understand the way subshells work and how they interact with your environment. You know now that a subshell can't change the value of a variable in a parent shell, nor can it change its current directory. Suppose that you want to write a program to set values for some variables that you like to use whenever you log on. For example, assume that you have the following file called vars:

```
$ cat vars
BOOK=/users/steve/book
UUPUB=/usr/spool/uucppublic
DOCS=/users/steve/docs/memos
DB=/usr2/data
$
```

You know that if you execute vars, the values assigned to these variables will not be accessible by you after this program has finished executing because vars will be run in a subshell:

```
$ vars
$ echo $BOOK

$
```

The . Command

Luckily, there is a shell built-in command called . (pronounced "dot") whose general format is

. *file*

and whose purpose is to execute the contents of *file* in the *current* shell. That is, commands from *file* are executed by the current shell just as if they were typed at that point. A subshell is not spawned to execute the program. The shell uses your PATH variable to find *file*, just like it does when executing other programs.

```
$ . vars                    Execute vars in the current shell
$ echo $BOOK
/users/steve/book           Hoorah!
$
```

Because a subshell isn't spawned to execute the program, any variable that gets assigned a value stays even after execution of the program is completed. It follows then that if you have a program called db that has the following commands in it:

```
$ cat db
DATA=/usr2/data
RPTS=$DATA/rpts
BIN=$DATA/bin
```

```
cd $DATA
$
```

executing db with the "dot" command

```
$ . db
$
```

defines the three variables DATA, RPTS, and BIN in the current shell and then changes you to the $DATA directory.

```
$ pwd
/usr2/data
$
```

This last example brings up an interesting point of discussion. If you're one of those Unix users who have to support a few different directory hierarchies, you can create programs like db to execute whenever you have to work on one of your directories. In that program, you can also include definitions for other variables; for example, you might want to change your prompt in PS1 to something like DB—to let you know that your database variables have been set up. You may also want to change your PATH to include a directory that has programs related to the database and your CDPATH variable so that directories in the database will be easily accessible with the cd command. You can even change HOME so that a cd without any arguments returns you directly to your database directory.

If you make these sorts of changes, you'll probably want to execute db in a subshell and not in the current shell because doing the latter leaves all the modified variables around after you've finished your work on the database. The trick to doing it right is to start up a *new* shell from inside the subshell, with all the modified variables exported to it. Then, when you're finished working with the database, you can "log off" the new shell by pressing *Ctrl+d*. Let's take a look at how this works. Here is a new version of db:

```
$ cat db
#
# Set up and export variables related to the data base
#

HOME=/usr2/data
BIN=$HOME/bin
RPTS=$HOME/rpts
DATA=$HOME/rawdata
```

```
PATH=$PATH$BIN
CDPATH=:$HOME:$RPTS

PS1="DB: "

export HOME BIN RPTS DATA PATH CDPATH PS1

#
# Start up a new shell
#

/usr/bin/sh
$
```

The HOME directory is set to /usr2/data, and then the variables BIN, RPTS, and DATA are defined relative to this HOME (a good idea in case you ever have to move the directory structure somewhere else: all you'd have to change in the program is the variable HOME).

Next, the PATH is modified to include the database bin directory, and the CDPATH variable is set to search the current directory, the HOME directory, and the RPTS directory (which presumably contains subdirectories).

After exporting these variables (which as you recall must be done to put the values of these variables into the environment of subsequently spawned subshells), the standard shell, /usr/bin/sh, is started. From that point on, this new shell processes commands typed in from the terminal. When *Ctrl+d* is typed to this shell, control returns to db, which in turn returns control to your login shell.

```
$ db                              Run it
DB: echo $HOME
/usr2/data
DB: cd rpts                       Try out CDPATH
/usr2/data/rpts                   It works
DB: ps                            See what processes are running
PID TTY TIME COMMAND
123 13  0:40 sh                   Your login shell
761 13  0:01 sh                   Subshell running db
765 13  0:01 sh                   New shell run from db
769 13  0:03 ps
DB: Ctrl+d                        Done for now
$ echo $HOME
/users/steve                      Back to normal
$
```

The execution of db is depicted in Figure 11.7 (where we've shown only the exported variables of interest, not necessarily all that exist in the environment).

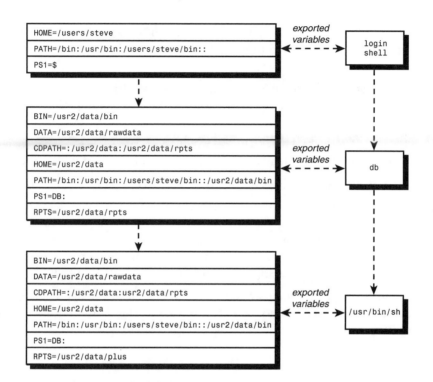

FIGURE 11.7   Executing db.

The exec **Command**

After you started up the new shell from db, you weren't interested in doing anything further after the shell finished, as evidenced by the fact that no commands followed /usr/bin/sh in the program. Instead of having db wait around for the new shell to finish, you can use the exec command to *replace the current program* (db) *with the new one* (/usr/bin/sh). The general format of exec is

exec *program*

where *program* is the name of the program to be executed. Because the exec'ed program replaces the current one, there's one less process hanging around; also, startup time of an exec'ed program is quicker, due to the way the Unix system executes processes.

To use `exec` in the `db` program, you simply replace the last line with

```
exec /usr/bin/sh
```

As noted, after this gets executed, `db` will be replaced by `/usr/bin/sh`. This means that it's pointless to have any commands follow the `exec` because they'll never be executed.

`exec` can be used to close standard input and reopen it with any file that you want to read. To change standard input to *file*, you use the `exec` command in the form

```
exec < file
```

Any commands that subsequently read data from standard input will read from *file*.

Redirection of standard output is done similarly. The command

```
exec > report
```

redirects all subsequent output written to standard output to the file `report`. Note here that `exec` is not used to start up execution of a new program as previously described; here it is used to reassign standard input or standard output.

If you use `exec` to reassign standard input and later want to reassign it someplace else, you can simply execute another `exec`. To reassign standard input back to the terminal, you would write

```
exec < /dev/tty
```

The same discussion applies to reassignment of standard output.

The (...) and { ...; } Constructs

Sometimes you may want to group a set of commands together for some reason. For example, you may want to send a `sort` followed by execution of your `plotdata` program into the background for execution. You can group a set of commands together by enclosing them in a set of parentheses or braces. The first form causes the commands to be executed by a subshell, the latter form by the current shell.

Here are some examples to illustrate how they work:

```
$ x=50
$ (x=100)                          Execute this in a subshell
$ echo $x
50                                 Didn't change
$ { x=100; }                       Execute this in the current shell
$ echo $x
```

```
100
$ pwd                              Where am I?
/users/steve
$ (cd bin; ls)                     Change to bin and do an ls
add
greetings
lu
number
phonebook
rem
rolo
$ pwd
/users/steve                       No change
$ { cd bin; }                      This should change me
$ pwd
/users/steve/bin
$
```

If the commands enclosed in the braces are all to be typed on the same line, a space must follow the left brace, and a semicolon must appear after the last command.

As the example

```
(cd bin; ls)
```

shows, the parentheses are useful for doing some commands without affecting your current environment. You can also use them for other purposes:

```
$ (sort 2002data -o 2002data; plotdata 2002data) &
[1]    3421
$
```

The parentheses group the sort and plotdata commands together so that they can both be sent to the background for execution, with their order of execution preserved.

Input and output can be piped to and from these constructs, and I/O can be redirected. In the next example, a

```
.ls 2
```

nroff command (for double-spaced output) is effectively tacked to the beginning of the file memo before being sent to nroff.

```
$ { echo ".ls 2"; cat memo; } | nroff -Tlp | lp
```

In the command sequence

```
$ { prog1; prog2; prog3; } 2> errors
```

all messages written to standard error by the three programs are collected into the file errors.

As a final example, let's return to the mon program from Chapter 9, "'Round and 'Round She Goes." As you'll recall, this program periodically checked for a user logging on to the system. One of the comments we made back then is that it would be nice if the program could somehow automatically "send itself" to the background for execution because that's how it's really meant to be run. Now you know how to do it: You simply enclose the until loop and the commands that follow inside parentheses and send it into the background:

```
$ cat mon
#
# Wait until a specified user logs on -- version 4
#

# Set up default values
mailopt=FALSE
interval=60


# process command options

while getopts mt: option
do
        case "$option"
        in
                        m)      mailopt=TRUE;;
                        t)      interval=$OPTARG;;
                        \?)     echo "Usage: mon [-m] [-t n] user"
                                echo" -m means to be informed by mail"
                                echo" -t means check every n secs."
                                exit 1;;
        esac
done


# Make sure a user name was specified

if [ "$OPTIND" -gt "$#" ]
then
        echo "Missing user name!"
```

```
        exit 2
fi

shiftcount=$(( OPTIND - 1 ))
shift $shiftcount
user=$1

#
# Send everything that follows into the background
#

(
    #
    # Check for user logging on
    #

    until who | grep "^$user " > /dev/null
    do
            sleep $interval
    done

    #
    # When we reach this point, the user has logged on
    #

    if [ "$mailopt" = FALSE]
    then
            echo "$user has logged on"
    else
            runner=$(who am i | cut -c1-8)
            echo "$user has logged on" | mail $runner
    fi
) &
```

The entire program could have been enclosed in parentheses, but we arbitrarily decided to do the argument checking and parsing first before sending the remainder to the background.

```
$ mon fred
$                                   Prompt comes back so you can continue working
  ...
fred has logged on
```

Note that a process id number is not printed by the shell when a command is sent to the background within a shell program.

Another Way to Pass Variables to a Subshell

If you want to send the value of a variable to a subshell, there's another way to do it besides setting the variable and then exporting it. On the command line, you can precede the name of the command with the assignment of as many variables as you want. For example,

```
DBHOME=/uxn2/data DBID=452 dbrun
```

places the variables DBHOME and DBID, and their indicated values, into the environment of dbrun and then dbrun gets executed. These variables will not be known to the current shell; they're created only for the execution of dbrun. In fact, execution of the preceding command behaves identically to typing

```
(DBHOME=/uxn2/data; DBID=452; export DBHOME DBID; dbrun)
```

Here's a short example:

```
$ cat foo1
echo :$x:
foo2
$ cat foo2
echo :$x:
$ foo1
::
::                          x not known to foo1 or foo2
$ x=100 foo1               Try it this way
:100:                       x  is known to foo1
:100:                       and to its subshells
$ echo :$x:
::                          Still not known to current shell
$
```

So variables defined this way otherwise behave as normal exported variables to the subshell.

Your .profile File

In Chapter 3, "What Is the Shell?," you learned about the login sequence. This sequence is completed when your shell displays your command prompt and waits for you to type your first command. Just before it does that, however, your login shell executes two special files on the system. The first is /etc/profile. This file is set up by the system administrator and usually does things like checking to see whether you have mail (Where do you think the "You have mail." message comes from?), setting your default file creation mask (your *umask*), assigning values to some standard exported variables, and anything else that the administrator wants to have executed whenever a user logs in.

The second file that gets automatically executed is .profile in your home directory. Your system administrator may have given you a default .profile file when you got your account. See what's in it now:

```
$ cat $HOME/.profile
PATH="/bin:/usr/bin:/usr/lbin:.:"
export PATH
$
```

Here you see a small .profile file that simply sets the PATH and exports it.

You can change your .profile file to include any commands that you want executed whenever you log in. You can even put commands in your .profile file that override settings (usually environment variables) made in /etc/profile. Note that the commands in /etc/profile and .profile are executed by your login shell (as if you typed in

```
$ . /etc/profile
$ . .profile
$
```

as soon as you logged in), which means that changes made to your environment remain after the programs are executed.

Here's a sample .profile that sets your PATH to include your own bin, sets your CDPATH, changes your primary and secondary command prompts, changes your erase character to a backspace *(Ctrl+h)* with the stty command, and prints a friendly message using the greetings program from Chapter 8, "Decisions, Decisions":

```
$ cat $HOME/.profile
PATH=/bin:/usr/bin:/usr/lbin:$HOME/bin:.:
CDPATH=.:$HOME:$HOME/misc:$HOME/documents

PS1="=> "
PS2="====> "

export PATH CDPATH PS1 PS2
```

```
stty echoe erase CTRL+h

echo
greetings
$
```

Here's what a login sequence would look like with this .profile:

```
login: steve
Password:

Good morning                        Output from greetings
=>                                  New PS1
```

The TERM Variable

If you tend to use more than one type of terminal, the .profile is a good place to put some code to prompt for the terminal type and then set the TERM variable accordingly. This variable is used by screen editors such as vi and other screen-based programs.

A sample section of code from a .profile file to prompt for the terminal type might look like this:

```
echo "What terminal are you using (xterm is the default)? \c"
read TERM
if [ -z "$TERM" ]
then
        TERM=xterm
fi
export TERM
```

Based on the terminal type entered, you may also want to do things such as set up the function keys or the tabs on the terminal.

Even if you always use the same terminal type, you should set the TERM variable in your .profile file.

The TZ Variable

The TZ variable is used by the date command and some Standard C library functions to determine time zone information. The simplest setting for TZ is a time zone name of three or more alphabetic characters followed by a number that specifies the number of hours that must be added to the local time to arrive at *Coordinated*

Universal Time, also known as Greenwich Mean Time. This number can be positive (local time zone is west of 0 longitude) or negative (local time zone is east of 0 longitude). For example, Eastern Standard Time can be specified as

```
TZ=EST5
```

The `date` command calculates the correct time based on this information and also uses the time zone name in its output:

```
$ TZ=EST5 date
Wed Sep 18 15:24:09 EST 2002
$ TZ=xyz3 date
Wed Sep 18 17:24:28 xyz 2002
$
```

A second time zone name can follow the number; if this time zone is specified, daylight savings time is assumed to apply (`date` automatically adjusts the time in this case when daylight saving is in effect) and is assumed to be one hour earlier than standard time. If a number follows the daylight saving time zone name, this value is used to compute the daylight savings time from the Coordinated Universal Time in the same way as the number previously described.

So, the following `TZ` settings are quivalent:

```
TZ=EST5EDT
TZ=EST5EDT6
```

The `TZ` variable is usually set in either the `/etc/profile` file or your `.profile` file. If not set, an implementation-specific default time zone is used, typically Coordinated Universal Time.

Exercises

1. Write a program called `myrm` that takes as arguments the names of files to be removed. If the global variable `MAXFILES` is set, take it as the maximum number of files to remove without question. If the variable is not set, use 10 as the maximum. If the number of files to be removed exceeds this count, ask the user for confirmation before removing the files:

```
$ ls | wc -l
25
$ myrm *                          Remove them all
Remove 25 files (y/n)? n
files not removed
```

```
$ MAXFILES=100 myrm *
$ ls
$                                    All files removed
```

If MAXFILES is set to zero, the check should be suppressed.

2. Here are two programs called prog1 and prog2:

```
$ cat prog1
e1=100
export e1
e2=200
e3=300 prog2
$ cat prog2
echo $e1 $e2 $e3 $e4
$
```

What output would you expect after typing the following:

```
$ e2=20; export e2
$ e4=40 prog1
```

3. Modify rolo from this chapter so that a person running the program can keep his or her phone book file in any directory and not just in the home directory. This can be done by requiring that the user set an exported variable called PHONEBOOK to the name of the phone book file before executing rolo. Check to make sure that this variable is set to a valid file. If the variable is not set, have the program assume that the phone book file is in the user's home directory as before.

Here are some examples:

```
$ PHONEBOOK=/users/steve/personal lu Gregory
Gregory        973-555-0370
$ PHONEBOOK=/users/pat/phonebook lu Toritos
El Toritos     973-555-2236
$
```

In the preceding example, we assume that the user steve has been granted read access to pat's phone book file.

12

More on Parameters

In this chapter, you'll learn some more about parameters. Technically, parameters include the arguments passed to a program (the *positional* parameters), the special shell variables such as $# and $?, and ordinary variables, also known as *keyword* parameters.

Positional parameters cannot be assigned values directly; however, they can be reassigned values with the set command. Keyword parameters are assigned values simply by writing

variable=value

The format is a bit more general than that shown; actually, you can assign several keyword parameters at once using the format

variable=value variable=value ...

as the following example illustrates:

```
$ x=100 y=200 z=50
$ echo $x $y $z
100 200 50
$
```

Parameter Substitution

In the simplest form, to have the value of a parameter substituted, you simply precede the parameter with a dollar sign, as in $i or $9.

${*parameter*}

If there's a potential conflict caused by the characters that follow the parameter name, you can enclose the name inside curly braces, as in

```
mv $file ${file}x
```

This command would add an x to the end of the filename specified by $file and could not be written as

```
mv $file $filex
```

because the shell would substitute the value of filex for the second argument.

As mentioned in Chapter 7, "Passing Arguments," to access positional parameters 10 and above, you must enclose the number inside the curly braces, as in ${11}.

${*parameter:-value*}

This construct says to substitute the value of *parameter* if it is not null, and to substitute *value* otherwise. For example, in the command line

```
echo Using editor ${EDITOR:-/bin/vi}
```

the shell substitutes the value of EDITOR if it's not null, and the value /bin/vi otherwise. It has the same effect as writing

```
if [ -n "$EDITOR" ]
then
        echo Using editor $EDITOR
else
        echo Using editor /bin/vi
fi
```

The command line

```
${EDITOR:-/bin/ed} /tmp/edfile
```

starts up the program stored in the variable EDITOR (presumably a text editor), or /bin/ed if EDITOR is null.

Here's a simple test of this construct from the terminal:

```
$ EDITOR=/bin/ed
$ echo ${EDITOR:-/bin/vi}
/bin/ed
$ EDITOR=                        Set it null
```

```
$ echo ${EDITOR:-/bin/vi}
/bin/vi
$
```

${*parameter*:=*value*}

This version is similar to the last, only if *parameter* is null; not only is *value* used, but it is also assigned to *parameter* as well (note the = in the construct). You can't assign values to positional parameters this way (that means that *parameter* can't be a number).

A typical use of this construct would be in testing to see whether an exported variable has been set and, if not, setting it to a default value, as in

```
${PHONEBOOK:=$HOME/phonebook}
```

This says that if PHONEBOOK is set to some value, leave it alone; otherwise, set it to $HOME/phonebook.

Note that the preceding example could not stand alone as a command because after the substitution was performed the shell would attempt to execute the result:

```
$ PHONEBOOK=
$ ${PHONEBOOK:=$HOME/phonebook}
sh: /users/steve/phonebook: cannot execute
$
```

To use this construct as a standalone command, the null command is often employed. If you write

```
: $ {PHONEBOOK:=$HOME/phonebook}
```

the shell still does the substitution (it evaluates the rest of the command line), yet executes nothing (the null command).

```
$ PHONEBOOK=
$ : ${PHONEBOOK:=$HOME/phonebook}
$ echo $PHONEBOOK                        See if it got assigned
/users/steve/phonebook
$ : ${PHONEBOOK:=foobar}                 Shouldn't change it
$ echo $PHONEBOOK
/users/steve/phonebook                   It didn't
$
```

${*parameter*:?*value*}

If *parameter* is not null, the shell substitutes its value; otherwise, the shell writes *value* to standard error and then exits (don't worry—if it's done from your login shell, you won't be logged off). If *value* is omitted, the shell writes the message

prog: *parameter*: `parameter null or not set`

Here's an example from the terminal:

```
$ PHONEBOOK=
$ : ${PHONEBOOK:?"No PHONEBOOK file!"}
No PHONEBOOK file!
$ : ${PHONEBOOK:?}                    Don't give a value
sh: PHONEBOOK: parameter null or not set
$
```

With this construct, you can easily check to see whether a set of variables needed by a program are all set and not null, as in

```
: ${TOOLS:?}  ${EXPTOOLS:?}  ${TOOLBIN:?}
```

${*parameter*:+*value*}

This one substitutes *value* if *parameter* is not null; otherwise, it substitutes nothing.

```
$ traceopt=T
$ echo options: ${traceopt:+"trace mode"}
options: trace mode
$ traceopt=
$ echo options: ${traceopt:+"trace mode"}
options:
$
```

The *value* part for any of the constructs in this section can be a command substitution; it's executed by the shell only if its value is to be used. In

```
WORKDIR=${DBDIR:-$(pwd)}
```

WORKDIR is assigned the value of DBDIR if it's not null; otherwise, the pwd command is executed and the result assigned to WORKDIR. pwd is executed *only if* DBDIR is null.

Pattern Matching Constructs

The POSIX standard shell provides four parameter substitution constructs that perform pattern matching. Note that some older shells do not support this feature.

In each case, the construct takes two arguments: a variable name (or parameter number) and a pattern. The shell searches through the contents of the specified variable to match the supplied pattern. If the pattern is matched, the shell substitutes the value of the variable on the command line, *with the matching portion of the pattern deleted*. If the pattern is not matched, the entire contents of the variable are substituted on the command line. In any case, the contents of the variable remain unchanged.

The term *pattern* is used here because the shell allows you to use the same pattern matching characters that it accepts in filename substitution and case values: * to match zero or more characters, ? to match any single character, [...] to match any single character from the specified set, and [!...] to match any single character not in the specified set.

When you write the construct

${*variable%pattern*}

the shell looks inside *variable* to see whether it *ends* with the specified *pattern*. If it does, the contents of *variable* are substituted on the command line with the shortest matching *pattern* removed from the right.

If you use the construct

${*variable%%pattern*}

the shell once again looks inside *variable* to see whether it ends with *pattern*. This time, however, it removes the *longest* matching pattern from the right. This is relevant only if the * is used in *pattern*. Otherwise, the % and %% behave the same way.

The # is used in a similar way to force the pattern matching to occur on the left rather than the right. So, the construct.

${*variable#pattern*}

tells the shell to substitute the value of *variable* on the command line, with *pattern* removed from the left.

Finally, the shell construct

${*variable##pattern*}

works like the # form, only the longest occurrence of *pattern* is removed from the left.

Remember that in all four cases, no permanent changes are made to the variable itself; you are affecting only what gets substituted on the command line. Also, remember that the pattern matches are *anchored.* In the case of the % and %% constructs, the variables must *end* with the specified pattern; in the case of the # and ## constructs, the variable must *begin* with it.

Here are some simple examples to show how these constructs work:

```
$ var=testcase
$ echo $var
testcase
$ echo ${var%e}              Remove e from right
testcas
$ echo $var                  Variable is unchanged
testcase
$ echo ${var%s*e}            Remove smallest match from right
testca
$ echo ${var%%s*e}           Remove longest match
te
$ echo ${var#?e}             Remove smallest match from left
stcase
$ echo ${var#*s}             Remove smallest match from left
tcase
$ echo ${var##*s}            Remove longest match from left
e
$ echo ${var#test}           Remove test from left
case
$ echo ${var#teas}           No match
testcase
$
```

There are many practical uses for these constructs, even though these examples don't seem to show it. For example, the following tests to see whether the filename stored inside the variable file ends in the two characters .o:

```
if [ ${file%.o} != $file ]
then
    # file ends in .o
        ...
fi
```

As another example, here's a shell program that works just like the Unix system's basename command:

```
$ cat mybasename
echo ${1##*/}
$
```

The program displays its argument with all the characters up to the last / removed:

```
$ mybasename /usr/spool/uucppublic
uucppublic
$ mybasename $HOME
steve
$ mybasename memos
memos
$
```

${#variable}

This construct gives you the ability to count the number of characters stored inside a variable. For example,

```
$ text='The shell'
$ echo ${#text}
9
$
```

Note that some older shells do not support this feature.

Each of the parameter substitution constructs described in this section is summarized in Table A.3 in Appendix A, "Shell Summary."

The $0 Variable

Whenever you execute a shell program, the shell automatically stores the name of the program inside the special variable $0. This can be used to advantage when you have two or more programs that are linked under different names and you want to know which one was executed. It's also useful for displaying error messages because it removes the dependency of the filename from the program. If the name of the program is referenced by $0, subsequently renaming the program will not require the program to be edited:

```
$ cat lu
#
# Look someone up in the phone book
#

if [ "$#" -ne 1 ]
then
        echo "Incorrect number of arguments"
        echo "Usage: $0 name"
```

```
        exit 1
fi

name=$1
grep "$name" $PHONEBOOK

if [ $? -ne 0 ]
then
        echo "I couldn't find $name in the phone book"
fi
```

```
$ PHONEBOOK=$HOME/phonebook
$ export PHONEBOOK
$ lu Teri
Teri Zak        201-555-6000
$ lu Teri Zak
Incorrect number of arguments
Usage: lu name
$ mv lu lookup                   Rename it
$ lookup Teri Zak                See what happens now
Incorrect number of arguments
Usage: lookup name
$
```

The set Command

The shell's set command is a dual-purpose command: it's used both to set various shell options as well as to reassign the positional parameters $1, $2, and so forth.

The -x Option

This option turns on trace mode in the shell. It does to the current shell what the command

```
sh -x ctype a
```

did for the execution of the ctype program in Chapter 8, "Decisions, Decisions." From the point that the

```
set -x
```

command is executed, all subsequently executed commands will be printed to standard error by the shell, after filename, variable, and command substitution and I/O redirection have been performed. The traced commands are preceded by plus signs.

```
$ x=*
$ set -x                          Set command trace option
$ echo $x
+ echo add greetings lu rem rolo
add greetings lu rem rolo
$ cmd=wc
+ cmd=wc
$ ls | $cmd -l
+ ls
+ wc -l
      5
$
```

You can turn off trace mode at any time simply by executing set with the +x option:

```
$ set +x
+ set +x
$ ls | wc -l
        5                         Back to normal
$
```

You should note that the trace option is *not* passed down to subshells. But you can trace a subshell's execution either by running the shell with the -x option followed by the name of the program to be executed, as in

```
sh -x rolo
```

or you can insert a set -x command inside the file itself. In fact, you can insert any number of set -x and set +x commands inside your program to turn trace mode on and off as desired.

set with No Arguments

If you don't give any arguments to set, you'll get an alphabetized list of all the variables that exist in your environment, be they local or exported:

```
$ set                            Show me all variables
CDPATH=:/users/steve:/usr/spool
EDITOR=/bin/vi
HOME=/users/steve
IFS=

LOGNAME=steve
MAIL=/usr/spool/mail/steve
```

```
MAILCHECK=600
PATH=/bin:/usr/bin:/users/steve/bin:.:
PHONEBOOK=/users/steve/phonebook
PS1=$
PS2=>
PWD=/users/steve/misc
SHELL=/usr/bin/sh
TERM=xterm
TMOUT=0
TZ=EST5EDT
cmd=wc
x=*
$
```

Using set to Reassign Positional Parameters

There is no way to directly assign a value to a positional parameter; for example,

```
1=100
```

does not work. These parameters are initially set on execution of the shell program. The only way they may be changed is with the shift or the set commands. If words are given as arguments to set on the command line, those words will be assigned to the positional parameters $1, $2, and so forth. The previous values stored in the positional parameters will be lost forever. So

```
set a b c
```

assigns a to $1, b to $2, and c to $3. $# also gets set to 3.

```
$ set one two three four
$ echo $1:$2:$3:$4
one:two:three:four
$ echo $#                    This should be 4
4
$ echo $*                    What does this reference now?
one two three four
$ for arg; do echo $arg; done
one
two
three
four
$
```

So after execution of the set, everything seems to work consistently: $#, $*, and the for loop without a list.

set is often used in this fashion to "parse" data read from a file or the terminal. Here's a program called words that counts the number of words typed on a line (using the shell's definition of a "word"):

```
$ cat words
#
# Count words on a line
#

read line
set $line
echo $#
$ words                          Run it
Here's a line for you to count.
7
$
```

The program stores the line read in the shell variable line and then executes the command

```
set $line
```

This causes each word stored in line to be assigned to the positional parameters. The variable $# is also set to the number of words assigned, which is the number of words on the line.

The -- Option

Try typing in a line to words that begins with a - and see what happens:

```
$ words
-1 + 5 = 4
words: -1: bad option(s)
$
```

After the line was read and assigned to line, the command

```
set $line
```

was executed. After the shell did its substitution, the command line looked like this:

```
set -1 + 5 = 4
```

When set executed, it saw the - and thought that an option was being selected, thus explaining the error message.

Another problem with words occurs if you give it a line consisting entirely of white-space characters, or if the line is null:

```
$ words
                              Just Enter is pressed
CDPATH=.:/users/steve:/usr/spool
EDITOR=/bin/vi
HOME=/users/steve
IFS=

LOGNAME=steve
MAIL=/usr/spool/mail/steve
MAILCHECK=600
PATH=/bin:/usr/bin:/users/steve/bin:.:
PHONEBOOK=/users/steve/phonebook
PS1=$
PS2=>
PWD=/users/steve/misc
SHELL=/usr/bin/sh
TERM=xterm
TMOUT=0
TZ=EST5EDT
cmd=wc
x=*
0
$
```

To protect against both of these problems occurring, you can use the -- option to set. This tells set not to interpret any subsequent arguments on the command line as options. It also prevents set from displaying all your variables if no other arguments follow, as was the case when you typed a null line.

So the set command in words should be changed to read

```
set -- $line
```

With the addition of a while loop and some integer arithmetic, the words program can be easily modified to count the total number of words on standard input, giving you your own version of wc -w:

```
$ cat words
#
```

```
# Count all of the words on standard input
#

count=0
while read line
do
        set -- $line
        count=$(( count + $# ))
done

echo $count
$
```

After each line is read, the set command is executed to take advantage of the fact that $# will be assigned the number of words on the line. The -- option is supplied to set just in case any of the lines read begins with a - or consists entirely of white-space characters.

The value of $# is then added into the variable count, and the next line is read. When the loop is exited, the value of count is displayed. This represents the total number of words read.

```
$ words < /etc/passwd
567
$ wc -w < /etc/passwd                Check against wc
567
$
```

(Our version is a lot slower than wc because the latter is written in C.)

Here's a quick way to count the number of files in your directory:[1]

```
$ set *
$ echo $#
8
$
```

This is much faster than

```
ls | wc -l
```

---

[1]*This technique may not work on very large directories because you may exceed the limit on the length of the command line (the precise length varies between Unix systems). Working with such directories may cause problems when using filename substitution in other commands as well, such as* echo * *or* for file in *.

because the first method uses only shell built-in commands. In general, your shell programs run much faster if you try to get as much done as you can using the shell's built-in commands.

Other Options to `set`

`set` accepts several other options, each of them enabled by preceding the option with a `-`, and disabled by preceding it with a `+`. The `-x` option that we have described here is perhaps the most commonly used. Others are summarized in Table A.9 in Appendix A.

The `IFS` Variable

There is a special shell variable called `IFS`, which stands for *Internal Field Separator*. The shell uses the value of this variable when parsing input from the `read` command, output from command substitution (the back-quoting mechanism), and when performing variable substitution. If it's typed on the command line, the shell treats it like a normal whitespace character (that is, as a word delimiter).

See what it's set to now:

```
$ echo "$IFS"


$
```

Well, that wasn't very illuminating! To determine the actual characters stored in there, pipe the output from `echo` into the `od` (*o*ctal *d*ump) command with the `-b` (byte display) option:

```
$ echo "$IFS" | od -b
0000000 040 011 012 012
0000004
$
```

The first column of numbers shown is the relative offset from the start of the input. The following numbers are the octal equivalents of the characters read by od. The first such number is 040, which is the ASCII value of the space character. It's followed by 011, the tab character, and then by 012, the newline character. The next character is another newline; this was written by the echo. These characters for IFS come as no surprise; they're the "whitespace" characters we've talked about throughout the book.

You can change your IFS to any character or characters you want. This is useful when you want to parse a line of data whose fields aren't delimited by the normal whitespace characters. For example, we noted that the shell normally strips any leading whitespace characters from the beginning of any line that you read with the read command. You can change your IFS to just a newline character before the read is executed, which has the effect of preserving the leading whitespace (because the shell won't consider it a field delimiter):

```
$ read line                        Try it the "old" way
          Here's a line
$ echo "$line"
Here's a line
$ IFS="
> "                                Set it to a just a newline
$ read line                        Try it again
          Here's a line
$ echo "$line"
          Here's a line            Leading spaces preserved
$
```

To change the IFS to just a newline, an open quote was typed, followed immediately by the pressing of the Enter key, followed by the closed quote on the next line. No additional characters can be typed inside those quotes because they'll be stored inside IFS and then used by the shell.

Now let's change the IFS to something more visible, like a colon:

```
$ IFS=:
$ read x y z
123:345:678
$ echo $x
123
$ echo $z
678
$ list="one:two:three"
$ for x in $list; do echo $x; done
one
two
three
$ var=a:b:c
$ echo "$var"
a:b:c
$
```

Because the IFS was changed to a colon, when the line was read, the shell divided the line into three words: 123, 345, and 678, which were stored into the three variables x, y, and z, respectively. In the next to last example, the shell used the IFS when substituting the value of list in the for loop. The last example shows that the shell doesn't use the IFS when performing variable assignment.

Changing the IFS is often done in conjunction with execution of the set command:

```
$ line="Micro Logic Corp.:Box 174:Hackensack, NJ 07602"
$ IFS=:
$ set $line
$ echo $#                      How many parameters were set?
3
$ for field; do echo $field; done
Micro Logic Corp.
Box 174
Hackensack, NJ 07602
$
```

This technique is a powerful one; it uses all built-in shell commands, which also makes it very fast. (An alternative approach might have been to echo the value of $line into the tr command, where all colons could have been translated into newlines, an approach that would have been much slower.) This technique is used in a final version of the rolo program that's presented in Chapter 14, "Rolo Revisited."

The following program, called number2, is a final version of the line numbering program presented in Chapter 10, "Reading and Printing Data." This program faith-fully prints the input lines to standard output, preceded by a line number. Notice the use of printf to right-align the line numbers.

```
$ cat number2
#
# Number lines from files given as argument or from
# standard input if none supplied (final version)
#

# Modify the IFS to preserve leading whitespace on input

IFS='
'    # Just a newline appears between the quotes

lineno=1

cat $* |
while read -r line
do
```

```
        printf "%5d:%s\n" $lineno "$line"
        lineno=$(( lineno + 1 ))
done
```

Here's a sample execution of number:

```
$ number2 words
   1:#
   2:# Count all of the words on standard input
   3:#
   4:
   5:count=0
   6:while read line
   7:do
   8:  set -- $line
   9:  count=$(( count + $# ))
  10:done
  11:
  12:echo $count
$
```

Because the IFS has an influence on the way things are interpreted by the shell, if you're going to change it in your program, it's usually wise to save the old value first in another variable (such as OIFS) and then restore it after you've finished the operations that depend on the changed IFS.

The readonly Command

The readonly command is used to specify variables whose values cannot be subsequently changed. For example,

```
readonly PATH HOME
```

makes the PATH and HOME variables read-only. Subsequently attempting to assign a value to these variables causes the shell to issue an error message:

```
$ PATH=/bin:/usr/bin:.:
$ readonly PATH
$ PATH=$PATH:/users/steve/bin
sh: PATH: is read-only
$
```

Here you see that after the variable PATH was made read-only, the shell printed an error message when an attempt was made to assign a value to it.

To get a list of your read-only variables, type **readonly -p** without any arguments:[2]

```
$ readonly -p
readonly PATH=/bin:/usr/bin:.:
$
```

unset removes both exported and local shell variables.

You should be aware of the fact that the read-only variable attribute is not passed down to subshells. Also, after a variable has been made read-only in a shell, there is no way to "undo" it.

The unset **Command**

Sometimes you may want to remove the definition of a variable from your environment. To do so, you type unset followed by the names of the variables:

```
$ x=100
$ echo $x
100
$ unset x            Remove x from the environment
$ echo $x

$
```

You can't unset a read-only variable. Furthermore, the variables IFS, MAILCHECK, PATH, PS1, and PS2 cannot be unset. Also, some older shells do not support the unset command.

Exercises

1. Given the following variable assignments:

```
$ EDITOR=/bin/vi
$ DB=
$ EDITFLAG=yes
$ PHONEBOOK=
$
```

---

[2]*By default, Bash produces output of the form* declare -r *variable. To get POSIX-compliant output, you must run Bash with the* –posix *command-line option or run the* set *command with the* -o posix *option.*

What will be the results of the following commands?

```
echo ${EDITOR}                    echo ${DB:=/users/pat/db}
echo ${EDITOR:-/bin/ed}           echo ${PHONEBOOK:?}
echo ${DB:-/users/pat/db}         ed=${EDITFLAG:+${EDITOR:-/bin/ed}}
```

2. Rewrite the home program from Exercise 5 in Chapter 7 to use the set command and the IFS to extract the home directory from /etc/passwd. What happens to the program if one of the fields in the file is null, as in

```
steve:*:203:100::/users/steve:/usr/bin/ksh
```

Here the fifth field is null (::).

3. Using the fact that the shell construct ${#*var*} gives the number of characters stored in *var*, rewrite wc in the shell. Be sure to use integer arithmetic! (Notes: Change your IFS variable to just a newline character so that leading whitespace characters on input are preserved, and also use the -r option to the shell's read command so that terminating backslash characters on the input are ignored.)

4. Write a function called rightmatch that takes two arguments as shown:

rightmatch *value pattern*

where *value* is a sequence of one or more characters, and *pattern* is a shell pattern that is to be removed from the right side of *value*. The *shortest* matching pattern should be removed from *value* and the result written to standard output. Here is some sample output:

```
$ rightmatch test.c .c
test
$ rightmatch /usr/spool/uucppublic '/*'
/usr/spool
$ rightmatch /usr/spool/uucppublic o
/usr/spool/uucppublic
$
```

The last example shows that the rightmatch function should simply echo its first argument if it does not end with the specified pattern.

5. Write a function called leftmatch that works similarly to the rightmatch function developed in Exercise 4. Its two arguments should be as follows:

leftmatch *pattern value*

Here are some example uses:

```
$ leftmatch /usr/spool/ /usr/spool/uucppublic
uucppublic
$ leftmatch s. s.main.c
main.c
$
```

6. Write a function called `substring` that uses the `leftmatch` and `rightmatch` functions developed in Exercises 4 and 5 to remove a pattern from the left and right side of a value. It should take three arguments as shown:

```
$ substring /usr/ /usr/spool/uucppublic /uucppublic
spool
$ substring s. s.main.c .c
main
$ substring s. s.main.c .o        Only left match
main.c
$ substring x. s.main.c .o        No matches
s.main.c
$
```

7. Modify the `substring`, `leftmatch`, and `rightmatch` functions developed in the previous exercises to take options that allow you to remove the *largest* possible matches of the specified pattern from the left or right side of the specified value.

13

Loose Ends

W e've put commands and features into this chapter that for one reason or another did not logically fit into earlier chapters. There's no particular rationale for their order of presentation.

The eval **Command**

This section describes another of the more unusual commands in the shell: eval. Its format is as follows:

eval *command-line*

where *command-line* is a normal command line that you would type at the terminal. When you put eval in front of it, however, the net effect is that the shell scans the command line *twice* before executing it.[1] For the simple case, this really has no effect:

```
$ eval echo hello
hello
$
```

But consider the following example without the use of eval:

```
$ pipe="|"
$ ls $pipe wc -l
|: No such file or directory
wc: No such file or directory
-l: No such file or directory
$
```

---

[1] *Actually, what happens is that* eval *simply executes the command passed to it as arguments; so the shell processes the command line when passing the arguments to* eval, *and then once again when* eval *executes the command. The net result is that the command line is scanned twice by the shell.*

Those errors come from 1s. The shell takes care of pipes and I/O redirection *before* variable substitution, so it never recognizes the pipe symbol inside pipe. The result is that the three arguments |, wc, and -1 are passed to 1s as arguments.

Putting eval in front of the command sequence gives the desired results:

```
$ eval ls $pipe wc -l
     16
$
```

The first time the shell scans the command line, it substitutes | as the value of pipe. Then eval causes it to rescan the line, at which point the | is recognized by the shell as the pipe symbol.

The eval command is frequently used in shell programs that build up command lines inside one or more variables. If the variables contain any characters that must be seen by the shell directly on the command line (that is, not as the result of substitution), eval can be useful. Command terminator (;, |, &), I/O redirection (<, >), and quote characters are among the characters that must appear directly on the command line to have any special meaning to the shell.

For the next example, consider writing a program last whose sole purpose is to display the last argument passed to it. You needed to get at the last argument in the mycp program in Chapter 10, "Reading and Printing Data." There you did so by shifting all the arguments until the last one was left. You can also use eval to get at it as shown:

```
$ cat last
eval echo \$$#
$ last one two three four
four
$ last *                          Get the last file
zoo_report
$
```

The first time the shell scans

```
echo \$$#
```

the backslash tells it to ignore the $ that immediately follows. After that, it encounters the special parameter $#, so it substitutes its value on the command line. The command now looks like this:

```
echo $4
```

(the backslash is removed by the shell after the first scan). When the shell rescans this line, it substitutes the value of $4 and then executes echo.

This same technique could be used if you had a variable called arg that contained a digit, for example, and you wanted to display the positional parameter referenced by arg. You could simply write

```
eval echo \$$arg
```

The only problem is that just the first nine positional parameters can be accessed this way; to access positional parameters 10 and greater, you must use the ${n} construct:

```
eval echo \${$arg}
```

Here's how the eval command can be used to effectively create "pointers" to variables:

```
$ x=100
$ ptrx=x
$ eval echo \$$ptrx            Dereference ptrx
100
$ eval $ptrx=50               Store 50 in var that ptrx points to
$ echo $x                     See what happened
50
$
```

The wait Command

If you submit a command line to the background for execution, that command line runs in a subshell independent of your current shell (the job is said to run *asynchronously)*. At times, you may want to wait for the background process (also known as a *child* process because it's spawned from your current shell—the *parent)* to finish execution before proceeding. For example, you may have sent a large sort into the background and now want to wait for the sort to finish because you need to use the sorted data.

The wait command is for such a purpose. Its general format is

```
wait process-id
```

where *process-id* is the process id number of the process you want to wait for. If omitted, the shell waits for all child processes to complete execution. Execution of your current shell will be suspended until the process or processes finish execution. You can try the wait command at your terminal:

```
$ sort big-data > sorted_data &        Send it to the background
[1] 3423                               Job number & process id from the shell
$ date                                 Do some other work
Wed Oct  2 15:05:42 EDT 2002
$ wait 3423                            Now wait for the sort to finish
$                                      When sort finishes, prompt is returned
```

The $! Variable

If you have only one process running in the background, then wait with no argument suffices. However, if you're running more than one command in the background and you want to wait on a particular one, you can take advantage of the fact that the shell stores the process id of the last command executed in the background inside the special variable $!. So the command

```
wait $!
```

waits for the last process sent to the background to complete execution. As mentioned, if you send several commands to the background, you can save the value of this variable for later use with wait:

```
prog1 &
pid1=$!
...
prog2 &
pid2=$!
...
wait $pid1        # wait for prog1 to finish
...
wait $pid2        # wait for prog2 to finish
```

The trap Command

When you press the Delete[2] or Break key at your terminal during execution of a shell program, normally that program is immediately terminated, and your command prompt returned. This may not always be desirable. For instance, you may end up leaving a bunch of temporary files that won't get cleaned up.

The pressing of the Delete key at the terminal sends what's known as a *signal* to the executing program. The program can specify the action that should be taken on receipt of the signal. This is done with the trap command, whose general format is

---

[2]*Some Unix systems use Ctrl+c rather than the Delete key for this purpose. You can determine which key sequence is used with the* stty *command.*

trap *commands signals*

where *commands* is one or more commands that will be executed whenever any of the signals specified by *signals* is received.

Numbers are assigned to the different types of signals, and the more commonly used ones are summarized in Table 13.1. A more complete list is given under the trap command in Appendix A, "Shell Summary."

TABLE 13.1   Commonly Used Signal Numbers

Signal	Generated for
0	Exit from the shell
1	Hangup
2	Interrupt (for example, Delete, *Ctrl+c* key)
15	Software termination signal (sent by kill by default)

As an example of the trap command, the following shows how you can remove some files and then exit if someone tries to abort the program from the terminal:

```
trap "rm $WORKDIR/work1$$ $WORKDIR/dataout$$; exit" 2
```

From the point in the shell program that this trap is executed, the two files work1$$ and dataout$$ will be automatically removed if signal number 2 is received by the program. So if the user interrupts execution of the program after this trap is executed, you can be assured that these two files will be cleaned up. The exit that follows the rm is necessary because without it execution would continue in the program at the point that it left off when the signal was received.

Signal number 1 is generated for hangup: Either someone intentionally hangs up the line or the line gets accidentally disconnected. You can modify the preceding trap to also remove the two specified files in this case by adding signal number 1 to the list of signals:

```
trap "rm $WORKDIR/work1$$ $WORKDIR/dataout$$; exit"  1 2
```

Now these files will be removed if the line gets hung up or if the Delete key gets pressed.

The commands specified to trap must be enclosed in quotes if they contain more than one command. Also note that the shell scans the command line at the time that the trap command gets executed and also again when one of the listed signals is received. So in the preceding example, the value of WORKDIR and $$ will be substituted at the time that the trap command is executed. If you wanted this substitution to occur at the time that either signal 1 or 2 was received (for example, WORKDIR may not have been defined yet), you can put the commands inside single quotes:

```
trap 'rm $WORKDIR/work1$$ $WORKDIR/dataout$$; exit'  1 2
```

The trap command can be used to make your programs more user friendly. In the next chapter, when we revisit the rolo program, the signal generated by the Delete key is caught by the program and brings the user back to the main menu. In this way, this key can be used to abort the current operation without exiting from the program.

trap with No Arguments

Executing trap with no arguments results in the display of any traps that you have changed.

```
$ trap 'echo logged off at $(date) >>$HOME/logoffs' 0
$ trap                          List changed traps
trap - 'echo logged off at $(date) >>$HOME/logoffs' EXIT
$ Ctrl+d                        Log off
login: steve                    Log back in
Password:
$ cat $HOME/logoffs             See what happened
logged off at Wed Oct  2 15:11:58 EDT 2002
$
```

A trap was set to be executed whenever signal 0 was received by the shell. This signal is generated whenever the shell is exited. Because this was set in the login shell, the trap will be taken when you log off. The purpose of this trap is to write the time you logged off into the file $HOME/logoffs. The command is enclosed in single quotes to prevent the shell from executing date when the trap is defined.

The trap command is then executed with no arguments, which results in the display of the changed action to be taken for signal 0 (EXIT). Next, steve logs off and then back on again to see whether the trap works. Displaying the contents of $HOME/logoffs verifies that the echo command was executed when steve logged off.

Ignoring Signals

If the command listed for trap is null, the specified signal will be ignored when received. For example, the command

```
trap "" 2
```

specifies that the interrupt signal is to be ignored. You might want to ignore certain signals when performing some operation that you don't want interrupted.

Note that the first argument must be specified for a signal to be ignored and is not equivalent to writing the following, which has a separate meaning of its own:

```
trap 2
```

If you ignore a signal, all subshells also ignore that signal. However, if you specify an action to be taken on receipt of a signal, all subshells will still take the default action on receipt of that signal. For the signals we've described, this means that the subshells will be terminated.

Suppose that you execute the command

```
trap "" 2
```

and then execute a subshell, which in turn executes other shell programs as subshells. If an interrupt signal is then generated, it will have no effect on the shells or subshells that are executing because they will all ignore the signal.

If instead of executing the previous trap command you execute

```
trap : 2
```

and then execute your subshells, then on receiving the interrupt signal the current shell will do nothing (it will execute the null command), but all active subshells will be terminated (they will take the default action—termination).

Resetting Traps

After you've changed the default action to be taken on receipt of a signal, you can change it back again with trap if you simply omit the first argument; so

```
trap 1 2
```

resets the action to be taken on receipt of signals 1 or 2 back to the default.

More on I/O

You know about the standard constructs <, >, and >> for input redirection, output redirection, and output redirection with append, respectively. You also know that you can redirect standard error from any command simply by writing

command 2> *file*

Sometimes you may want to explicitly write to standard error in your program. You can redirect the standard output for a command to standard error by writing

command >&   2

The notation >& specifies output redirection to a file associated with the *file descriptor* that follows. File descriptor 0 is standard input, descriptor 1 is standard output, and descriptor 2 is standard error. Note that no space is permitted between the > and the &.

So to write an error message to standard error, you write

```
echo "Invalid number of arguments" >&   2
```

Frequently, you may want to collect the standard output and the standard error output from a program into the same file. If you know the name of the file, this is straightforward enough:

command >foo 2>>foo

Here, both the standard output and the standard error output from *command* will be written to foo.

You can also write

command >foo 2>&1

to achieve the same effect; standard output is redirected to foo, and standard error is redirected to standard output (which has already been redirected to foo). Note that because the shell evaluates redirection from left to right on the command line, the last example cannot be written

command 2>&1 > foo

because this would first redirect standard error to standard output (your terminal by default) and then standard output to foo.

You recall that you can also dynamically redirect standard input or output in a program using the exec command:

```
exec < datafile
```

redirects standard input from the file datafile. Subsequent commands executed that read from standard input will read from datafile instead. The command

```
exec > /tmp/output
```

does the same thing with standard output: All commands that subsequently write to standard output will write to /tmp/output (unless explicitly redirected elsewhere). Naturally, standard error can be reassigned this way as well:

```
exec 2> /tmp/errors
```

Here, all output to standard error will go to /tmp/errors.

<&- **and** >&-

The characters >&- have the effect of closing standard output. If preceded by a file descriptor, the associated file is closed instead. So writing (the impractical)

```
ls >&-
```

causes the output from ls to go nowhere because standard output is closed by the shell before ls is executed.

The same thing applies for input using <&-.

```
$ wc <&-
     0    0    0
$
```

Inline Input Redirection

If the << characters follow a command in the format

command <<*word*

the shell uses the lines that follow as the standard input for *command*, until a line that contains just *word* is found. Here's a small example at the terminal:

```
$ wc -l <<ENDOFDATA              Use lines up to ENDOFDATA as standard input
> here's a line
> and another
> and yet another
> ENDOFDATA
     3
$
```

Here the shell fed every line typed into the standard input of wc until it encountered the line containing just ENDOFDATA.

Inline input redirection is a powerful feature when used inside shell programs. It lets you specify the standard input to a command directly in the program, thus obviating the need to write it into a separate file first, or to use echo to get it into the standard input of the command.

```
$ cat mailmsg
mail $* <<END-OF-DATA

Attention:

Our monthly computer users group meeting
will take place on Friday, October 4, 2002 at
8am in Room 1A-308. Please try to attend.

END-OF-DATA
$
```

To execute this program for all members of the group that are contained in the file users_list, you could write

```
mailmsg $(cat users_list)
```

The shell performs parameter substitution for the redirected input data, executes back-quoted commands, and recognizes the backslash character. However, any other special characters, such as *, |, and ", are ignored. If you have dollar signs, back quotes, or backslashes in these lines that you don't want interpreted by the shell, you can precede them with a backslash character. Alternatively, if you want the shell to leave the input lines completely untouched, you can precede the word that follows the << with a backslash.

```
$ cat <<FOOBAR
> $HOME
> *****
>       \$foobar
> `date`
> FOOBAR                          Terminates the input
/users/steve
*****
    $foobar
Wed Oct  2 15:23:15 EDT 2002
$
```

Here the shell supplies all the lines up to FOOBAR as the input to cat. It substitutes the value for HOME but not for foobar because it's preceded by a backslash. The date command is also executed because back quotes are interpreted.

```
$ cat <<\FOOBAR
> \\\\
> `date`
> $HOME
> FOOBAR
\\\\
`date`
$HOME
$
```

The backslash before FOOBAR tells the shell to leave the following lines alone. So it ignores the dollar signs, backslashes, and back quotes.

Use care when selecting the word that follows the <<. Generally, just make sure that it's weird enough so that the chances of it accidentally appearing in the following lines are remote.

If the first character that follows the << is a dash (-), leading tab characters in the input will be removed by the shell. This is useful for visually indenting the redirected text.

```
$ cat <<-END
>           Indented lines
>           So there you have it
> END
Indented lines
So there you have it
$
```

Shell Archives

One of the best uses of the inline input redirection feature is for creating shell *archive* files. With this technique, one or more related shell programs can be put into a single file and then shipped to someone else using the standard Unix mail commands. When the archive is received, it can be easily "unpacked" by simply running the shell on it.

For example, here's an archived version of the lu, add, and rem programs used by rolo:

```
$ cat rolosubs
#
# Archived programs used by rolo.
#

echo Extracting lu
```

```
cat >lu <<\THE-END-OF-DATA
#
# Look someone up in the phone book
#

if [ "$#" -ne 1 ]
then
        echo "Incorrect number of arguments"
        echo "Usage: lu name"
        exit 1
fi

name=$1
grep "$name" $PHONEBOOK

if [ $? -ne 0 ]
then
        echo "I couldn't find $name in the phone book"
fi
THE-END-OF-DATA

echo Extracting add
cat >add <<\THE-END-OF-DATA
#
# Program to add someone to the phonebook file
#

if [ "$#" -ne 2 ]
then
        echo "Incorrect number of arguments"
        echo "Usage: add name number"
        exit 1
fi

echo "$1     $2" >> $PHONEBOOK
sort -o $PHONEBOOK $PHONEBOOK
THE-END-OF-DATA

echo Extracting rem
cat >rem <<\THE-END-OF-DATA
#
# Remove someone from the phone book
```

```
#

if [ "$#" -ne 1 ]
then
        echo "Incorrect number of arguments"
        echo "Usage: rem name"
        exit 1
fi

name=$1

#
# Find number of matching entries
#

matches=$(grep "$name" $PHONEBOOK | wc -l)

#
# If more than one match, issue message, else remove it
#

if [ "$matches" -gt 1 ]
then
        echo "More than one match; please qualify further"
elif [ "$matches" -eq 1 ]
then
        grep -v "$name" $PHONEBOOK > /tmp/phonebook
        mv /tmp/phonebook $PHONEBOOK
else
        echo "I couldn't find $name in the phone book"
fi
THE-END-OF-DATA
$
```

To be complete, this archive should probably include rolo as well, but we didn't here to conserve space.

Now you have one file, rolosubs, that contains the source for the three programs lu, add, and rem, which can be sent to someone else using mail:

```
$ mail tony@aisystems.com < rolosubs          Mail the archive
$ mail tony@aisystems.com                     Mail tony a message
Tony,
```

```
      I mailed you a shell archive containing the programs
      lu, add, and rem. rolo itself will be sent along shortly.
Pat
```
Ctrl+d
```
$
```

When tony receives the file in his mail, he can extract the three programs simply by running the shell on the file (after having first removed some header lines that mail sticks at the beginning of the file):

```
$ sh rolosubs
Extracting lu
Extracting add
Extracting rem
$ ls lu add rem
add
lu
rem
$
```

The shar program used to create the rolosubs archive file is simple:

```
$ cat shar
#
# Program to create a shell archive
# from a set of files
#

echo "#"
echo "# To restore, type sh archive"
echo "#"

for file
do
    echo
    echo "echo Extracting $file"
    echo "cat >$file <<\THE-END-OF-DATA"
    cat $file
    echo "THE-END-OF-DATA"
done
```

Refer to the contents of the rolosubs file when studying the operation of this shar program. Remember, shar actually creates a shell program.

More sophisticated archiving programs allow entire directories to be archived and also check to make sure that no data is lost in the transmission (see Exercises 2 and 3 at the end of this chapter). The Unix sum command can be used to generate a checksum for a program. This checksum can be generated on the sending end for each file in the archive, and then commands included in the shell archive can verify the sum on the receiving end. If they don't match, an error message can be displayed.

Functions

The POSIX standard shell supports the concept of functions; note that older shells may not support this feature.

To define a function, you use the general format:

name () { *command*; ... *command*; }

where *name* is the name of the function, the parentheses denote to the shell that a function is being defined, and the commands enclosed between the curly braces define the body of the function. These commands will be executed whenever the function is executed. Note that at least one whitespace character must separate the { from the first command, and that a semicolon must separate the last command from the closing brace if they occur on the same line.

The following defines a function called nu that displays the number of logged-in users:

```
nu () { who | wc -l; }
```

You execute a function the same way you execute an ordinary command: simply by typing its name to the shell:

```
$ nu
     22
$
```

Arguments listed after the function on the command line are assigned to the positional parameters $1, $2, ..., just as with any other command. Here's a function called nrrun that runs tbl, nroff, and lp on the file given as its argument:

```
$ nrrun () { tbl $1 | nroff -mm -Tlp | lp; }
$ nrrun memo1                    Run it on memo1
request id is laser1-33 (standard input)
$
```

Functions exist only in the shell in which they're defined; that is, they can't be passed down to subshells. Further, because the function is executed in the current

shell, changes made to the current directory or to variables remain after the function
has completed execution:

```
$ db () {
>        PATH=$PATH:/uxn2/data
>        PS1=DB:
>        cd /uxn2/data
>        }
$ db                              Execute it
DB:
```

As you see, a function definition can continue over as many lines as necessary. The
shell displays your secondary command prompt until you close the definition with
the }.

You can put definitions for commonly used functions inside your .profile so that
they'll be available whenever you log in. Alternatively, you can group the definitions
in a file, say myfuncs, and then execute the file in the current shell by typing

```
. myfuncs
```

This has the effect of causing any functions defined inside myfuncs to be read in and
defined to the current shell.

The following function, called mycd, takes advantage of the fact that functions are
run in the current environment. It mimics the operation of the Korn shell's cd
command, which has the capability to substitute portions of the current directory's
path with something else (see the discussion of cd in Chapter 15, "Interactive and
Nonstandard Shell Features," for more details).

```
$ cat myfuncs                    See what's inside
#
# new cd function:
#       mycd dir Switches dir
#       mycd old new  Substitute new for old in current directory's path
#
mycd ()
{
        if [ $# -le 1 ]
        then
                # normal case -- 0 or 1 argument
                cd $1
        elif [ $# -eq 2 ]
        then
                # special case -- substitute $2 for $1
```

```
               cd $(echo $PWD | sed "s|$1|$2|")
        else
               # cd can't have more than two arguments
               echo mycd: bad argument count
               exit 1
        fi
}
```

```
$ . myfuncs                  Read in definition
$ pwd
/users/steve
$ mycd /users/pat            Change directory
$ pwd                        Did it work?
/users/pat
$ mycd pat tony              Substitute tony for pat
$ pwd
/users/tony
$
```

After a function has been defined, its execution will be faster than an equivalent shell program file. That's because the shell won't have to search the disk for the program, open the file, and read its contents into memory.

Another advantage of functions is the capability to group all your related shell programs in a single file if desired. For example, the add, lu, and rem programs from Chapter 11, "Your Environment," can be defined as functions inside rolo. The template for such an approach is shown:

```
$ cat rolo
#
# rolo program written in function form
#


#
# Function to add someone to the phonebook file
#


add () {
        # put commands from add program here
}


#
# Function to look someone up in the phone book
```

```
#

lu () {
        # put commands from lu program here
}

#
# Function to remove someone from the phone book
#

rem () {
        # put commands from rem program here
}

#
# rolo - rolodex program to look up, add, and
#        remove people from the phone book
#

# put commands from rolo here
$
```

None of the commands inside the original add, lu, rem, or rolo programs would
have to be changed. These first three programs are turned into functions by including them inside rolo, sandwiched between the function header and the closing curly
brace. Note that defining them as functions this way now makes them inaccessible
as standalone commands.

Removing a Function Definition

To remove the definition of a function from the shell, you use the unset command
with the –f option. This is the same command you use to remove the definition of a
variable to the shell.

```
$ unset -f nu
$ nu
sh: nu: not found
$
```

The return Command

If you execute an exit command from inside a function, its effect is not only to
terminate execution of the function but also of the shell program that called the

function. If you instead want to just terminate execution of the function, you can use the `return` command, whose format is

```
return n
```

The value n is used as the return status of the function. If omitted, the status returned is that of the last command executed. This is also what gets returned if you don't execute a `return` at all in your function. The return status is in all other ways equivalent to the exit status: You can access its value through the shell variable $?, and you can also test it in `if`, `while`, and `until` commands.

The `type` Command

When you type in the name of a command to execute, it's frequently useful to know where that command is coming from. In other words, is the command actually defined as a function? Is it a shell program? Is it a shell built-in? Is it a standard Unix command? This is where the `type` command comes in handy. The `type` command takes one or more command names as its argument and tells you what it knows about it. Here are some examples:

```
$ nu () { who | wc -l; }
$ type pwd
pwd is a shell builtin
$ type troff
troff is /usr/bin/troff
$ type cat
cat is /bin/cat
$ type nu
nu is a function
$
```

Exercises

1. Using `eval`, write a program called `recho` that prints its arguments in reverse order. So

   ```
   recho one two three
   ```

   should produce

   ```
   three two one
   ```

   Assume that more than nine arguments can be passed to the program.

2. Modify the shar program presented in this chapter to handle directories. shar should recognize input files from different directories and should make sure that the directories are created if necessary when the archive is unpacked. Also allow shar to be used to archive an entire directory.

```
$ ls rolo
lu
add
rem
rolo
$ shar rolo/lu rolo/add rolo/rem > rolosubs.shar
$ shar rolo > rolo.shar
```

In the first case, shar was used to archive three files from the rolo directory. In the last case, shar was used to archive the entire rolo directory.

3. Modify shar to include in the archive the character count for each file and commands to compare the count of each extracted file against the count of the original file. If a discrepancy occurs, an error should be noted, as in

```
add: expected 345 characters, extracted 343.
```

14

Rolo Revisited

T his chapter presents a final version of the `rolo` program. This version is enhanced with additional options and also allows for more general types of entries (other than just names and numbers). The sections in this chapter discuss the individual programs in `rolo`, starting with `rolo` itself. At the end of this chapter, sample output is shown.

Design Considerations

A more practical type of rolodex program would permit more than just the names and numbers to be stored in the phone book. You'd probably want to keep addresses (maybe even electronic mail addresses) there as well. The new `rolo` program allows entries in the phone book to consist of multiple lines. For example, a typical entry might be

```
Steve's Ice Cream
444 6th Avenue
New York City 10003
212-555-3021
```

To increase the flexibility of the program, we're allowing an individual entry to contain as many lines as desired. So another entry in the phone book might read

```
YMCA
(201) 555-2344
```

To logically separate one entry from the next inside the phone book file, each entry is "packed" into a single line. This is done by replacing the terminating newline characters in an entry with a special character. We arbitrarily chose the caret ^. The only restriction here is that this character not be used as part of the entry itself.

Using this technique, the first entry shown would be stored in the phone book file as

```
Steve's Ice Cream^444 6th Avenue^New York City 10003^212-555-3021^
```

and the second entry shown as

```
YMCA^(201) 555-2344^
```

You'll shortly see how convenient it becomes to process the entries when they're stored in this format. Now we'll describe each program written for the rolodex program.

rolo

```
#
# rolo - rolodex program to look up, add,
#        remove and change entries from the phone book
#


#
# Set PHONEBOOK to point to the phone book file
# and export it so other progs know about it
# if it's set on entry, then leave it alone
#

: ${PHONEBOOK:=$HOME/phonebook}
export PHONEBOOK
if [ ! -e "$PHONEBOOK" ]
then
        echo "$PHONEBOOK does not exist!"
        echo "Should I create it for you (y/n)? \c"
        read answer

        if [ "$answer" != y ]
        then
                exit 1
        fi

        > $PHONEBOOK || exit 1        # exit if the creation fails
fi

#
```

```
# If arguments are supplied, then do a lookup
#

if [ "$#" -ne 0 ]
then
        lu "$@"
        exit
fi

#
# Set trap on interrupt (DELETE key) to continue the loop
#

trap "continue" 2

#
# Loop until user selects 'exit'
#

while true
do
        #
        # Display menu
        #

        echo '
        Would you like to:

                1. Look someone up
                2. Add someone to the phone book
                3. Remove someone from the phone book
                4. Change an entry in the phone book
                5. List all names and numbers in the phone book
                6. Exit this program

        Please select one of the above (1-6): \c'

        #
        # Read and process selection
        #

        read choice
```

```
        echo
        case "$choice"
        in
            1) echo "Enter name to look up: \c"
               read name

               if [ -z "$name" ]
               then
                       echo "Lookup ignored"
               else
                       lu "$name"
               fi;;
            2) add;;
            3) echo "Enter name to remove: \c"
               read name
               if [ -z "$name" ]
               then
                       echo "Removal ignored"
               else
                       rem "$name"
               fi;;
            4) echo "Enter name to change: \c"
               read name
               if [ -z "$name" ]
               then
                       echo "Change ignored"
               else
                       change "$name"
               fi;;
            5) listall;;
            6) exit 0;;
            *) echo "Bad choice\a";;
        esac
    done
```

Instead of requiring that the user have a phone book file in his or her home directory, the program checks on startup to see whether the variable PHONEBOOK has been
set. If it has, it's assumed that it contains the name of the phone book file. If it
hasn't, it's set to $HOME/phonebook as the default. In either case, the program then
checks to see whether the file exists, and if it doesn't, instead of immediately exiting,
asks the user whether he would like to have an initial file created. This was added so
that first-time users of rolo can have an empty phone book file created for them by
the program.

This version of rolo also has a couple of new items added to the menu. Because individual entries can be rather long, an editing option has been added to allow you to edit a particular entry. Formerly, the only way to change an entry was to first remove it and then add a new one, a strategy that was perfectly acceptable when the entries were small.

Another option allows for listing of the entire phone book. With this option, just the first and last lines of each entry are displayed. This assumes that the user follows some convention such as putting the name on the first line and the number on the last.

The entire menu selection process was placed inside a while loop so that rolo will continue to display menus until the "exit" option is picked from the menu.

A trap command is executed before the loop is entered. This trap specifies that a continue command is to be executed if signal number 2 is received. So if the user presses the Delete key in the middle of an operation (such as listing the entire phone book), the program won't exit but will abort the current operation and simply continue with the loop. This will result in the redisplay of the menu.

Because entries can now span as many lines as desired, the action performed when add is selected has been changed. Instead of asking for the name and number, rolo executes the add program to get the entry from the user.

For the lookup, change, and remove options, a check is made to ensure that the user doesn't simply press the Enter key when asked to type in the name. This avoids the RE error that grep issues if it's given a null first argument.

Now let's look at the individual programs that rolo executes. Each of the original programs has been changed to accommodate the new entry format and also to be more user friendly.

add

```
#
# Program to add someone to the phonebook file
#

echo "Type in your new entry"
echo "When you're done, type just a single Enter on the line."

first=
entry=

while true
do
```

```
        echo ">> \c"
        read line

        if [ -n "$line" ]
        then
                entry="$entry$line^"

                if [ -z "$first" ]
                then
                        first=$line
                fi
        else
                break
        fi
done


echo "$entry" >> $PHONEBOOK
sort -o $PHONEBOOK $PHONEBOOK
echo
echo "$first has been added to the phone book"
```

This program adds an entry to the phone book. It continually prompts the user to enter lines until a line with just an Enter is typed (that is, a null line). Each line that is entered is concatenated to the variable entry, with the special ^ character used to logically separate one line from the next.

When the while loop is exited, the new entry is added to the end of the phone book, and the file is sorted.

lu

```
#
# Look someone up in the phone book
#

name=$1
grep "$name" $PHONEBOOK > /tmp/matches$$

if [ ! -s /tmp/matches$$ ]
then
```

```
        echo "I can't find $name in the phone book"
else
        #
        # Display each of the matching entries
        #

        while read line
        do
                display "$line"
        done < /tmp/matches$$
fi

rm /tmp/matches$$
```

This is the program to look up an entry in the phone book. The matching entries are written to the file /tmp/matches$$. If the size of this file is zero, no match was found. Otherwise, the program enters a loop to read each line from the file (remember an entry is stored as a single line in the file) and then display it at the terminal. A program called display is used for this purpose. This program is also used by the rem and change programs to display entries at the terminal.

display

```
#
# Display entry from the phonebook
#

echo
echo "------------------------------------"

entry=$1
IFS="^"
set $entry

for line in "$1" "$2" "$3" "$4" "$5" "$6"
do
        printf "| %-34.34s |\n" $line
done
echo "|          o                o       |"
echo "------------------------------------"
echo
```

As noted, this program displays an entry passed as its argument. To make the output more aesthetically pleasing, the program actually "draws" a rolodex card. So typical output from `display` would look like this:

```
--------------------------------------
| Steve's Ice Cream                  |
| 444 6th Avenue                     |
| New York City  10003               |
| 212-555-3021                       |
|                                    |
|                                    |
|       o                   o        |
--------------------------------------
```

After skipping a line and then displaying the top of the card, `display` changes `IFS` to `^` and then executes the `set` command to assign each "line" to a different positional parameter. For example, if `entry` is equal to

```
Steve's Ice Cream^444 6th Avenue^New York City 10003^212-555-3021^
```

executing the set command assigns `Steve's Ice Cream` to `$1`, `444 6th Avenue` to `$2`, `New York City 10003` to `$3`, and `212-555-3021` to `$4`.

After executing the `set`, the program enters a `for` loop that will be executed exactly six times, no matter how many lines are contained in the entry (this ensures uniformity of our rolodex cards—the program can be easily modified to "draw" larger-sized cards if needed). If the `set` command was executed on `Steve's Ice Cream` as shown previously, `$5` and `$6` would be null, thus resulting in two blank lines to "fill out" the bottom of the card.

The `printf` command displays a line exactly 38 characters wide: the leading | followed by a space followed by the first 34 characters of `$line` followed by a space and a |.

rem

```
#
# Remove someone from the phone book
#

name=$1

#
```

```
# Get matching entries and save in temp file
#

grep "$name" $PHONEBOOK > /tmp/matches$$
if [ ! -s /tmp/matches$$ ]
then
        echo "I can't find $name in the phone book"
        exit 1
fi



#
# Display matching entries one at a time and confirm removal
#

while read line
do
        display "$line"
        echo "Remove this entry (y/n)? \c"
        read answer < /dev/tty

        if [ "$answer" = y ]
        then
                break
        fi
done < /tmp/matches$$

rm /tmp/matches$$

if [ "$answer" = y ]
then
        if grep -v "^$line$" $PHONEBOOK > /tmp/phonebook$$
        then
                mv /tmp/phonebook$$ $PHONEBOOK
                echo "Selected entry has been removed"
        else
                echo "Entry not removed"
        fi
fi
```

The rem program collects all matching entries into a temporary file. If the size of the file is zero, no match was found and an appropriate message is issued. Otherwise, for each matching entry, the program displays the entry and asks the user whether that entry is to be removed. This provides reassurance to the user that the entry the user intends to remove is the same one that the program intends to remove, even in the single match case.

After a y has been typed to the program, a break command is executed to exit from the loop. Outside the loop, the program tests the value of answer to determine how the loop was exited. If its value is not equal to y, then the user doesn't want to remove an entry after all (for whatever reason). Otherwise, the program proceeds with the removal by greping out all lines but the desired one (and here the pattern specified to grep is made to match only entire lines by anchoring it to the start and end of the line).

change

```
#
# Change an entry in the phone book
#

name=$1

#
# Get matching entries and save in temp file
#

grep "$name" $PHONEBOOK > /tmp/matches$$
if [ ! -s /tmp/matches$$ ]
then
        echo "I can't find $name in the phone book"
        exit 1
fi

#
# Display matching entries one at a time and confirm change
#

while read line
do
        display "$line"
        echo "Change this entry (y/n)? \c"
        read answer < /dev/tty
```

```
        if [ "$answer" = y ]
        then
                break
        fi
done < /tmp/matches$$

rm /tmp/matches$$

if [ "$answer" != y ]
then
        exit
fi

#
# Start up editor on the confirmed entry
#

echo "$line\c" | tr '^' '\012' > /tmp/ed$$

echo "Enter changes with ${EDITOR:=/bin/ed}"
trap "" 2            # don't abort if DELETE hit while editing
$EDITOR /tmp/ed$$

#
# Remove old entry now and insert new one
#

grep -v "^$line$" $PHONEBOOK > /tmp/phonebook$$
{ tr '\012' '^' < /tmp/ed$$; echo; } >> /tmp/phonebook$$
# last echo was to put back trailing newline translated by tr

sort /tmp/phonebook$$ -o $PHONEBOOK
rm /tmp/ed$$ /tmp/phonebook$$
```

The change program allows the user to edit an entry in the phone book. The initial code is virtually identical to rem: it finds the matching entries and then prompts the user to select the one to be changed.

The selected entry is then written into the temporary file /tmp/ed$$, with the ^ characters translated to newlines. This "unfolds" the entry into separate lines for convenient editing. The program then displays the message

```
echo "Enter changes with ${EDITOR:=/bin/ed}"
```

which serves a dual purpose: It tells the user what editor will be used to make the change while at the same time setting the variable EDITOR to /bin/ed if it's not already set. This technique allows the user to use his or her preferred editor by simply assigning its name to the variable EDITOR and exporting it before executing rolo:

```
$ EDITOR=vi; export EDITOR; rolo
```

The signal generated by the Delete key (2) is ignored so that if the user presses this key while in the editor, the change program won't abort. The editor is then started to allow the user to edit the entry. After the user makes his changes, writes the file, and quits the editor, control is given back to change. The old entry is then removed from the phone book with grep, and the modified entry is converted into the special internal format with tr and tacked onto the end. An extra newline character must be added here to make sure that a real newline is stored in the file after the entry. This is done with an echo with no arguments.

The phone book file is then sorted, and the temporary files removed.

listall

```
#
# list all of the entries in the phone book
#

IFS='^'      # to be used in set command below
echo "----------------------------------------------------"
while read line
do
        #
        # Get the first and last fields, presumably names and numbers
        #

        set $line

        #
        # display 1st and last fields (in reverse order!)
        #

        eval printf "\"%-40.40s %s\\n\"" "\"$1\"" "\"\${$#}\""
done < $PHONEBOOK
echo "----------------------------------------------------"
```

The listall program lists all entries in the phone book, printing just the first and last lines of each entry. The internal field separator characters (IFS) is set to a ^, to be used later inside the loop. Each line from the phone book file is then read and assigned to the variable line. The set command is used to assign each field to the positional parameters.

The trick now is to get the value of the first and last positional parameters because that's what we want to display. The first one is easy because it can be directly referenced as $1. To get the last one, you use eval as you saw in Chapter 13, "Loose Ends." The command

```
eval echo \${$#}
```

has the effect of displaying the value of the last positional parameter. The command

```
eval printf "\"%-40.40s %-s\\n\"" "\"$1\"" "\"\${$#}\""
```

gets evaluated to

```
printf "%-40.40s %-s\n" "Steve's Ice Cream" "${4}"
```

using the entry shown previously as the example, and then the shell rescans the line to substitute the value of ${4} before executing printf.

Sample Output

Now it's time to see how rolo works. We'll start with an empty phone book and add a few entries to it. Then we'll list all the entries, look up a particular one, and change one (using the default editor ed—remember that the variable EDITOR can always be set to a different editor and then exported). To conserve space, we'll show only the full menu that rolo displays the first time.

```
$ PHONEBOOK=/users/steve/misc/book
$ export PHONEBOOK
$ rolo                          Start it up
/users/steve/misc/book does not exist!
Should I create it for you (y/n)? y

    Would you like to:

        1. Look someone up
        2. Add someone to the phone book
        3. Remove someone from the phone book
        4. Change an entry in the phone book
```

```
             5. List all names and numbers in the phone book
             6. Exit this program

Please select one of the above (1-6): 2

Type in your new entry
When you're done, type just a single Enter on the line.
>> Steve's Ice Cream
>> 444 6th Avenue
>> New York City 10003
>> 212-555-3021
>>

Steve's Ice Cream has been added to the phone book

      Would you like to:
        ...
      Please select one of the above (1-6): 2

Type in your new entry
When you're done, type just a single Enter on the line.
>> YMCA
>> 973-555-2344
>>

YMCA has been added to the phone book
      Would you like to:
        ...
      Please select one of the above (1-6): 2

Type in your new entry
When you're done, type just a single Enter on the line.
>> Maureen Connelly
>> Hayden Book Companu
>> 10 Mulholland Drive
>> Hasbrouck Heights, N.J. 07604
>> 201-555-6000
>>

Maureen Connelly has been added to the phone book

      Would you like to:
```

```
        ...
    Please select one of the above (1-6): 2


Type in your new entry
When you're done, type just a single Enter on the line.
>> Teri Zak
>> Hayden Book Company
>> (see Maureen Connelly for address)
>> 201-555-6060
>>


Teri Zak has been added to the phone book

        Would you like to:
        ...
    Please select one of the above (1-6): 5



------------------------------------------------------------
Maureen Connelly                    201-555-6000
Steve's Ice Cream                   212-555-3021
Teri Zak                            201-555-6060
YMCA                                973-555-2344
------------------------------------------------------------


        Would you like to:
        ...
    Please select one of the above (1-6): 1
Enter name to look up: Maureen



------------------------------------
| Maureen Connelly                 |
| Hayden Book Companu              |
| 10 Mulholland Drive              |
| Hasbrouck Heights, NJ 07604      |
| 201-555-6000                     |
|      o                 o         |
------------------------------------
```

```
--------------------------------------
| Teri Zak                           |
| Hayden Book Company                |
| (see Maureen Connelly for address)|
| 201-555-6060                       |
|                                    |
|      o                 o           |
--------------------------------------
```

```
        Would you like to:
          ...
        Please select one of the above (1-6): 4
```

```
Enter name to change: Maureen
```

```
--------------------------------------
| Maureen Connelly                   |
| Hayden Book Companu                |
| 10 Mulholland Drive                |
| Hasbrouck Heights, NJ 07604        |
| 201-555-6000                       |
|      o                 o           |
--------------------------------------
```

```
Change this person (y/n)? y
Enter changes with /bin/ed
101
1,$p
Maureen Connelly
Hayden Book Companu
10 Mulholland Drive
Hasbrouck Heights, NJ 07604
201-555-6000
2s/anu/any                              Change the misspelling
Hayden Book Company
w
101
q
```

```
        Would you like to:
          ...
        Please select one of the above (1-6): 6
$
```

The only function not tested here is removal of an entry.

Hopefully this example has given you some insight on how to develop larger shell programs, and how to use the many different programming tools provided by the system. Other than the shell built-ins, rolo relies on tr, grep, an editor, sort, and the standard file system commands such as mv and rm to get the job done. The simplicity and elegance that enable you to easily tie all these tools together account for the deserved popularity of the Unix system.

See Appendix B for more information on downloading the rolo programs.

Chapter 15, "Interactive and Nonstandard Shell Features," introduces you to interactive features of the shell and two shells that have some nice features not found in the POSIX standard shell.

Exercises

1. Modify rolo so that upper- and lowercase letters are not distinguished when doing a lookup in the phone book.

2. Add a -m command-line option to rolo to send mail to the person who follows on the command line. Have rolo look up the person in the phone book and then look for the string mail:*mailaddr* in the matching entry, where *mailaddr* is the person's mail address. Then start up an editor (as in change mode) to allow the user to enter the mail message. When the editing is complete, mail the message to the user. If no mail address is found in the phone book, prompt for it.

   Also add a mail option to the menu so that it can be selected interactively. Prompt for the name of the person to send mail to.

3. After adding the -m option, add a -f option to specify that the mail message is to be taken from the file that follows on the command line. So

   ```
   rolo -m tony -f memo
   ```

   should look up tony and mail him the contents of the file memo.

4. Can you think of other ways to use rolo? For example, can it be used as a small general-purpose database program (for example, for storing recipes or employee data)?

5. Modify rolo to use the following convention instead of the exported PHONEBOOK variable: the file .rolo in each rolo user's home directory contains the pathname to that user's phone book file, for example:

   ```
   $ cat $HOME/.rolo
   /users/steve/misc/phonebook
   $
   ```

Then add an option to `rolo` to allow you to look up someone in another user's phone book (provided that you have read access to it). This option should be added to the command line (as a `-u` option) as well as to the menu. For example,

```
$ rolo -u pat Pizza
```

would look up `Pizza` in `pat`'s phone book, no matter who is running `rolo`. The program can find `pat`'s phone book by looking at `.rolo` in `pat`'s home directory.

6. What happens with `rolo` if the user adds an entry containing a ^ or [character?

7. Add a –s (send) option to `rolo` to mail a rolodex entry to a specified user. So

```
$ rolo -s tom pizza
```

should send the rolodex card entry for `pizza` to the user `tom`.

15

Interactive and Nonstandard Shell Features

In this chapter you'll learn about shell features that are either useful to interactive users or not part of the POSIX shell standard. These features are available in Bash and the Korn shell, the two most commonly available POSIX-compliant shells.

The Korn shell was developed by David Korn of AT&T Bell Laboratories. It was designed to be "upward compatible" with the System V Bourne shell and the POSIX standard shell. It is available in the standard Unix distributions from Sun, HP, and IBM, and is the default shell on MIPS workstations.

Bash (short for Bourne-Again Shell) was developed by Brian Fox for the Free Software Foundation. It was also designed to be upward compatible with the System V Bourne shell and the POSIX standard shell, and also contains many extensions from the Korn and C shells. Bash is the standard shell on Linux systems.

Except for a few minor differences, Bash and the Korn shell provide all the POSIX standard shell's features, as well as many new ones. To give you an idea of the compatibility of these shells with the POSIX standard, all shell programs in the previous chapters work under both Bash and the Korn shell.

We'll note any nonstandard features that we discuss in this chapter, and Table 15.4 at the end of this chapter lists the features supported by the different shells.

Getting the Right Shell

Most shells follow a convention that allows you to select a specific program to run a file. If the first two characters on the first line of a file are #!, the remainder of the line specifies an interpreter for the file. So

```
#!/usr/bin/ksh
```

specifies the Korn shell and

```
#!/usr/bin/bash
```

specifies Bash. If you use constructs specific to one shell, you can use this feature to force that shell to run your programs, avoiding compatibility problems.

Note that you can put any program you want here, so a Perl program beginning with

```
#!/usr/bin/perl
```

forces the shell to execute /usr/bin/perl on it.

You have to use this feature with caution, however, because many programs, such as Perl, don't reside in a standard place on every Unix system. Also, this is not a feature specified by the POSIX standard, even though it's found in every modern shell we've seen and is even implemented at the operating system level on many Unix versions.

The ENV File

When you start the shell, one of the first things it does is look in your environment for a variable called ENV. If it finds it, the file specified by ENV will be executed, much like the profile is executed when logging in. The ENV file usually contains commands to set up the shell's environment. Throughout this chapter, we'll mention various things that you may want to put into this file.

If you do decide to have an ENV file, you should set and export the ENV variable inside your .profile file:

```
$ cat .profile
 ...
ENV=$HOME/.alias
export ENV
 ...
$
```

For Bash users, the ENV file is read only when Bash is invoked with the name sh or with the --posix command-line option, or after set -o posix is executed (all of which force POSIX standard compliance). By default, when a noninteractive Bash shell is started (for example, when you run a shell program), it reads commands from the file specified by the BASH_ENV environment variable, and when an interactive Bash shell is started (for example, by typing bash at the command prompt), it doesn't.

You should also set and export inside your .profile file a variable called SHELL.

```
$ cat .profile
   ...
SHELL=/usr/bin/ksh
export SHELL
   ...
$
```

This variable is used by certain applications (such as vi) to determine what shell to start up when you execute a shell escape. In such cases, you want to make sure that each time you start up a new shell, you get the shell you want and not an older Bourne shell.

Command-Line Editing

Line edit mode is a feature of the shell that allows you to edit a command line using built-in commands that mimic those found in two popular screen editors. The POSIX standard shell provides the capability to mimic vi; however, both Bash and the Korn shell also support an emacs line edit mode. We list the complete set of vi commands in Table A.4 in Appendix A, "Shell Summary."

If you've used either of these screen editors, you'll find that the built-in line editors in the shell are faithful reproductions of their full-screen counterparts. If you've never used a screen editor, don't be intimidated. This capability is one of the most useful features in the shell. In fact, after learning how to use one of the shell's built-in editors, you'll be able to learn vi or emacs with little effort.

To turn on a line edit mode, you use the set command with the -o *mode* option, where *mode* is either vi or emacs:

```
$ set -o vi              Turn on vi mode
```

Note that you can put this in your .profile or ENV file to automatically start up the shell with one of the edit modes turned on.

Command History

As we said before, the shell keeps a history of previously entered commands. Each time you press the Enter key to execute a command, that command gets added to the end of this history list. This command list is actually stored inside a file, which means that you can access previously entered commands across login sessions. By default, the history list is kept in a file in your home directory under the name .sh_history (.bash_history for Bash, unless it is started with the --posix option). You can change this filename to anything you want by setting the variable HISTFILE to the name of your history file. This variable can be set and exported in your .profile file.

Naturally, there is a limit to the number of commands the shell records. The default value of this limit varies by implementation, but the POSIX standard requires it to be at least 128; the default value for the Korn shell is 128; the default value for Bash is 500. Each time you log in, the shell automatically truncates your history file to this length.

You can control the size of your history file through the HISTFILE variable. You may find that the default size isn't adequate for your needs, in which case you may want to set the HISTFILE variable to a larger value, such as 500 or 1000. The value you assign to HISTSIZE can be set and exported in your .profile file:

```
$ cat .profile
...
HISTSIZE=500
export HISTSIZE
...
$
```

Be reasonable about the values that you assign to HISTSIZE. The larger the value, the more disk space you will need to store the history file, and the longer it will take the shell to search through the entire history file.

The vi Line Edit Mode

After turning on the vi line editor, you will be placed in *input* mode. You probably won't even notice anything different about input mode because you can type in and execute commands almost the same as before you started the vi line editor:

```
$ set -o vi
$ echo hello
hello
$ pwd
/users/pat
$
```

To make use of the line editor, you must enter *command* mode by pressing the ESCAPE or Esc key, usually in the upper-left corner of the keyboard. When you enter command mode, the cursor moves to the left one space, to the last character typed in. The *current character* is whatever character the cursor is on; we'll say more about the current character in a moment. When in command mode, you can enter vi commands. *Note that vi commands are not followed by an Enter.*

One problem often encountered when typing in long commands is that you may notice an error in a command line after you finish typing it in. Invariably, the error is at the beginning of the line. In command mode, you can move the cursor around without disturbing the command line. After you've moved the cursor to the place where the error is, you can change the letter or letters to whatever you want.

In the following examples, the underline (_) represents the cursor. A command line will be shown, followed by one or more keystrokes, followed by what the line looks like after applying the keystrokes:

before keystrokes after

First, let's look at moving the cursor around. The H key moves the cursor to the left and the L key moves it to the right. Try this out by entering command mode and pressing the H and L keys a few times. The cursor should move around on the line. If you try to move the cursor past the left or right side of the line, the shell "beeps" at you.

```
$ mary had a little larb_    Esc    $ mary had a little larb
$ mary had a little larb     h      $ mary had a little larb
$ mary had a little larb     h      $ mary had a little larb
$ mary had a little larb     l      $ mary had a little larb
```

After the cursor is on the character you want to change, you can use the x command to delete the current character ("X" it out).

```
$ mary had a little larb     x      $ mary had a little lab
```

Note that the b moved to the left when the r was deleted and is now the current character.

To add characters to the command line, you can use the i and a commands. The i command inserts characters *before* the current character, and the a command adds characters *after* the current character. Both of these commands put you back into input mode; you must press Esc again to go back to command mode.

```
$ mary had a little lab      im     $ mary had a little lamb
$ mary had a little lamb     m      $ mary had a little lammb
$ mary had a little lammb    Esc    $ mary had a little lammb
$ mary had a little lammb    x      $ mary had a little lamb
$ mary had a little lamb     a      $ mary had a little lamb_
$ mary had a little lamb_    da     $ mary had a little lambda_
```

If you think that moving the cursor around by repeatedly pressing h and l is slow, you're right. The h and l commands may be preceded by a number that specifies the number of spaces to move the cursor.

```
$ mary had a little lambda_    Esc    $ mary had a little lambda
$ mary had a little lambda     10h    $ mary had a little lambda
$ mary had a little lambda     13h    $ mary had a little lambda
$ mary had a little lambda     5x     $ had a little lambda
```

As you can see, the x command can also be preceded by a number to tell it how many characters to delete.

You can easily move to the end of the line by typing the $ command:

```
$ had a little lambda          $      $ had a little lambda
```

To move to the beginning of the line, you use the 0 (that's a zero) command:

```
$ had a little lambda          0      $ had a little lambda
```

Two other commands useful in moving the cursor are the w and b commands. The w command moves the cursor forward to the beginning of the next word, where a word is a string of letters, numbers, and underscores delimited by blanks or punctuation. The b command moves the cursor backward to the beginning of the previous word. These commands may also be preceded by a number to specify the number of words to move forward or backward.

```
$ had a little lambda          w      $ had a little lambda
$ had a little lambda          2w     $ had a little lambda
$ had a little lambda          3b     $ had a little lambda
```

At any time you can press Enter and the current line will be executed as a command.

```
$ had a little lambda          Hit Enter
ksh: had:  not found
$ _
```

After a command is executed, you are placed back in input mode.

Accessing Commands from Your History

So far, you've learned how to edit the current line. You can use the vi commands k and j to retrieve commands from your history. The k command replaces the current line on your terminal with the previously entered command, putting the cursor at the beginning of the line. Let's assume that these commands have just been entered:

```
$ pwd
/users/pat
```

```
$ cd /tmp
$ echo this is a test
this is a test
$ _
```

Now go into command mode and use k to access them:

```
$ _                        Esc k      $ echo this is a test
```

Every time k is used, the current line is replaced by the previous line from the command history.

```
$ echo this is a test      k          $ cd /tmp
$ cd /tmp                  k          $ pwd
```

To execute the command being displayed, just press the Enter key.

```
$ pwd                      Hit Enter
/tmp
$ _
```

The j command is the reverse of the k command and is used to display the next command in the history.

The / command is used to search through the command history for a command containing a string. If the / is entered, followed by a string, the shell searches backward through its history to find the most recently executed command that contains that string anywhere on the command line. The command will then be displayed. If no line in the history contains the string, the shell "beeps" the terminal. When the / is entered, the current line is replaced by a /.

```
/tmp
$ _                        Esc /test    /test_
```

The search is begun when the Enter key is pressed.

```
/test_                     Enter      $ echo this is a test
```

To execute the command that results from the search, Enter must be pressed again.

```
$ echo this is a test      Hit Enter again
this is a test
$ _
```

If the command that's displayed isn't the one you're interested in, you can continue the search through the command history by simply typing / and pressing Enter. The shell uses the string that you entered the last time you executed the search command.

When you've found the command in the history (either by k, j, or /), you can edit the command using the other vi commands we've already discussed. Note that you don't actually change the command in the history: That command cannot be changed after it is entered. Instead, you are editing a copy of the command in the history, which will itself be entered in the history when you press Enter.

Table 15.1 summarizes the basic vi line edit commands.

TABLE 15.1   Basic vi Line Edit Commands

Command	Meaning
h	Move left one character.
l	Move right one character.
b	Move left one word.
w	Move right one word.
0	Move to start of line.
$	Move to end of line.
x	Delete character at cursor.
dw	Delete word at cursor.
r*c*	Change character at cursor to *c*.
a	Enter input mode and enter text after the current character.
i	Enter input mode and insert text before the current character.
k	Get previous command from history.
j	Get next command from history.
/*string*	Search history for the most recent command containing *string*; if *string* is null, the previous string will be used.

The Line Edit Mode

After turning on the emacs line editor, you probably won't even notice anything different because you can type in and execute commands the same way as before:

```
$ set -o emacs
$ echo hello
hello
$ pwd
/users/pat
$
```

To use the line editor, you enter emacs *commands*. emacs commands are either *control* characters—that is, characters typed in by holding down the Ctrl key and pressing another character—or they are characters preceded by the ESCAPE or Esc key. You may enter emacs commands anytime you want; there are no separate modes like the vi line editor. *Note that* emacs *commands are not followed by an Enter.* We cover only a few of them here; for a complete list of commands, refer to the documentation for Bash or the Korn shell.

First, let's look at moving the cursor around. The *Ctrl+b* command moves the cursor to the left, and the *Ctrl+f* command moves it to the right. Try this out by pressing *Ctrl+b* and *Ctrl+f* a few times. The cursor should move around on the line. If you try to move the cursor past the left or right side of the line, the shell simply ignores you.

```
$ mary had a little larb_      Ctrl+b     $ mary had a little larb
$ mary had a little larb       Ctrl+b     $ mary had a little larb
$ mary had a little larb       Ctrl+b     $ mary had a little larb
$ mary had a little larb       Ctrl+f     $ mary had a little larb
```

After the cursor is on the character you want to change, you can use the *Ctrl+d* command to delete the current character.

```
$ mary had a little larb       Ctrl+d     $ mary had a little lab
```

Note that the b moved to the left when the r was deleted and is now the current character.

To add characters to the command line, you simply type them in. The characters are inserted *before* the current character.

```
$ mary had a little lab        m          $ mary had a little lamb
$ mary had a little lamb       m          $ mary had a little lammb
$ mary had a little lammb      Ctrl+h     $ mary had a little lamb
```

Note that the current erase character (usually either # or *Ctrl+h*) will *always* delete the character to the left of the cursor.

The *Ctrl+a* and *Ctrl+e* commands may be used to move the cursor to the beginning and end of the command line, respectively.

```
$ mary had a little lamb       Ctrl+a     $ mary had a little lamb
$ mary had a little lamb       Ctrl+e     $ mary had a little lamb_
```

Note that the *Ctrl+e* command places the cursor one space to the right of the last character on the line. (When you're not in emacs mode, the cursor is always at the end of the line, one space to the right of the last character typed in.) When you're at the end of the line, anything you type will be appended to the line.

```
$ mary had a little lamb_      da         $ mary had a little lambda_
```

Two other commands useful in moving the cursor are the `Esc f` and `Esc b` commands. The `Esc f` command moves the cursor forward to the end of the current word, where a word is a string of letters, numbers, and underscores delimited by blanks or punctuation. The `Esc b` command moves the cursor backward to the beginning of the previous word.

```
$ mary had a little lambda_    Esc b        $ mary had a little lambda
$ mary had a little lambda     Esc b        $ mary had a little lambda
$ mary had a little lambda     Esc b        $ mary had a little lambda
$ mary had a little lambda     Esc f        $ mary had a_little lambda
$ mary had a_little lambda     Esc f        $ mary had a little_lambda
```

At any time you can press the Enter key and the current line will be executed as a command.

```
$ mary had a little_lambda     Hit Enter; enter command
ksh: mary: not found
$ _
```

Accessing Commands from Your History

So far, you've learned how to edit the current line. As we said before, the shell keeps a history of recently entered commands. To access these commands, you can use the emacs commands *Ctrl+p* and *Ctrl+n*. The *Ctrl+p* command replaces the current line on your terminal with the previously entered command, putting the cursor at the end of the line. Let's assume that these commands have just been entered:

```
$ pwd
/users/pat
$ cd /tmp
$ echo this is a test
this is a test
$ _
```

Now use *Ctrl+p* to access them:

```
$ _                         Ctrl+p        $ echo this is a test_
```

Every time *Ctrl+p* is used, the current line is replaced by the previous line from the command history.

```
$ echo this is a test_      Ctrl+p        $ cd /tmp_
$ cd /tmp_                   Ctrl+p        $ pwd_
```

To execute the command being displayed, just press Enter.

```
$ pwd_                    Hit Enter
/tmp
$ _
```

The *Ctrl+n* command is the reverse of the *Ctrl+p* command and is used to display the next command in the history.

The *Ctrl+r* command is used to search through the command history for a command containing a string. The *Ctrl+r* is entered followed by the string to search for, followed by the Enter key. The shell then searches the command history for the most recently executed command that contains that string on the command line. If found, the command line is displayed; otherwise, the shell "beeps" the terminal. When the *Ctrl+r* is typed, the shell replaces the current line with ^R:

```
$ _                       Ctrl+r test    $ ^Rtest_
```

The search is initiated when Enter is pressed.

```
$ ^Rtest_                 Enter          $ echo this is a test_
```

To execute the command that is displayed as a result of the search, Enter must be pressed again.

```
$ echo this is a test_    Hit Enter again
this is a test
$ _
```

To continue the search through the command history, you simply type *Ctrl+r* followed by an Enter.

Bash handles *Ctrl+r* a little differently. When you type *Ctrl+r*, Bash replaces the current line with (reverse-i-search)`':

```
$ _                       Ctrl+r       (reverse-i-search)`': _
```

As you type text, the line is updated inside the `' with the text you type, and the rest of the line is updated with the matching command:

```
(reverse-i-search)`': _ c (reverse-i-search)`c': echo this is a test
(reverse-i-search)`c': echo this is a test   d   (reverse-i-search)`cd': cd /tmp
```

Note how Bash highlights the matching part of the command by placing the cursor on it. As with the Korn shell, the command is executed by pressing Enter.

When you've found the command in the history (either by *Ctrl+p*, *Ctrl+n*, or *Ctrl+r*), you can edit the command using the other emacs commands we've already discussed. Note that you don't actually change the command in the history: That command cannot be changed after it is entered. Instead, you are editing a copy of the command in the history, which will itself be entered in the history when you press Enter.

Table 15.2 summarizes the basic line edit commands.

TABLE 15.2 Basic emacs Line Edit Commands

Command	Meaning
Ctrl+b	Move left one character
Ctrl+f	Move right one character
Esc+f	Move forward one word
Esc+b	Move back one word
Ctrl+a	Move to start of line
Ctrl+e	Move to end of line
Ctrl+d	Delete current character
Esc+d	Delete current word
erase char	(User-defined erase character, usually # or *Ctrl+h*), delete previous character
Ctrl+p	Get previous command from history
Ctrl+n	Get next command from history
Ctrl+r string	Search history for the most recent command line containing *string*

Other Ways to Access Your History

There are several other ways to access your command history that are worth noting.

The history Command

The operation of the history command differs between the Korn shell and Bash because it is not part of the POSIX standard.

The Korn shell history command writes your last 16 commands to standard output:

```
$ history
507   cd shell
508   cd ch15
509   vi int
510   ps
511   echo $HISTSIZE
512   cat $ENV
513   cp int int.sv
514   history
```

```
515   exit
516   cd shell
517   cd ch16
518   vi all
519   run -n5 all
520   ps
521   lpr all.out
522   history
```

The numbers to the left are simply relative command numbers (command number 1 would be the first, or oldest, command in your history).

Without any arguments, the Bash history command lists your entire history (as specified by the HISTSIZE variable) to standard output. If you just want to see the last few commands, you must specify the number of commands to display as an argument:

```
$ history 10
  513   cp int int.sv
  514   history
  515   exit
  516   cd shell
  517   cd ch16
  518   vi all
  519   run -n5 all
  520   ps
  521   lpr all.out
  522   history 10
$
```

The fc Command

The fc command allows you to start up an editor on one or more commands from your history or to simply write a list of history commands to your terminal. In the latter form, which is indicated by giving the -l option to fc, it is like typing in history, only more flexible (you can specify a range of commands to be listed or can get fewer or more than the last 16 commands listed). For example, the command

```
fc -l 510 515
```

writes commands 510 through 515 to standard output, whereas the command

```
fc -n -l -20
```

writes the last 20 commands to standard output, not preceded by line numbers (-n). Suppose that you've just executed a long command line and then decide that it would be nice to turn that command line into a shell program called `runx`. You can use `fc` to get the command from your history and I/O redirection to write that command to a file:

```
fc -n -l -1 > runx
```

(That's the letter l followed by the number -1.) `fc` is described in full detail in Appendix A.

The `r` Command

A simple Korn shell command allows you to re-execute previous commands using even a fewer number of keystrokes than described. If you simply type in the `r` command, the Korn shell re-executes your last command:

```
$ date
Thu Oct 24 14:24:48 EST 2002
$ r                             Re-execute previous command
date
Thu Oct 24 14:25:13 EST 2002
$
```

When you type in the `r` command, the Korn shell redisplays the previous command and then immediately executes it.

If you give the `r` command the name of a command as an argument, the Korn shell re-executes the most recent command line from your history that *begins* with the specified argument:

```
$ cat docs/planA
...
$ pwd
/users/steve
$ r cat                         Rerun last cat command
cat docs/planA
$
```

Once again, the Korn shell redisplays the command line from its history before automatically re-executing it.

The final form of the `r` command allows you to substitute the first occurrence of one string with the next. To re-execute the last `cat` command on the file `planB` instead of `planA`, you could type:

```
$ r cat planA=planB
cat docs/planB
...
$
```

or even more simply, you could have typed:

```
$ r cat A=B
cat docs/planB
...
$
```

Bash has the ! built-in command; !! re-executes the previous command, and !*string* re-executes the most recent command line from your history that begins with *string*:

```
$ !!
cat docs/planB
...
$ !d
date
Thu Oct 24 14:39:40 EST 2002
$
```

Note that no spaces can exist between ! and *string*.

The fc command can be used with the -s option to do the same thing with any POSIX-compliant shell (the r command is actually an *alias* to the fc command in the Korn shell—more on that later in this chapter):

```
$ fc -s cat
cat docs/planB
...
$ fc -s B=C
cat docs/planC
...
$
```

Functions

Bash and the Korn shell both have function features not available in the POSIX standard shell.

Local Variables

Bash and Korn shell functions can have local variables, making recursive functions possible. They are defined with the typeset command, as in

```
typeset i j
```

If a variable of the same name as a local function variable exists, it is saved when the typeset is executed and restored when the function exits. Note that the typeset command is not part of the POSIX standard shell.

After using the shell for a while, you may develop a set of functions that you like to use during your interactive work sessions. A good place to define such functions is inside your ENV file so that they will be defined whenever you start up a new shell.

Automatically Loaded Functions

The Korn shell allows you to set up a special variable called FPATH that is similar to your PATH variable. If you try to execute a function that is not yet defined, the Korn shell searches the colon-delimited list of directories in your FPATH variable for a file that matches the function name. If it finds such a file, it executes it in the current shell. Presumably, somewhere inside the file will be a definition for the specified function.

Integer Arithmetic

Both Bash and the Korn shell support evaluating arithmetic expressions without arithmetic expansion. The syntax is similar to $((...)) but without the dollar sign. Because expansion is not performed, the construct can be used without variable assignment or the colon operator:

```
$ x=10
$ ((x = x * 12))
$ echo $x
120
$
```

The real value of this construct is that it allows arithmetic expressions to be used rather than test in if, while, and until commands. The comparison operators set the exit status to a nonzero value if the result of the comparison is false and to a zero value if the result is true. So writing

```
(( i == 100 ))
```

has the effect of testing i to see whether it is equal to 100 and setting the exit status appropriately. This knowledge makes integer arithmetic ideal for inclusion in if commands:

```
if (( i == 100 ))
then
       ...
fi
```

The ((i == 100)) returns an exit status of zero (true) if i equals 100 and one (false) otherwise, and has the same effect as writing

```
if [ "$i" -eq 100 ]
then
        ...
fi
```

One advantage of using ((...)) rather than test is the capability to perform arithmetic as part of the test:

```
if (( i / 10 != 0 ))
then
    ...
fi
```

Here the comparison returns a true if i divided by 10 is not equal to zero.

while loops can also benefit from integer arithmetic. For example,

```
x=0
while ((x++ < 100))
do
        commands
done
```

executes *commands* 100 times. (Note that some older versions of the Korn shell and Bash do not support the ++ and -- operators.)

Integer Types

The Korn shell and Bash both support an integer data type. You can declare variables to be integers by using the typeset command with the -i option

typeset -i *variables*

where *variables* are any valid shell variable names. Initial values can be assigned to the variables at the time they are declared.

Arithmetic performed on integer variables with the ((...)) construct is slightly faster than on noninteger ones because the shell internally stores the value of an integer variable as a binary number and not as a character string.

An integer variable cannot be assigned anything but an integer value or an integer expression. If you attempt to assign a noninteger to it, the message bad number is printed by the Korn shell:

```
$ typeset -i i
$ i=hello
ksh: i: bad number
```

Bash simply ignores any strings that don't contain numeric values and generates an error for anything that contains both numbers and other characters:

```
$ typeset -i i
$ i=hello
$ echo $i
0
$ i=1hello
bash: 1hello: value too great for base (error token is "1hello")
$ i=10+15
$ echo $i
25
$
```

The preceding example shows that integer-valued expressions can be assigned to an integer variable, without even having to use the ((...)) construct. This holds true for both Bash and the Korn shell.

Numbers in Different Bases

The Korn shell and Bash allow you to perform arithmetic in different bases. To write a number in a different base with these shells, you use the notation

base#number

For example, to express the value 100 in base 8 (octal) you write

```
8#100
```

You can write constants in different bases anywhere an integer value is permitted. To assign octal 100 to the integer variable i, you can write

```
typeset -i i=8#100
```

Note that with the Korn shell the base of the first value assigned to an integer variable fixes the base of all subsequent substitutions of that variable. In other words, if the first value you assign to the integer variable i is an octal number, each time you subsequently substitute the value of i on the command line, the Korn shell substitutes the value as an octal number using the notation 8#*value*.

```
$ typeset -i i=8#100
$ echo $i
8#100
$ i=50
$ echo $i
8#62
```

```
$ (( i = 16#a5 + 16#120 ))
$ echo $i
8#705
$
```

Because the first value assigned to i in this example is an octal number (8#100), all further substitutions of i will be in octal. When the base 10 value of 50 is next assigned to i and then i is subsequently displayed, we get the value 8#62, which is the octal equivalent of 50 in base 10.

In the preceding example, the ((...)) construct is used to add together the two hexadecimal values a5 and 120. The result is then displayed, once again in octal.

Bash uses both the *base#number* syntax for arbitrary bases and the C language syntax for octal and hexadecimal numbers—octal numbers are preceded by 0 (zero), and hexadecimal numbers are preceded by 0x:

```
$ typeset -i i=0100
$ echo $i
64
$ i=0x80
$ echo $i
128
$ i=2#1101001
$ echo $i
105
$ (( i = 16#a5 + 16#120 ))
$ echo $i
453
$
```

Unlike the Korn shell, Bash doesn't keep track of the variable's base; integer variables are displayed as decimal numbers. You can always use printf to print integers in octal or hexadecimal format.

As you can see, with Bash and the Korn shell it's easy to work with different bases. This makes it possible to easily write functions to perform base conversion and arithmetic, for example.

The alias Command

An *alias* is a shorthand notation provided by the shell to allow customization of commands. The shell keeps a list of aliases that is searched when a command is entered. If the first word of a command line is an alias, it is replaced by the text of the alias. An alias is defined by using the alias command. The format is

alias *name=string*

where *name* is the name of the alias, and *string* is any string of characters. For example,

```
alias ll='ls -l'
```

assigns ls -l to the alias ll. Now when the alias ll is typed in, the shell replaces it with ls -l. You can type arguments after the alias name on the command line, as in

```
ll *.c
```

which looks like this after alias substitution has been performed:

```
ls -l *.c
```

The shell performs its normal command-line processing both when the alias is set and when it is used, so quoting can be tricky. For example, recall that the shell keeps track of your current working directory inside a variable called PWD:

```
$ cd /users/steve/letters
$ echo $PWD
/users/steve/letters
$
```

You can create an alias called dir that gives you the base directory of your current working directory by using the PWD variable and one of the parameter substitution constructs described in an earlier section of this chapter:

```
alias dir="echo ${PWD##*/}"
```

Let's see how this alias works:

```
$ alias dir="echo ${PWD##*/}"        Define alias
$ pwd                                Where are we?
/users/steve
$ dir                                Execute alias
steve
$ cd letters                         Change directory
$ dir                                Execute the alias again
steve
$ cd /usr/spool                      One more try
$ dir
steve
$
```

It seems that no matter what the current directory is, the dir alias prints out steve. That's because we weren't careful about our quotes when we defined the dir alias.

Recalling that the shell performs parameter substitution inside double quotes, the shell evaluated

${PWD##*/}

at the time the alias was defined. This means, that for all intents and purposes, the dir alias was defined as though we typed in the following:

```
$ alias dir="echo steve"
```

The solution is to use single rather than double quotes when defining the dir alias to defer the parameter substitution until the time the alias is executed:

```
$ alias dir='echo ${PWD##*/}'        Define alias
$ pwd                                Where are we?
/users/steve
$ dir                                Execute alias
steve
$ cd letters                         Change directory
$ dir                                Execute alias again
letters
$ cd /usr/spool                      One more try
$ dir
spool
$
```

Now the alias works just fine.

If an alias ends with a space, the word following the alias is also checked for alias substitution. For example:

```
alias nohup="/bin/nohup "
nohup ll
```

causes the shell to perform alias checking on the string ll after replacing nohup with /bin/nohup.

Quoting a command prevents alias substitution. For example:

```
$ 'll'
ksh: ll: command not found
$
```

The format

alias *name*

causes the value of the alias *name* to be listed, and the alias command without arguments causes all aliases to be listed.

The following aliases are automatically defined when the Korn shell starts up:

```
autoload='typeset -fu'
functions='typeset -f'
history='fc -l'
integer='typeset -i'
local=typeset
nohup='nohup '
r='fc -e -'
suspend='kill -STOP $$'
```

Note from the preceding example that r is actually an alias for the fc command with the -e option, and history is an alias for fc -l. Bash doesn't automatically define any aliases by default.

Removing Aliases

The unalias command is used to remove aliases from the alias list. The format is

unalias *name*

which removes the alias *name* and

unalias -a

which removes all aliases.

This concludes this section on aliases. If you develop a set of alias definitions that you like to use during your login sessions, you may want to define them inside your ENV file so that they will always be available for you to use.

Arrays

The Korn shell and Bash provide a limited array capability (arrays are not a part of the POSIX standard shell). Bash arrays may contain an unlimited number of elements (subject to memory limitations); Korn shell arrays are limited to 4096 elements. Array indexing in both shells starts at zero. An array element is accessed with a *subscript*, which is an integer-valued expression enclosed inside a pair of brackets. You don't declare the maximum size of a shell array; you simply assign values to elements as you need them. The values that you can assign are the same as for ordinary variables.

```
$ arr[0]=hello
$ arr[1]="some text"
$ arr[2]=/users/steve/memos
$
```

To retrieve an element from an array, you write the array name followed by the element number, enclosed inside a pair of brackets as before. The entire construct must be enclosed inside a pair of curly braces, which is then preceded by a dollar sign.

```
$ echo ${array[0]}
hello
$ echo ${array[1]}
some text
$ echo ${array[2]}
/users/steve/memos
$ echo $array
hello
$
```

As you can see from the preceding example, if no subscript is specified, element zero is used.

If you forget the curly braces when performing the substitution, here's what happens:

```
$ echo $array[1]
hello[1]
$
```

In the preceding example, the value of array is substituted (hello—the value inside array[0]) and then echoed along with [1]. (Note that because the shell does filename substitution after variable substitution, the shell would attempt to match the pattern hello[1] against the files in your current directory.)

The construct [*] can be used as a subscript to substitute all the elements of the array on the command line, with each element delimited by a single space character.

```
$ echo ${array[*]}
hello some text /users/steve/memos
$
```

The construct ${#*array*[*]} can be used to substitute the number of elements in the array *array*.

```
$ echo ${#array[*]}
3
$
```

Note that the number reported here is the actual number of values stored inside the array, not the largest subscript used to store an element inside the array.

```
$ array[10]=foo
$ echo ${array[*]}                  Display all elements
hello some text /users/steve/memos foo
$ echo ${#array[*]}                 Number of elements
4
$
```

You can declare an array of integers to the shell simply by giving the array name to typeset -i:

```
typeset -i data
```

Integer calculations can be performed on array elements using the ((...)) construct:

```
$ typeset -i array
$ array[0]=100
$ array[1]=50
$ (( array[2] = array[0] + array[1] ))
$ echo ${array[2]}
150
$ i=1
$ echo ${array[i]}
50
$ array[3]=array[0]+array[2]
$ echo ${array[3]}
250
$
```

Note that not only can you omit the dollar signs and the curly braces when referencing array elements inside double parentheses, you also can omit them outside when the array is declared to be of integer type. Also note that dollar signs are not needed before variables used in subscript expressions.

The following program, called reverse, reads in up to 4096 lines from standard input and then writes them back out to standard output in reverse order:

```
$ cat reverse
# read lines to array buf

typeset -i line=0

while (( line < 4096 )) && read buf[line]
do
    (( line = line + 1 ))
done

# now print the lines in reverse order
```

```
while (( line > 0 )) do
   (( line = line - 1 ))
   echo "${buf[line]}"
done
```

```
$ reverse
line one
line two
line three
Ctrl+d
line three
line two
line one
$
```

The first while loop executes as long as 4096 or fewer lines have been read and there is more data to be read from standard input (recall the && described at the end of Chapter 8, "Decisions, Decisions").

The following function, cdh, changes the current directory like cd but uses an array to keep a history of previous directories. It allows the user to list the directory history and change back to any directory in it:

```
$ cat cdh
CDHIST[0]=$PWD                          # initialize CDHIST[0]

cdh ()
{
        typeset -i cdlen i
        if [ $# -eq 0 ]                 # default to HOME with no arguments
        then
                set -- $HOME
        fi

        cdlen=${#CDHIST[*]}             # number of elements in CDHIST

        case "$@" in
        -l)                             # print directory list
                i=0
                while ((i < cdlen))
                do
                        printf "%3d %s\n" $i ${CDHIST[i]}
                        ((i = i + 1))
                done
                return ;;
        -[0-9]|-[0-9][0-9])             # cd to dir in list
                i=${1#-}                # remove leading '-'
```

```
            cd ${CDHIST[i]} ;;
    *)                              # cd to new dir
            cd $@ ;;
    esac

    CDHIST[cdlen]=$PWD
}
$
```

The CDHIST array stores each directory visited by cdh, and the first element, CDHIST[0], is initialized with the current directory when the cdh file is run:

```
$ pwd
/users/pat
$ . cdh                            Define cdh function
$ cdh /tmp
$ cdh -1
  0 /users/pat
  1 /tmp
$
```

When the cdh file was run, CDHIST[0] was assigned /users/pat, and the cdh function was defined; when cdh /tmp was executed, cdlen was assigned the number of elements in CDHIST (one), and CDHIST[1] was assigned /tmp. The cdh -1 caused printf to display each element of CDHIST (on this invocation, cdlen was set to 2, because elements 0 and 1 of CDHIST contained data).

Note that the if statement at the beginning of the function sets $1 to $HOME if no arguments are passed. Let's try that out:

```
$ cdh
$ pwd
/users/pat
$ cdh -1
  0 /users/pat
  1 /tmp
  2 /users/pat
$
```

Well, it worked, but now /users/pat shows up twice in the list. One of the exercises at the end of this chapter asks you to remedy this.

Okay, the most useful feature of cdh is the -*n* option, which causes it to change the current directory to the one specified in the list:

```
$ cdh /usr/spool/uucppublic
$ cdh -1
  0 /users/pat
```

```
    1 /tmp
    2 /users/pat
    3 /usr/spool/uucppublic
$ cdh -1
$ pwd
/tmp
$ cdh -3
$ pwd
/usr/spool/uucppublic
$
```

We can make cdh replace our cd command by using the fact that alias lookup is performed before built-in commands are executed. So if we create a cd alias to cdh, we can have an enhanced cd. In that case, we have to quote every use of cd in the cdh function to prevent recursion:

```
$ cat cdh
CDHIST[0]=$PWD                      # initialize CDHIST[0]
alias cd=cdh

cdh ()
{
        typeset -i cdlen i
        if [ $# -eq 0 ]            # default to HOME with no arguments
        then
                set -- $HOME
        fi

        cdlen=${#CDHIST[*]}        # number of elements in CDHIST

        case "$@" in
        -l)                        # print directory list
                i=0
                while ((i < cdlen))
                do
                        printf "%3d %s\n" $i ${CDHIST[i]}
                        ((i = i + 1))
                done
                return ;;
        -[0-9]|-[0-9][0-9])        # cd to dir in list
                i=${1#-}           # remove leading '-'
                'cd' ${CDHIST[i]} ;;
        *)                         # cd to new dir
```

```
              'cd' $@ ;;
        esac

        CDHIST[cdlen]=$PWD
}
$ . cdh                        Define cdh function and cd alias
$ cd /tmp
$ cd -l
  0 /users/pat
  1 /tmp
$ cd /usr/spool
$ cd -l
  0 /users/pat
  1 /tmp
  2 /usr/spool
$
```

Table 15.3 summarizes the various array constructs in the Korn shell and Bash.

TABLE 15.3   Array Constructs

Construct	Meaning
${*array*[*i*]}	Substitute value of element *i*
$*array*	Substitute value of first element (*array*[0])
${*array*[*]}	Substitute value of all elements
${#array[*]}	Substitute number of elements
array[*i*]=*val*	Store *val* into *array*[*i*]

Job Control

The shell provides facilities for controlling *jobs*. A job is any command sequence. For example:

```
who | wc
```

When a command is started in the background (that is, with &), the shell prints out the job number inside brackets ([ ]) as well as the process number:

```
$ who | wc &
[1]      832
$
```

When a job finishes, the shell prints the message

[*n*]   +   *sequence*

where *n* is the job number of the finished job, and *sequence* is the text of the
command sequence used to create the job.

The jobs command may be used to print the status of jobs that haven't yet finished.

```
$ jobs
[3] + Running        make ksh &
[2] - Running        monitor &
[1]   Running        pic chapt2 | troff > aps.out &
```

The + and - after the job number mark the current and previous jobs, respectively.
The current job is the last job sent to the background, and the previous job is the
next-to-the-last job sent to the background. Several built-in commands may be given
a job number or the current or previous job as arguments.

The shell's built-in kill command can be used to terminate a job running in the
background. The argument to it can be a process number or a percent sign (%)
followed by a job number, a + (current job), a – (previous job), or another % (also
current job).

```
$ pic chapt1 | troff > aps.out &
[1]      886
$ jobs
[1] + Running             pic chapt1 | troff > aps.out &
$ kill %1
[1]    Done               pic chapt1 | troff > aps.out &
$
```

The preceding kill could have used %+ or %% to refer to the same job.

The first few characters of the command sequence can also be used to refer to a job;
for example, kill %pic would have worked in the preceding example.

Stopped Jobs and the fg and bg Commands

If you are running a job in the foreground (without an &) and you want to suspend
it, you can press the Ctrl+z key. The job stops executing, and the shell prints the
message

[*n*]   + Stopped (SIGTSTP)   *sequence*

The stopped job is made the current job. To have it continue executing, you must
use the fg or bg command. The fg command with no arguments causes the current
job to resume execution in the foreground, and bg causes the current job to resume
execution in the background. You can also use a job number, the first few characters

of the pipeline, a +, a -, or a % preceded by a to specify any job to the `fg` and `bg` commands. These commands print out the command sequence to remind you what is being brought to the foreground or sent to the background.

```
$ troff memo | photo
Ctrl+z
[1] + Stopped (SIGTSTP)        troff memo | photo
$ bg
[1]         troff memo | photo &
$
```

The preceding sequence is one of the most often used with job control: sending a job mistakenly started in the foreground to the background.

If a job running in the background tries to read from the terminal, it is stopped, and the message

```
[n] - Stopped (SIGTTIN)   sequence
```

is printed. It can then be brought to the foreground with the `fg` command. After entering input to the job, it can be stopped (with the Ctrl+z) and returned to the background until it again requests input from the terminal.

Output from a background job normally goes directly to the terminal. The command

```
stty tostop
```

causes any background job that attempts to write to the terminal to be stopped and the message

```
[n] - Stopped (SIGTTOU)   sequence
```

to be printed. (Note that Bash generates slightly different messages than the ones shown here.)

The following shows how job control might be used:

```
$ stty tostop
$ rundb                        Start up data base program
??? find green red             Find green and red objects
Ctrl+z                         This may take a while
[1] + Stopped        rundb
$ bg                           So put it in the background
[1]        rundb &
...                            Do some other stuff
$ jobs
[1] + Stopped(tty output)      rundb &
$ fg                           Bring back to foreground
```

```
rundb
1973 Ford      Mustang       red
1975 Chevy     Monte Carlo   green
1976 Ford      Granada       green
1980 Buick     Century       green
1983 Chevy     Cavalier      red
??? find blue                       Find blue objects
Ctrl+z                              Stop it again
[1] + Stopped        rundb
$ bg                                Back to the background
[1]     rundb &
...                                 Keep working until it's ready
```

The Restricted Shell rsh

Although the restricted shell is not part of the POSIX standard, it is supported by every Bourne shell variant we know of.

The restricted shell is almost the same as the regular shell, but it's designed to *restrict* a user's capabilities by disallowing certain actions that the standard shell allows. This allows an administrator to let users who should not have complete access to the system use the shell. It is usually found in /usr/lib/rsh and is started as the login shell for a user who should not have full capabilities on a system—for example, a game user or data-entry clerk. The list of actions disallowed is very short:

- Cannot change directory (cd)
- Cannot change PATH, ENV, or SHELL variables
- Cannot specify a path to a command
- Cannot redirect output (> and >>)
- Cannot exec programs

These restrictions are enforced *after* the .profile is executed when logging in, and the user is logged off if he presses Break or Delete while the .profile is being interpreted.

These simple restrictions allow the writer of a restricted user's .profile to have control over what commands that user can use. The following example shows a simple setup for a restricted environment:

```
$ cat .profile                      User restrict's .profile
PATH=/usr/rbin:/users/restrict/bin
export PATH
SHELL=/usr/lib/rsh                  Some commands use SHELL variable
export SHELL
cd /users/restrict/restdir          Don't leave user in HOME directory
```

```
$ ls -l .profile              Restricted user shouldn't own his .profile
-rw-r--r--  1 pat  group1  179 Sep 14 17:50 .profile
$ ls /usr/rbin                Directory of restricted commands
cat                           Harmless commands
echo
ls
mail                          Let them send us mail
red                           Restricted editor
write
$ ls /users/restrict/bin      restrict's command directory
adventure                     Lots of games
backgammon
chess
hearts
poker
rogue
$
```

Here we have a restricted environment for a user. When this user logs in, his PATH is changed to search just the directories /usr/rbin and /users/restrict/bin. He can run only commands found in these two directories. Any other command will get a *command:* not found response. The user is effectively bottled up in the directory /users/restrict/restdir and cannot cd out of it. The .profile is owned by a user other than the restricted one, and the permissions are such that only the owner can change the file. (Don't let a restricted user alter his or her .profile because the .profile is executed before any restrictions are applied.)

One quick note about the commands in /usr/rbin: They were simply copied from the /bin and /usr/bin directories. You can put almost any command from /bin and /usr/bin in /usr/rbin; just use common sense in choosing the commands you allow restricted users to use. For example, don't give them access to the shell, a compiler, or chmod because these may be used to bypass the restricted shell. The mail and write commands are safe even though they have shell escapes because the shell looks at the SHELL variable and runs restricted if the first character of its name is "r." The restricted editor red is the same as ed, except it doesn't allow shell escapes, and it only allows editing of files in the current directory.

Note that most restricted shells are not really very secure. They should not be used to contain hostile users. Even though some restricted shells are more secure than others, if you give a restricted user certain commands (such as env), he will be able to break out into a nonrestricted shell.

If you can't find the restricted shell on your system, you can copy or link your Bash, Korn shell, or even old Bourne shell to any filename that begins with "r" and make that file the login shell of the restricted user. When the shell starts up, it checks the first letter of the command name that was used to invoke it; if that letter is "r," it will be a restricted shell.

Miscellaneous Features

Other Features of the cd Command

The - argument to cd always means "the previous directory."

```
$ pwd
/usr/src/cmd
$ cd /usr/spool/uucp
$ pwd
/usr/spool/uucp
$ cd -                          cd to previous directory
/usr/src/cmd                    cd prints out name of new directory
$ cd -
/usr/spool/uucp
$
```

As you can see, cd - can be used to toggle between two directories with no effort at all.

The Korn shell's cd command has the capability to substitute portions of the current directory's path with something else. (Bash and the POSIX standard shell do not support this feature.) The format is

cd *old new*

cd attempts to replace the first occurrence of the string *old* in the current directory's path with the string *new*.

```
$ pwd
/usr/spool/uucppublic/pat
$ cd pat steve                  Change pat to steve and cd
/usr/spool/uucppublic/steve     cd prints out name of new directory
$ pwd                           Confirm location
/usr/spool/uucppublic/steve
$
```

Tilde Substitution

If a word on a command line begins with the tilde (~) character, the shell scans the rest of the word and performs the following substitutions: If the tilde is the only character in the word or if the character following the tilde is a slash (/),the value of the HOME variable is substituted:

```
$ echo ~
/users/pat
$ grep Korn ~/shell/chapter9/ksh
The Korn shell is a new shell developed
```

```
by David Korn at AT&T
for the Bourne shell would also run under the Korn
the one on System V, the Korn shell provides you with
idea of the compatibility of the Korn shell with Bourne's,
the Bourne and Korn shells.
The main features added to the Korn shell are:
$
```

If the rest of the word up to a slash is a user's login name in /etc/passwd, the tilde and the user's login name are substituted with the HOME directory of that user.

```
$ echo ~steve
/users/steve
$ echo ~pat
/users/pat
$ grep Korn -pat/shell/chapter9/ksh
The Korn shell is a new shell developed
by David Korn at AT&T
for the Bourne shell would also run under the Korn
the one on System V, the Korn shell provides you with
idea of the compatibility of the Korn shell with Bourne's,
the Bourne and Korn shells.
The main features added to the Korn shell are:
$
```

In the Korn shell and Bash, if the ~ is followed by a + or a -, the value of the variable PWD or OLDPWD is substituted, respectively. PWD and OLDPWD are set by cd and are the full pathnames of the current and previous directories, respectively. ~+ and ~- are not supported by the POSIX standard shell.

```
$ pwd
/usr/spool/uucppublic/steve
$ cd
$ pwd
/users/pat
$ echo ~+
/users/pat
$ echo ~-
/usr/spool/uucppublic/steve
$
```

In addition to the preceding substitutions, the shell also checks for a tilde after a colon (:) and performs tilde substitution on that as well (for PATH interpretation).

Order of Search

It's worthwhile listing the order of searching the shell uses when you type a command name:

1. The shell first checks to see whether the command is a reserved word (such as for and do).

2. If it's not a reserved word and is not quoted, the shell next checks its alias list, and if it finds a match, performs the substitution. If the alias definition ends in a space, it attempts alias substitution on the next word. The final result is then checked against the reserved word list, and if it's not a reserved word, the shell proceeds to step 3.

3. Next, the shell checks the command against its function list and executes it if found.

4. The shell checks to see whether the command is a built-in command (such as cd and pwd).

5. Finally, the shell searches the PATH to locate the command.

6. If the command still isn't found, a "command not found" error message is issued.

Compatibility Summary

Table 15.4 summarizes the compatibility of the POSIX standard shell, the Korn shell, and Bash with the features described in this chapter. In this table, an "X" denotes a supported feature, "UP," an optional feature in the POSIX shell (these are also known as "User Portability" features in the POSIX shell specification), and "POS," a feature supported only by Bash when it is invoked with the name sh or with the --posix command-line option, or after set -o posix is executed.

TABLE 15.4   POSIX Shell, Korn Shell, and Bash Compatibility

	POSIX Shell	Korn Shell	Bash
ENV file	X	X	POS
vi line edit mode	X	X	X
emacs line edit mode		X	X
fc command	X	X	X
r command		X	
!!			X
!string			X
Functions	X	X	X
local variables		X	X
autoload via FPATH		X	

TABLE 15.4   Continued

	POSIX Shell	Korn Shell	Bash
Integer expressions with ((...))		X	X
Integer data type		X	X
integers in different bases		X	X
0x*hexnumber*, 0*octalnumber*			X
Aliases	UP	X	X
Arrays		X	X
Job control	UP	X	X
cd -	X	X	X
cd *old new*		X	
~*username*, ~/	X	X	X
~+, ~-		X	X

Exercises

1. Using only shell built-in commands, write a function that prints all filenames in a specified directory hierarchy. Its output should be similar to the output of the `find` command:

```
$ myfind /users/pat
/users/pat
/users/pat/bin
/users/pat/bin/ksh
/users/pat/bin/lf
/users/pat/bin/pic
/users/pat/chapt1
/users/pat/chapt1/intro
/users/pat/rje
/users/pat/rje/file1
```

(Hint: Bash and Korn shell functions can be recursive.)

2. Write a shell function called `octal` that converts octal numbers given as command-line arguments to decimal numbers and prints them out, one per line:

```
$ octal 10 11 12
8
9
10
$
```

(Hint for Korn shell users: If you assign a decimal number to a variable when it's declared—for example, `typeset -i d=10#0`—assignments to this variable from other bases are converted to decimal first.)

3. Modify the `cdh` function to filter out multiple occurrences of the same directory; for example:

```
$ cdh -l
  0 /users/pat
$ cdh
$ cdh
$ cdh -l
  0 /users/pat
$
```

4. Modify the `cdh` function to set the prompt (PS1) to show the current directory; for example:

```
/users/pat: cdh /tmp
/tmp: cdh
/users/pat:
```

5. Modify the `cdh` function to allow the user to specify a partial name of a directory in the history file preceded by a dash:

```
/etc: cdh -l
  0 /users/pat
  1 /tmp
  2 /users/steve
  3 /usr/spool/uucppublic
  4 /usr/local/bin
  5 /etc
/etc: cdh -pub
/usr/spool/uucppublic: cdh -bin
/usr/local/bin:
```

6. (Bash users only) Add the Korn shell's `cd` *old* *new* feature to the `cdh` function.

A

Shell Summary

This appendix summarizes the main features of the standard POSIX shell as per IEEE Std 1003.1-2001.

Startup

The shell can be given the same options on the command line as can be specified with the set command. In addition, the following options can be specified:

-c *commands*	*commands* are executed.
-i	The shell is interactive. Signals 2, 3, and 15 are ignored.
-s	Commands are read from standard input.

Commands

The general format of a command typed to the shell is

command arguments

where *command* is the name of the program to be executed, and *arguments* are its arguments. The command name and the arguments are delimited by *whitespace* characters, normally the space, tab, and newline characters (changing the variable IFS affects this).

Multiple commands can be typed on the same line if they're separated by semicolons (;).

Every command that gets executed returns a number known as the *exit status*; zero is used to indicate success, and nonzero indicates a failure.

The pipe symbol | can be used to connect the standard output from one command to the standard input of another, as in

```
who | wc -l
```

The exit status is that of the last command in the pipeline. Placing a ! at the beginning of the pipeline causes the exit status of the pipeline to be the logical negation of the last command in the pipeline.

If the command sequence is terminated by an ampersand character (&), it is run asynchronously in the background. The shell displays the process id number and job id of the command at the terminal.

Typing of a command can continue to the next line if the last character on the line is a backslash character (\).

The characters && cause the command that follows to be executed only if the preceding command returns a zero exit status. The characters || cause the command that follows to be executed only if the preceding command returns a nonzero exit status. As an example, in

```
who | grep "fred" > /dev/null && echo "fred's logged on"
```

the echo is executed only if the grep returns a zero exit status.

Comments

If a word begins with the character #, the shell treats the remainder of the line as a comment and simply ignores it.

Parameters and Variables

There are three different "types" of *parameters*: shell variables, special parameters, and positional parameters.

Shell Variables

A shell variable name must start with an alphabetic or underscore (_) character, and can be followed by any number of alphanumeric or underscore characters. Shell variables can be assigned values on the command line by writing:

variable=value variable=value ...

Filename substitution is not performed on *value*.

Positional Parameters

Whenever a shell program is executed, the name of the program is assigned to the variable $0 and the arguments typed on the command line to the variables $1, $2, and ..., respectively. Positional parameters can also be assigned values with the set command. Parameters 1 through 9 can be explicitly referenced. Parameters greater than nine must be enclosed inside braces, as in ${10}.

Special Parameters

Table A.1 summarizes the special shell parameters.

TABLE A.1   Special Parameter Variables

Parameter	Meaning
$#	The number of arguments passed to the program; or the number of parameters set by executing the set statement
$*	Collectively references all the positional parameters as $1, $2, ...
$@	Same as $*, except when double-quoted ("$@") collectively references all the positional parameters as "$1", "$2", ...
$0	The name of the program being executed
$$	The process id number of the program being executed
$!	The process id number of the last program sent to the background for execution
$?	The exit status of the last command not executed in the background
$-	The current option flags in effect (see the set statement)

In addition to these parameters, the shell has some other variables that it uses. Table A.2 summarizes the more important of these variables.

TABLE A.2   Other Variables Used by the Shell

Variable	Meaning
CDPATH	The directories to be searched whenever cd is executed without a full path as argument.
ENV	The name of a file that the shell executes in the current environment when started interactively.
FCEDIT	The editor used by fc. If not set, ed is used.
HISTFILE	If set, it specifies a file to be used to store the command history. If not set or if the file isn't writable, $HOME/.sh_history is used.
HISTSIZE	If set, specifies the number of previously entered commands accessible for editing. The default value is at least 128.
HOME	The user's home directory; the directory that cd changes to when no argument is supplied.

TABLE A.2   Continued

Variable	Meaning
IFS	The Internal Field Separator characters; used by the shell to delimit words when parsing the command line, for the read and set commands, when substituting the output from a back-quoted command, and when performing parameter substitution. Normally, it contains the three characters space, horizontal tab, and newline.
LINENO	Set by the shell to the line number in the script it is executing. This value is set before the line gets executed and starts at 1.
MAIL	The name of a file that the shell periodically checks for the arrival of mail. If new mail arrives, the shell displays a You have mail message. See also MAILCHECK and MAILPATH.
MAILCHECK	The number of seconds specifying how often the shell is to check for the arrival of mail in the file in MAIL or in the files listed in MAILPATH. The default is 600. A value of 0 causes the shell to check before displaying each command prompt.
MAILPATH	A list of files to be checked for the arrival of mail. Each file is delimited by a colon and can be followed by a percent sign (%) and a message to be displayed when mail arrives in the indicated file. (You have mail is often the default.)
PATH	A colon-delimited list of directories to be searched when the shell needs to find a command to be executed. The current directory is specified as :: or :.: (if it heads or ends the list, : suffices).
PPID	The process id number of the program that invoked this shell (that is, the parent process).
PS1	The primary command prompt, normally "$ ".
PS2	The secondary command prompt, normally "> ".
PS4	Prompt used during execution trace (-x option to shell or set -x). Default is "+ ".
PWD	Pathname of the current working directory.

Parameter Substitution

In the simplest case, the value of a parameter can be accessed by preceding the parameter with a dollar sign ($). Table A.3 summarizes the different types of parameter substitution that can be performed. Parameter substitution is performed by the shell before filename substitution and before the command line is divided into arguments.

The presence of the colon after *parameter* in Table A.3 indicates that *parameter* is to be tested to see whether it's set and not null. Without the colon, a test is made to check whether *parameter* is set only.

TABLE A.3 Parameter Substitution

Parameter	Meaning
$parameter or ${parameter}	Substitute the value of *parameter*.
${parameter:-value}	Substitute the value of *parameter* if it's set and non-null; otherwise, substitute *value*.
${parameter-value}	Substitute the value of *parameter* if it's set; otherwise, substitute *value*.
${parameter:=value}	Substitute the value of *parameter* if it's set and non-null; otherwise, substitute *value* and also assign it to *parameter*.
${parameter=value}	Substitute the value of *parameter* if it's set; otherwise, substitute *value* and also assign it to *parameter*.
${parameter:?value}	Substitute the value of *parameter* if it's set and non-null; otherwise, write *value* to standard error and exit. If *value* is omitted, write *parameter:* parameter null or not set instead.
${parameter?value}	Substitute the value of *parameter* if it's set; otherwise, write *value* to standard error and exit. If *value* is omitted, write *parameter:* parameter null or not set instead.
${parameter:+value}	Substitute *value* if *parameter* is set and non-null; otherwise, substitute null.
${parameter+value}	Substitute *value* if *parameter* is set; otherwise, substitute null.
${#parameter}	Substitute the length of *parameter*. If *parameter* is * or @, the result is not specified.
${parameter#pattern}	Substitute the value of *parameter* with *pattern* removed from the left side. The smallest portion of the contents of *parameter* matching *pattern* is removed. Shell filename substitution characters (*, ?, [...], !, and @) may be used in *pattern*.
${parameter##pattern}	Same as #*pattern* except the largest matching *pattern* is removed.
${parameter%pattern}	Same as #*pattern* except *pattern* is removed from the right side.
${parameter%%pattern}	Same as ##*pattern* except the largest matching *pattern* is removed from the right side.

Command Re-entry

The shell keeps a list, or history, of recently entered commands. The number of commands available is determined by the HISTSIZE variable (default at least 128), and the file in which the history is kept is determined by the HISTFILE variable (default $HOME/.sh_history). Because the command history is stored in a file, these commands are available after you log off and back on.

There are three ways you can access the command history.

The `fc` Command

The built-in command `fc` allows you to run an editor on one or more commands in the command history. When the edited command(s) is written and you leave the editor, the edited version of the command(s) is executed. The editor is determined by the FCEDIT variable (default ed). The -e option may be used with `fc` to specify the editor rather than FCEDIT.

The -s option causes commands to be executed without first invoking an editor. A simple editing capability is built in to the `fc` -s command; an argument of the form

old=new

may be used to change the first occurrence of the string *old* to the string *new* in the command(s) to be re-executed.

`vi` Line Edit Mode

The shell has a built-in implementation of the `vi` screen editor, scaled down to work on single lines. When `vi` mode is turned on, you are by default placed in a state similar to `vi`'s *input* mode. Commands can be typed just the same as when `vi` mode is off. At any time, however, you can press the Esc key to be placed in *edit* mode. At this point, most `vi` commands will be interpreted by the shell. The current command line can be edited, as can any of the lines in the command history. Pressing Enter at any point in either command or input mode causes the command being edited to be executed.

Table A.4 lists all the editing commands in `vi` mode. Note: [*count*] is any integer and may be omitted.

TABLE A.4   `vi` Editing Commands

Input Mode Commands

Command	Meaning
erase	(Erase character, usually *Ctrl+h* or #); delete previous character.
Ctrl+w	Delete the previous blank-separated word.
kill	(Line kill character, normally *Ctrl+u* or @); delete the entire current line.
eof	(End-of-file character, normally *Ctrl+d*); terminate the shell if the current line is empty.
Ctrl+v	Quote next character; editing characters and the erase and kill characters may be entered in a command line or in a search string if preceded by a *Ctrl+v*.
Enter	Execute the current line.
Esc	Enter edit mode.

TABLE A.4   Continued

Edit Mode Commands

Command	Meaning
[*count*]k	Get previous command from history.
[*count*]-	Get previous command from history.
[*count*]j	Get next command from history.
[*count*]+	Get next command from history.
[*count*]G	Get the command number *count* from history; the default is the oldest stored command.
/*string*	Search history for the most recent command containing *string*; if *string* is null, the previous string will be used *(string* is terminated by an Enter or a *Ctrl+j)*; if *string* begins with ^, search for line beginning with *string*.
?*string*	Same as / except that the search will be for the least recent command.
n	Repeat the last / or ? command.
N	Repeat the last / or ? command but reverse the direction of the search.
[*count*]l *or* [*count*]*space*	Move cursor right one character.
[*count*]w	Move cursor right one alphanumeric word.
[*count*]W	Move cursor right to next blank-separated word.
[*count*]e	Move cursor to end of word.
[*count*]E	Move cursor to end of current blank-separated word.
[*count*]h	Move cursor left one character.
[*count*]b	Move cursor left one word.
[*count*]B	Move cursor left to previous blank-separated word.
0	Move cursor to start of line.
^	Move cursor to first nonblank character.
$	Move cursor to end of line.
[*count*]|	Move cursor to column *count*; 1 is default.
[*count*]f*c*	Move cursor right to character *c*.
[*count*]F*c*	Move cursor left to character *c*.
[*count*]t*c*	Same as f*c* followed by h.
[*count*]T*c*	Same as F*c* followed by l.
;	Repeat the last f, F, t, or T command.
,	Reverse of ;.
a	Enter input mode and enter text after the current character.
A	Append text to the end of the line; same as $a.
[*count*]c *motion*	Delete current character through character specified by *motion* and enter input mode; if *motion* is c, the entire line is deleted.
C	Delete current character through end of line and enter input mode.
S	Same as cc.
[*count*]d *motion*	Delete current character through the character specified by *motion*; if *motion* is d, the entire line is deleted.
D	Delete current character through the end of line; same as d$.

TABLE A.4   Continued

Edit Mode Commands

Command	Meaning
i	Enter input mode and insert text before the current character.
I	Enter input mode and insert text before the first word on the line.
[*count*]P	Place the previous text modification before the cursor.
[*count*]p	Place the previous text modification after the cursor.
[*count*]y *motion*	Copy current character through character specified by *motion* into buffer used by p and P; if *motion* is y, the entire line is copied.
Y	Copy current character through the end of line; same as y$.
R	Enter input mode and overwrite characters on the line.
[*count*]rc	Replace the current character with *c*.
[*count*]x	Delete current character.
[*count*]X	Delete preceding character.
[*count*].	Repeat the previous text modification command.
~	Invert the case of the current character and advance the cursor.
[*count*]_	Append the *count* word from the previous command and enter input mode; the last word is the default.
*	Attempt filename generation on the current word; if a match is found, replace the current word with the match and enter input mode.
=	List files that begin with current word.
\	Complete pathname of current word; if current word is a directory, append a /; if current word is a file, append a space.
u	Undo the last text modification command.
U	Restore the current line to its original state.
@*letter*	Soft function key—if an alias of the name _*letter* is defined, its value will be executed.
[*count*]v	Execute vi editor on line *count*; if *count* is omitted, the current line is used.
Ctrl+l	Linefeed and print current line.
L	Reprint the current line.
Ctrl+j	Execute the current line.
Ctrl+m	Execute the current line.
Enter	Execute the current line.
#	Insert a # at the beginning of the line and enter the line into the command history (same as I#Enter).

Quoting

Four different types of quoting mechanisms are recognized. These are summarized in Table A.5.

TABLE A.5   Summary of Quotes

Quote	Description
'...'	Removes special meaning of all enclosed characters
"..."	Removes special meaning of all enclosed characters except $, `, and \
\c	Removes special meaning of character *c* that follows; inside double quotes removes special meaning of $, `, ", newline, and \ that follows, but is otherwise not interpreted; used for line continuation if appears as last character on line (newline is removed)
`command` or $(command)	Executes *command* and inserts standard output at that point

Tilde Substitution

Each word and shell variable on a command line is checked to see whether it begins with an unquoted ~. If it does, the rest of the word or variable up to a / is considered a login name and is looked up in a system file, typically /etc/passwd. If that user exists, his home directory replaces the ~ and his login name. If that user doesn't exist, the text is unchanged. A ~ by itself or followed by a / is replaced by the HOME variable.

Arithmetic Expressions

General Format: $((*expression*))

The shell evaluates the integer arithmetic *expression*. *expression* can contain constants, shell variables (which don't have to be preceded by dollar signs), and operators. The operators, in order of decreasing precedence, are

-	unary minus
~	bitwise NOT
!	logical negation
* / %	multiplication, division, remainder
+ -	addition, subtraction
<< >>	left shift, right shift
<= >= < >	comparison
== !=	equal, not equal
&	bitwise AND
^	bitwise exclusive OR
|	bitwise OR

&&	logical AND
||	logical OR
expr₁ ? *expr₂* : *expr₃*	conditional operator
=, *=, /=, %=	assignment
+=, <<=, >>=, &=,	
^=, |=	

Parentheses may be used to override operator precedence.

The exit status is zero (true) if the last expression is nonzero and one (false) if the last expression is zero.

The C operators `sizeof`, `++`, and `--` may be available in your shell implementation but are not required by the standard.

Examples

```
y=$((22 * 33))
```

```
z=$((y * y / (y - 1)))
```

Filename Substitution

After parameter substitution (and command substitution) is performed on the command line, the shell looks for the special characters *, ?, and [. If they're not quoted, the shell searches the current directory, or another directory if preceded by a /, and substitutes the names of all files that match (these names are first alphabetized by the shell). If no match is found, the characters remain untouched.

Note that filenames beginning with a . must be explicitly matched (so echo * won't display your hidden files; echo .* will).

The filename substitution characters are summarized in Table A.6.

TABLE A.6   Filename Substitution Characters

Character(s)	*Meaning*
?	Matches any single character.
*	Matches zero or more characters.
[*chars*]	Matches any single character in *chars*; the format C_1-C_2 can be used to match any character in the range C_1 through C_2, inclusive (for example, [A-Z] matches any uppercase letter).
[!*chars*]	Matches any single character *not* in *chars*; a range of characters may be specified previously.

I/O Redirection

When scanning the command line, the shell looks for the special redirection characters < and >. If found, they are processed and removed (with any associated arguments) from the command line. Table A.7 summarizes the different types of I/O redirection that the shell supports.

TABLE A.7   I/O Redirection

Construct	Meaning
< *file*	Redirect standard input from *file*.
> *file*	Redirect standard output to *file*; *file* is created if it doesn't exist and zeroed if it does.
>| *file*	Redirect standard output to *file*; *file* is created if it doesn't exist and zeroed if it does; the noclobber (-C) option to set is ignored.
>> *file*	Like >, only output is appended to *file* if it already exists.
<< *word*	Redirect standard input from lines that follow up until a line containing just *word*; parameter substitution occurs on the lines, and back-quoted commands are executed and the backslash character interpreted; if any character in *word* is quoted, none of this processing occurs and the lines are passed through unaltered; if *word* is preceded by a -, leading tabs on the lines are removed.
<& *digit*	Standard input is redirected from the file associated with file descriptor *digit*.
>& *digit*	Standard output is redirected to the file associated with file descriptor *digit*.
<&-	Standard input is closed.
>&-	Standard output is closed.
<> *file*	Open *file* for both reading and writing.

Note that filename substitution is not performed on *file*. Any of the constructs listed in the first column of the table may be preceded by a file descriptor number to have the same effect on the file associated with that file descriptor.

The file descriptor 0 is associated with standard input, 1 with standard output, and 2 with standard error.

Exported Variables and Subshell Execution

Commands other than the shell's built-in commands are normally executed in a "new" shell, called a *subshell*. Subshells cannot change the values of variables in the parent shell, and they can only access variables from the parent shell that were *exported* to them—either implicitly or explicitly—by the parent. If the subshell changes the value of one of these variables and wants to have its own subshells know about it, it must explicitly export the variable before executing the subshell.

When the subshell finishes execution, any variables that it may have set are inaccessible by the parent.

The (...) Construct

If one or more commands are placed inside parentheses, those commands will be executed in a subshell.

The { ...; } Construct

If one or more commands are placed inside curly braces, those commands will be executed by the *current* shell.

With this construct and the (...) construct, I/O can be redirected and piped into and out of the set of enclosed commands, and the set can be sent to the background for execution by placing an & at the end. For example,

```
(prog1; prog2; prog3) 2>errors &
```

submits the three listed programs to the background for execution, with standard error from all three programs redirected to the file errors.

More on Shell Variables

A shell variable can be placed into the environment of a command by preceding the command name with the assignment to the parameter on the command line, as in

```
PHONEBOOK=$HOME/misc/phone rolo
```

Here the variable PHONEBOOK will be assigned the indicated value and then placed in rolo's environment. The environment of the current shell remains unchanged, as if

```
(PHONEBOOK=$HOME/misc/phone; export PHONE BOOK; rolo)
```

had been executed instead.

Functions

Functions take the following form:

name () *compound-command*

where *compound-command* is a set of commands enclosed in (...), {...} or can be a for, case, until, or while command. Most often, the function definition takes this form:

name () { *command*; *command*; ...*command*; }

where *name* is the name of the function defined to the *current* shell (functions can't be exported). The function definition can span as many lines as necessary. A return command can be executed to cause execution of the function to be terminated without also terminating the shell (see the `return` command description).

For example,

```
nf () { ls | wc -l; }
```

defines a function called `nf` to count the number of files in your current directory.

Job Control

Shell Jobs

Every command sequence run in the background is assigned a job number, starting at one. The lowest available number not in use is assigned. A job may be referred to by a *job_id*, which is a `%` followed by the job number, `%+`, `%-`, `%%`, `%` followed by the first few letters of the pipeline, or `%?`*string*. The following built-in commands may be given a *job_id* as an argument: `kill`, `fg`, `bg`, and `wait`. The special conventions `%+` and `%-` refer to the current and previous jobs, respectively; `%%` also refers to the current job. The current job is the most recent job placed in the background or the job running in the foreground. The previous job is the previous current job. The convention `%`*string* refers to the job whose name begins with *string*; `%?`*string* refers to the job whose name contains *string*. The `jobs` command may be used to list the status of all currently running jobs.

If the `monitor` option of the `set` command is turned on, the shell prints a message when each job finishes. If you still have jobs when you try to exit the shell, a message is printed to alert you of this. If you immediately try to exit again, the shell exits. The monitor option is enabled by default for interactive shells.

Stopping Jobs

If the shell is running on a system with job control, and the `monitor` option of the `set` command is turned on, jobs that are running in the foreground may be placed in the background and vice versa. Normally, *Ctrl+z* stops the current job. The `bg` command puts a stopped job in the background. The `fg` command brings a background or stopped job to the foreground.

Whenever a job in the background attempts to read from the terminal, it is stopped until it is brought to the foreground. Output from background jobs normally comes to the terminal. If `stty tostop` is executed, output from background jobs is disabled, and a job writing to the terminal is stopped until it is brought to the foreground. When the shell exits, all stopped jobs are killed.

Command Summary

This section summarizes the shell's built-in commands. Actually, some of these commands (such as echo and test) may not be built in to the shell but must be provided as a utility by a POSIX-compliant system. They are built in to Bash and the Korn shell and are so often used in shell scripts that we decided to list them here anyway.

The following commands are organized alphabetically for easy reference.

The : Command

General Format: :

This is essentially a *null* command. It is frequently used to satisfy the requirement that a command appear.

Example

```
if who | grep jack > /dev/null
then
        :
else
        echo "jack's not logged in"
fi
```

The : command returns an exit status of zero.

The . Command

General Format: . *file*

The "dot" command causes the indicated file to be read and executed by the shell, just as if the lines from the file were typed at that point. Note that *file* does not have to be executable, only readable. Also, the shell uses the PATH variable to find *file*.

Example

```
. progdefs
```
                    Execute commands in progdefs

The preceding command causes the shell to search the current PATH for the file progdefs. When it finds it, it reads and executes the commands from the file.

Note that because *file* is not executed by a subshell, variables set and/or changed within *file* remain in effect after execution of the commands in *file* is complete.

The `alias` Command

General Format: `alias` *name=string* [*name=string* ...]

The `alias` command assigns *string* to the alias *name*. Whenever *name* is used as a command, the shell substitutes *string*, performing command-line substitution after *string* is in place.

Examples

```
alias ll='ls -l'

alias dir='basename $(pwd)'
```

If an alias ends with a blank, the word following the alias is also checked to see whether it's an alias.

The format

```
alias name
```

causes the alias for *name* to be printed out.

`alias` with no arguments lists all aliases.

`alias` returns an exit status of zero unless a *name* is given (as in `alias` *name)* for which no alias has been defined.

The `bg` Command

General Format: `bg` *job_id*

If job control is enabled, the job identified by *job_id* is put into the background. If no argument is given, the most recently suspended job is put into the background.

Example

```
bg %2
```

The `break` Command

General Format: `break`

Execution of this command causes execution of the innermost `for`, `while`, or `until` loop to be immediately terminated. Execution continues with the commands that immediately follow the loop.

If the format

```
break n
```

is used, where *n* is an integer greater than or equal to 1, execution of the *n* inner-most loops is automatically terminated.

The case **Command**

General Format:

```
case value in
      pat₁)  command
             command
             . . .
             command;;
      pat₂)  command
             command
             . . .
             command;;
             . . .
      patₙ)  command
             command
             . . .
             command;;
esac
```

The word *value* is successively compared against pat_1, pat_2, ..., pat_n until a match is found. The commands that appear immediately after the matching pattern are then executed until a double semicolon (;;) is encountered. At that point, execution of the case is terminated.

If no pattern matches *value*, none of the commands inside the case are executed. The pattern * matches *anything* and is often used as the last pattern in a case as the "catchall" case.

The shell metacharacters * (match zero or more characters), ? (match any single character), and [...] (match any single character enclosed between the brackets) can be used in patterns. The character | can be used to specify a logical ORing of two patterns, as in

pat_1 | pat_2

which means to match either pat_1 or pat_2.

Examples

```
case $1 in
      -l) lopt=TRUE;;
      -w) wopt=TRUE;;
```

```
        -c)  copt=TRUE;;
         *)  echo "Unknown option";;
esac

case $choice in
    [1-9])  valid=TRUE;;
         *)  echo "Please choose a number from 1-9";;
esac
```

The cd Command

General Format: cd *directory*

Execution of this command causes the shell to make *directory* the current directory. If directory is omitted, the shell makes the directory specified in the HOME variable the current directory.

If the shell variable CDPATH is null, directory must be a full directory path (for example, /users/steve/documents) or relative to the current directory (for example, documents, ../pat).

If CDPATH is non-null and *directory* is not a full path, the shell searches the colon-delimited directory list in CDPATH for a directory containing *directory*.

Examples

$ **cd documents/memos**   *Change to* documents/memos *directory*

$ **cd**   *Change to* HOME *directory*

An argument of - causes the shell to make the previous directory the current directory. The pathname of the new current directory is printed out.

Examples

```
$ pwd
/usr/lib/uucp
$ cd /
$ cd -
/usr/lib/uucp
$
```

The cd command sets the shell variable PWD to the new current directory, and OLDPWD to the previous directory.

The continue **command**

General Format: continue

Execution of this command from within a for, while, or until loop causes any commands that follow the continue to be skipped. Execution of the loop then continues as normal.

If the format

continue *n*

is used, the commands within the *n* innermost loops are skipped. Execution of the loops then continue as normal.

The echo **Command**

General Format: echo *args*

This command causes *args* to be written to standard output. Each word from *args* is delimited by a blank space. A newline character is written at the end. If *args* is omitted, the effect is to simply skip a line.

Certain backslashed characters have a special meaning to echo as shown in Table A.8.

TABLE A.8   echo Escape Characters

Character	Prints
\a	Alert
\b	Backspace
\c	The line without a terminating newline
\f	Formfeed
\n	Newline
\r	Carriage return
\t	Tab character
\v	Vertical tab character
\\	Backslash character
\0*nnn*	The character whose ASCII value is *nnn*, where *nnn* is a one- to three-digit octal number that starts with a zero

Remember to quote these characters so that the echo command interprets them and not the shell.

Examples

```
$ echo *                    List all files in the current directory
bin docs mail mise src
```

```
$ echo                              Skip a line

$ echo 'X\tY'                       Print X and Y, separated by a tab
X       Y
$ echo "\n\nSales Report"           Skip two lines before displaying Sales Report


Sales Report
$ echo "Wake up!!\a"                Print message and beep terminal
Wake up!!
$
```

The eval Command

General Format: eval *args*

Execution of this command causes the shell to evaluate *args* and then execute the results. This is useful for causing the shell to effectively "double-scan" a command line.

Example

```
$ x='abc def'
$ y='$x'                 Assign $x to y
$ echo $y
$x
$ eval echo $y
abc def
$
```

The exec Command

General Format: exec *command args*

When the shell executes the exec command, it initiates execution of the specified *command* with the indicated arguments. Unlike other commands executed as a new process, *command* replaces the current process (that is, no new process is created). After *command* starts execution, there is no return to the program that initiated the exec.

If just I/O redirection is specified, the input and/or output for the shell is accordingly redirected.

Examples

```
exec /bin/sh             Replace current process with sh
```

```
exec < datafile          Reassign standard input to datafile
```

The `exit` Command

General Format: `exit` *n*

Execution of `exit` causes the current shell program to be immediately terminated. The exit status of the program is the value of the integer *n*, if supplied. If *n* is not supplied, the exit status is that of the last command executed prior to the `exit`.

An exit status of zero is used by convention to indicate "success," and nonzero to indicate "failure" (such as an error condition). This convention is used by the shell in evaluation of conditions for `if`, `while`, and `until` commands, and with the `&&` and `||` constructs.

Examples

```
who | grep $user > /dev/null
exit                           Exit with status of last grep

exit 1                         Exit with status of 1
if finduser                    If finduser returns an exit status of zero then...
then
   ...
fi
```

Note that executing `exit` from a login shell has the effect of logging you off.

The `export` Command

General Format: `export` *variables*

The export command tells the shell that the indicated variables are to be marked as exported; that is, their values are to be passed down to subshells.

Examples

```
export PATH PS1

export dbhome x1 y1 date
```

Variables may be set when exported using the form

`export` *variable=value...*

So lines such as

```
PATH=$PATH:$HOME/bin; export PATH
CDPATH=.:$HOME:/usr/spool/uucppublic; export CDPATH
```

can be rewritten as

```
export PATH=$PATH:$HOME/bin CDPATH=.:$HOME:/usr/spool/uucppublic
```

The output of export with a -p argument is a list of the exported variables and their values in the form

export *variable=value*

or

export *variable*

if *variable* has been exported but not yet set.

The false **Command**

General Format: false

The false command simply returns a nonzero exit status.

The fc **Command**

General Format: fc   -e *editor* -lnr *first last*

fc -s *old=new first*

The fc command is used to edit commands in the command history. A range of commands is specified from *first* to *last*, where *first* and *last* can be either command numbers or strings; a negative number is taken as an offset from the current command number; a string specifies the most recently entered command beginning with that string. The commands are read into the editor and executed upon exit from the editor. If no editor is specified, the value of the shell variable FCEDIT is used; if FCEDIT is not set, ed is used.

The -l option lists the commands from *first* to *last* (that is, an editor is not invoked). If the -n option is also selected, these commands are not preceded by command numbers.

The -r option to fc reverses the order of the commands.

If *last* is not specified, it defaults to *first*. If *first* is also not specified, it defaults to the previous command for editing and to -16 for listing.

The -s option causes the selected command to be executed without editing it first. The format

fc -s *old=new first*

causes the command *first* to be re-executed after the string *old* in the command is replaced with *new*. If *first* isn't specified, the previous command is used, and if *old=new* isn't specified, the command is not changed.

Examples

`fc -l`	*List the last 16 commands*
`fc -e vi sed`	*Read the last* `sed` *command into* `vi`
`fc 100 110`	*Read commands 100 to 110 into* `$FCEDIT`
`fc -s`	*Re-execute the previous command*
`fc -s abc=def 104`	*Re-execute command 104, replacing* `abc` *with* `def`

The `fg` Command

General Format: `fg job_id`

If job control is enabled, the job specified by *job_id* is brought to the foreground. If no argument is given, the most recently suspended job, or the job last sent to the background is brought to the foreground.

Example

`fg %2`

The `for` Command

General Format:

for *var* in *word$_1$ word$_2$ ... word$_n$*
do
    command
    command
    ...
done

Execution of this command causes the commands enclosed between the do and done to be executed as many times as there are words listed after the in.

The first time through the loop, the first word—*word$_1$*—is assigned to the variable *var* and the commands between the do and done executed. The second time through the loop, the second word listed—*word$_2$*—is assigned to *var* and the commands in the loop executed again. This process continues until the last variable in the list—

word~*n*~—is assigned to *var* and the commands between the do and done executed. At that point, execution of the for loop is terminated. Execution then continues with the command that immediately follows the done.

The special format

```
for var
do
   ...
done
```

indicates that the positional parameters "$1", "$2", ... are to be used in the list and is equivalent to

```
for var in "$@"
do
   ...
done
```

Example

```
# nroff all of the files in the current directory
for file in *
do
      nroff -Tlp $file | lp
done
```

The getopts **Command**

General Format: getopts *options var*

This command processes command-line arguments. *options* is a list of valid single letter options. If any letter in *options* is followed by a :, that option takes a following argument on the command line, which must be separated from the option by at least one whitespace character.

Each time getopts is called, it processes the next command-line argument. If a valid option is found, getopts stores the matching option letter inside the specified variable *var* and returns a zero exit status.

If an invalid option is specified (that is, one not listed in options), getopts stores a ? inside *var* and returns with a zero exit status. It also writes an error message to standard error.

If an option takes a following argument, getopts stores the matching option letter inside *var* and stores the following command-line argument inside the special

variable OPTARG. If no arguments are left on the command line, getopts stores a ?
inside *var* and writes an error message to standard error.

If no more options remain on the command line (that is, if the next command-line
argument does not begin with a -), getopts returns a nonzero exit status.

The special variable OPTIND is also used by getopts. It is initially set to 1 and is
adjusted each time getopts returns to indicate the number of the next command-
line argument to be processed.

The argument - - can be placed on the command line to specify the end of the
command-line arguments.

getopts supports stacked arguments, as in

```
repx -iau
```

which is equivalent *to*

```
repx -i -a -u
```

Options that take following arguments may not be stacked.

If the format

getopts *options var args*

is used, getopts parses the arguments specified by *args rather than* the command-line
arguments.

Example
```
usage="Usage: foo [-r] [-O outfile] infile"

while getopts ro: opt
do
        case "$opt"
        in
                r) rflag=1;;
                O) oflag=1
                   ofile=$OPTARG;;
                \?) echo "$usage"
                    exit 1;;
        esac
done

if [ $OPTIND -gt $# ]
```

```
then
        echo "Needs input file!"
        echo "$usage"
        exit 2
fi

shift $(( OPTIND - 1 ))
ifile=$1
...
```

The hash Command

General Format: hash *commands*

This command tells the shell to look for the specified commands and to remember what directories they are located in. If *commands* is not specified, a list of the hashed commands is displayed.

If the format

```
hash -r
```

is used, the shell removes all commands from its hash list. Next time any command is executed, the shell uses its normal search methods to find the command.

Examples

hash rolo whoq	*Add* rolo *and* whoq *to hash list*
hash	*Print hash list*
hash -r	*Remove hash list*

The if Command

General Format:

```
if  command
then
        command
        command
        ...
fi
```

command₁ is executed and its exit status tested. If it is zero, the commands that follow up to the `fi` are executed. Otherwise, the commands that follow up to the `fi` are skipped.

Example

```
if grep $sys sysnames > /dev/null
then
        echo "$sys is a valid system name"
fi
```

If the `grep` returns an exit status of zero (which it will if it finds $sys in the file sysnames), the `echo` command is executed; otherwise it is skipped.

The built-in command `test` is often used as the command following the `if`.

Example

```
if [ $# -eq 0 ]
then
        echo "Usage: $0 [-l] file ..."
        exit 1
fi
```

An `else` clause can be added to the `if` to be executed if the command returns a nonzero exit status. In this case, the general format of the `if` becomes

```
if command₁
then
        command
        command
        ...
else
        command
        command
        ...
fi
```

If *command₁* returns an exit status of zero, the commands that follow up to the `else` are executed, and the commands between the `else` and the `fi` are skipped. Otherwise, *command₁* returns a nonzero exit status and the commands between the `then` and the `else` are skipped, and the commands between the `else` and the `fi` are executed.

Example

```
if [ -z "$line" ]
then
        echo "I couldn't find $name"
else
        echo "$line"
fi
```

In the preceding example, if line has zero length, the echo command that displays the message I couldn't find $name is executed; otherwise, the echo command that displays the value of line is executed.

A final format of the if command is useful when more than a two-way decision has to be made. Its general format is

```
if command₁
then
        command
        command
        . . .
elif command₂
then
        command
        command
        . . .
elif commandₙ
then
        command
        command
        . . .
else
        command
        command
        . . .
fi
```

command₁, command₂, ..., commandₙ are evaluated in order until one of the commands returns an exit status of zero, at which point the commands that immediately follow the then (up to another elif, else, or fi) are executed. If none of the commands returns an exit status of zero, the commands listed after the else (if present) are executed.

Example

```
if [ "$choice" = a ]
then
        add $*
elif [ "$choice" = d ]
then
        delete $*
elif [ "$choice" = l ]
then
        list
else
        echo "Bad choice!"
        error=TRUE
fi
```

The jobs **Command**

General Format: jobs

The list of active jobs is printed. If the -l option is specified, detailed information about each job, including its process id, is listed as well. If the -p option is specified, only process ids are listed.

If an optional *job_id* is supplied to the jobs command, just information about that job is listed.

Example

```
$ sleep 100 &
[1] 1104
$ jobs
[1] + Running         sleep 100 &
$
```

The kill **Command**

General Format: kill -*signal job*

The kill command sends the signal *signal* to the specified process, where *job* is a process id number or *job_id*, and *signal* is a number or one of the signal names specified in <signal.h> (see the description of trap later in the chapter). kill -l lists these names. A signal number supplied with the –l option lists the corresponding signal name. A process id used with the –l option lists the name of the signal that terminated the specified process (if it was terminated by a signal).

The -s option can also be used when a signal name is supplied, in which case the dash before the name is not used (see the following example).

If *signal* isn't specified, TERM is used.

Examples

```
kill -9 1234
kill -HUP %2
kill -s TERM %2
kill %1
```

Note that more than one process id can be supplied to the kill command on the command line.

The newgrp Command

General Format: newgrp *group*

This command changes your real group id (GID) to *group*. If no argument is specified, it changes you back to your default group.

Examples

newgrp shbook   *Change to group* shbook

newgrp   *Change back to default group*

If a password is associated with the new group, and you are not listed as a member of the group, you will be prompted to enter it.

newgrp -l changes you back to your login group.

The pwd Command

General Format: pwd

This command tells the shell to print your working directory, which is written to standard output.

Examples

```
$ pwd
/users/steve/documents/memos
$ cd
$ pwd
/users/steve
$
```

The read Command

General Format: read *vars*

This command causes the shell to read a line from standard input and assign successive whitespace-delimited words from the line to the variables *vars*. If fewer variables are listed than there are words on the line, the excess words are stored in the last variable.

Specifying just one variable has the effect of reading and assigning an entire line to the variable.

The exit status of read is zero unless an end-of-file condition is encountered.

Examples

```
$ read hours mins
10 19
$ echo "$hours:$mins"
10:19

$ read num rest
39 East 12th Street, New York City 10003
$ echo "$num\n$rest"
39
East 12th Street, New York City 10003

$ read line
        Here     is an entire        line \r
$ echo "$line"
Here     is an entire        line r
$
```

Note in the final example that any leading whitespace characters get "eaten" by the shell when read. You can change IFS if this poses a problem.

Also note that backslash characters get interpreted by the shell when you read the line, and any that make it through (double backslashes will get through as a single backslash) get interpreted by echo if you display the value of the variable.

A –r option to read says to not treat a \ character at the end of a line as line continuation.

The readonly Command

General Format: readonly *vars*

This command tells the shell that the listed variables cannot be assigned values. These variables may be optionally assigned values on the readonly command line. If you subsequently try to assign a value to a readonly variable, the shell issues an error message.

readonly variables are useful for ensuring that you don't accidentally overwrite the value of a variable. They're also good for ensuring that other people using a shell program can't change the values of particular variables (for example, their HOME directory or their PATH). The readonly attribute is not passed down to subshells.

readonly with a -p option prints a list of your readonly variables.

Example

```
$ readonly DB=/users/steve/database          Assign value to DB and make it readonly
$ DB=foo                                      Try to assign it a value
sh: DB: is read-only                          Error message from the shell
$ echo $DB                                    But can still access its value
/users/steve/database
$
```

The return **Command**

General Format: return *n*

This command causes the shell to stop execution of the current function and immediately return to the caller with an exit status of *n*. If *n* is omitted, the exit status returned is that of the command executed immediately prior to the return.

The set **Command**

General Format: set *options args*

This command is used to turn on or off options as specified by *options*. It is also used to set positional parameters, as specified by *args*.

Each single letter option in *options* is enabled if the option is preceded by a minus sign (-), or disabled if preceded by a plus sign (+). Options can be grouped, as in

```
set -fx
```

which enables the f and x options.

Table A.9 summarizes the options that can be selected.

TABLE A.9   set Options

Meaning	Option
- -	Don't treat subsequent *args* preceded by a - as options. If there are no arguments, the positional parameters are unset.
-a	Automatically export all variables that are subsequently defined or modified.
-b	If supported by the implementation, cause the shell to notify you when background jobs finish.
-C	Don't allow output redirection to overwrite existing files. >| can still be used to force individual files to be overwritten even if this option is selected.
-e	Exit if any command that gets executed fails or has a nonzero exit status.
-f	Disable filename generation.
-h	Add commands inside functions to the hash list as they are defined, and not as they are executed.
-m	Turn on the job monitor.
-n	Read commands without executing them (useful for checking for balanced do...dones, and if...fis).
+o	Write current option mode settings in command format.
-o *m*	Turn on option mode *m* (see Table A.10).
-u	Issue an error if a variable is referenced without having been assigned a value or if a positional parameter is referenced without having been set.
-v	Print each shell command line as it is read.
-x	Print each command and its arguments as it is executed, preceded by a +.

Shell modes are turned on or off by using the -o and +o options, respectively, followed by an option name. These options are summarized in Table A.10.

TABLE A.10   Shell Modes

Mode	Meaning
allexport	Same as -a.
errexit	Same as -e.
ignoreeof	The exit command must be used to leave the shell.
monitor	Same as -m.
noclobber	Same as -C.
noexec	Same as -n.
noglob	Same as -f.
nolog	Don't put function definitions in the history.
nounset	Same as -u.
verbose	Same as -v.
vi	The inline editor is set to vi.
xtrace	Same as -x.

The command `set -o` without any following options has the effect of listing all shell modes and their settings.

The shell variable `$-` contains the current options setting.

Each word listed in *args* is set to the positional parameters $1, $2, ..., respectively. If the first word might start with a minus sign, it's safer to specify the `--` option to `set` to avoid interpretation of that value.

If *args* is supplied, the variable `$#` will be set to the number of parameters assigned after execution of the command.

Examples

`set -vx`	*Print all command lines as they are read, and each command and its arguments as it is executed*
`set "$name" "$address" "$phone"`	*Set* $1 *to* $name, $2 *to* $address, *and* $3 *to* $phone
`set -- -1`	*Set* $1 *to* -1
`set -o vi`	*Turn on* vi *mode*
`set +o verbose -o noglob`	*Turn* verbose *mode off,* noglob *on*

The `shift` Command

General Format: `shift`

This command causes the positional parameters $1, $2, ..., $*n* to be "shifted left" one place. That is, $2 is assigned to $1, $3 to $2, ..., and $*n* to $*n-1*. $# is adjusted accordingly.

If the format

`shift` *n*

is used instead, the shift is to the left *n* places.

Examples

```
$ set a b c d
$ echo "$#\n$*"
4
a b c d
```

```
$ shift
$ echo "$#\n$*"
3
b c d
$ shift 2
$ echo "$#\n$*"
1
d
$
```

The `test` Command

General Format:

test *condition*

or

[*condition*]

The shell evaluates *condition* and if the result of the evaluation is *TRUE*, returns a zero exit status. If the result of the evaluation is *FALSE*, a nonzero exit status is returned. If the format [*condition*] is used, a space must appear immediately after the [and before the].

condition is composed of one or more operators as shown in Table A.11. The -a operator has higher precedence than the -o operator. In any case, parentheses can be used to group subexpressions. Just remember that the parentheses are significant to the shell and so must be quoted. Operators and operands (including parentheses) must be delimited by one or more spaces so that `test` sees them as separate arguments.

`test` is often used to test conditions in an `if`, `while`, or `until` command.

Examples

```
# see if perms is executable

if test -x /etc/perms
then
        ...
fi

# see if it's a directory or a normal file that's readable

if [ -d $file -o \( -f $file -a -r $file \) ]
```

```
then
        ...
fi
```

TABLE A.11   test Operators

Operator	Returns TRUE (zero exit status) if
File Operators	
-b *file*	*file* is a block special file
-c *file*	*file* is a character special file
-d *file*	*file* is a directory
-e *file*	*file* exists
-f *file*	*file* is an ordinary file
-g *file*	*file* has its set group id (SGID) bit set
-h *file*	*file* is a symbolic link
-k *file*	*file* has its sticky bit set
-L *file*	*file* is a symbolic link
-p *file*	*file* is a named pipe
-r *file*	*file* is readable by the process
-S *file*	*file* is a socket
-s *file*	*file* has nonzero length
-t *fd*	*fd* is open file descriptor associated with a terminal (1 is default)
-u *file*	*file* has its set user id (SUID) bit set
-w *file*	*file* is writable by the process
-x *file*	*file* is executable
String Operators	
string	*string* is not null
-n *string*	*string* is not null (and *string* must be seen by test)
-z *string*	*string* is null (and *string* must be seen by test)
string$_1$ = *string$_2$*	*string$_1$* is identical to *string$_2$*
string$_1$!= *string$_2$*	*string$_1$* is *not* identical to *string$_2$*
Integer Comparison Operators	
int$_1$ -eq *int$_2$*	*int$_1$* is equal to *int$_2$*
int$_1$ -ge *int$_2$*	*int$_1$* is greater than or equal to *int$_2$*
int$_1$ -gt *int$_2$*	*int$_1$* is greater than *int$_2$*
int$_1$ -le *int$_2$*	*int$_1$* is less than or equal to *int$_2$*
int$_1$ -lt *int$_2$*	*int$_1$* is less than *int$_2$*
int$_1$ -ne *int$_2$*	*int$_1$* is not equal to *int$_2$*
Boolean Operators	
! *expr*	*expr* is *FALSE*; otherwise, returns *TRUE*
expr$_1$ -a *expr$_2$*	*expr$_1$* is *TRUE*, and *expr$_2$* is *TRUE*
expr$_1$ -o *expr2*	*expr$_1$* is *TRUE*, or *expr$_2$* is *TRUE*

The `times` **Command**

General Format: `times`

Execution of this command causes the shell to write to standard output the total amount of time that has been used by the shell and by all its child processes. For each, two numbers are listed: first the accumulated user time and then the accumulated system time.

Note that `times` does not report the time used by built-in commands.

Example

```
$ times             Print time used by processes
1m5s 2m9s           1 min., 5 secs. user time, 2 mins., 9 secs. system time
8m22.23s 6m22.01s   Time used by child processes
$
```

The `trap` **Command**

General Format: `trap` *commands signals*

This command tells the shell to execute *commands* whenever it receives one of the signals listed in *signals*. The listed signals can be specified by name or number.

`trap` with no arguments prints a list of the current trap assignments.

If the first argument is the null string, as in

`trap "" ` *signals*

the signals in *signals* are ignored when received by the shell.

If the format

`trap ` *signals*

is used, processing of each signal listed in *signals* is reset to the default action.

Examples

`trap "echo hangup >> $ERRFILE; exit" 2`   *Log message and exit on hangup*

`trap "rm $TMPFILE; exit" 1 2 15`   *remove $TMPFILE on signals l, 2, or 15*

`trap "" 2`   *Ignore interrupts*

`trap 2`   *Reset default processing of interrupts*

Table A.12 lists values that can be specified in the signal list.

TABLE A.12   Signal Numbers and Names for `trap`

Signal #	Signal Name	Generated for
0	EXIT	Exit from the shell
1	HUP	Hangup
2	INT	Interrupt (for example, Delete key, *Ctrl+c*)
3	QUIT	Quit
6	ABRT	Abort
9	KILL	Kill
14	ALRM	Alarm timeout
15	TERM	Software termination signal (sent by `kill` by default)

The shell scans *commands* when the `trap` command is encountered and again when one of the listed signals is received. This means, for example, that when the shell encounters the command

```
trap "echo $count lines processed >> $LOGFILE; exit" HUP INT TERM
```

it substitutes the value of count at that point, and *not when one of the signals is received*. You can get the value of count substituted when one of the signals is received if you instead enclose the commands in single quotes:

```
trap 'echo $count lines processed >> $LOGFILE; exit' HUP INT TERM
```

The `true` Command

General Format: `true`

This command returns a zero exit status.

The `type` Command

General Format: `type` *commands*

This command prints information about the indicated commands.

Examples

```
$ type troff echo
troff is /usr/bin/troff
echo is a shell builtin
$
```

The umask **Command**

General Format: umask *mask*

umask sets the default file creation mask to *mask*. Files that are subsequently created are ANDed with this mask to determine the mode of the file.

umask with no arguments prints the current mask. The -s option says to produce symbolic output.

Examples

```
$ umask                    Print current mask
0002                       No write to others
$ umask 022                No write to group either
$
```

The unalias **Command**

General Format: unalias *names*

The alias's *names* are removed from the alias list. The -a option says to remove all aliases.

The unset **Command**

General Format: unset *names*

This causes the shell to erase definitions of the variables or functions listed in *names*. Read-only variables cannot be unset. The -v option to unset specifies that a variable name follows, whereas the -f option specifies a function name. If neither option is used, it is assumed that variable name(s) follow.

Example

```
unset dblist files         Remove definitions of variables dblist and files
```

The until **Command**

General Format:

```
until command_t
do
        command
        command
        ...
done
```

command_t is executed and its exit status tested. If it is nonzero, the commands enclosed between the do and done are executed. Then *command_t* is executed again and its status tested. If it is nonzero, the commands between the do and done are once again executed. Execution of *command_t* and subsequent execution of the commands between the do and done continues until *command_t* returns a zero exit status, at which point the loop is terminated. Execution then continues with the command that follows the done.

Note that because *command_t* gets evaluated immediately on entry into the loop, the commands between the do and done may never be executed if it returns a zero exit status the first time.

Example

```
# sleep for 60 seconds until jack logs on
until who | grep jack > /dev/null
do
        sleep 60
done

echo jack has logged on
```

The preceding loop continues until the grep returns a zero exit status (that is, finds jack in who's output). At that point, the loop is terminated, and the echo command that follows is executed.

The wait **Command**

General Format: wait *job*

This command causes the shell to suspend its execution until the process identified as *job* finishes executing. Job can be a process id number or a *job_id*. If *job* is not supplied, the shell waits for all child processes to finish executing. If more than one process id is listed, wait will wait for them all to complete.

wait is useful for waiting for processes to finish that have been sent to the background for execution.

Example

```
sort large_file > sorted_file &      sort in the background
    . . .                            Continue processing
wait                                 Now wait for sort to finish
plotdata sorted_file
```

The variable $! can be used to obtain the process id number of the last process sent to the background.

The while **Command**

General Format:

```
while command_t
do
        command
        command
        ...
done
```

command_t is executed and its exit status tested. If it is zero, the commands enclosed between the do and done are executed. Then *command_t* is executed again and its status tested. If it is zero, the commands between the do and done are once again executed. Execution of *command_t* and subsequent execution of the commands between the do and done continues until *command_t* returns a nonzero exit status, at which point the loop is terminated. Execution then continues with the command that follows the done.

Note that because *command_t* gets evaluated immediately on entry into the loop, the commands between the do and done may never be executed if it returns a nonzero exit status the first time.

Example

```
# fill up the rest of the buffer with blank lines

while [ $lines -le $maxlines ]
do
        echo >> $BUFFER
        lines=$((lines + 1))
done
```

B

For More Information

IN THIS APPENDIX

- Online Documentation
- Documentation on the Web
- Books

Many sources of information on the Unix system are available; however, we have selectively listed some titles and Web sites here of particular value to shell programmers. All Web sites and URLs are valid as of the publication of this book, but as is often the case on the Internet, some may not be available by the time you read this.

There is one reference that you cannot do without. This is the Unix documentation for your particular system. It gives detailed descriptions on the syntax and various options for each of the commands.

Online Documentation

If a printed version of your system's documentation isn't available, you can use the man command to get information (referred to as the "man pages" by Unix users) about any specific Unix command. The format is

man *command*

Some systems have an interactive documentation command called info. To invoke it, simply type info. After it starts up, just type h for a tutorial.

Note that some smaller systems may not have online documentation due to disk space limitations. However, almost all this information is also available on the Web and in printed form.

Documentation on the Web

The authors of this book maintain the Web site at www.kochan-wood.com. You can purchase other books by the authors; download the rolo program; get answers to the exercises; and find out more about Unix, the C programming language, and shell programming there.

The best place on the Web for information on the POSIX standard is at www.unix.org. This site is maintained by The Open Group, an international consortium that worked with the IEEE to create the current POSIX specification. The complete specification is available on its Web site. You must register first to read it, but registration is free. The URL for accessing the documentation is www.unix.org/online.html. You can also purchase for download a printable copy of the Open Group Unix documentation at www.opengroup.org/pubs/catalog/un.htm. (The standards publications are only available for download or on CD-ROM, although you may still be able to find some older, out-of-print hard-copy versions at Amazon.com.)

The Free Software Foundation maintains online documentation for a variety of Unix utilities, including Bash, at www.fsf.org/manual.

David Korn, the developer of the Korn shell, maintains www.kornshell.com. It contains documentation, downloads, information on books on the Korn shell, and links to information on other shells.

If you want to experiment with the Korn shell, or you're using a system that doesn't have a POSIX compliant shell, you can download the Korn shell executable for a variety of Unix systems for free from www.research.att.com/sw/download/.

If you only have access to Microsoft Windows systems but still want to try your hand at shell programming, or you just want to get a taste of Unix, install the Cygwin package from www.cygwin.com. The base system includes Bash, and you can also download other shells such as zsh. The total feel of the system is remarkably like Unix, even though it's running on Windows. There's even an X Window System available to enhance the Unix look and feel. Best of all, the entire Cygwin package is free.

Books

O'Reilly & Associates

One of the best sources of books on Unix-related topics is O'Reilly and Associates (www.ora.com). Their books cover a wide variety of subjects and are available from their Web site, from booksellers online, and in book stores. Their Web site also has many useful articles on Unix and Linux.

Two good references on Unix and Linux, respectively:

Unix in a Nutshell: System V Edition, 3rd Edition, A. Robbins, O'Reilly & Associates, 1999 (ISBN 1565924274).

Linux in a Nutshell, 3rd Edition, E. Siever, S. Spainhour, J. P. Hekman, and S. Figgins,

O'Reilly & Associates, 2000 (ISBN 0596000251).

Four good books on Perl programming, from beginner to advanced:

Learning Perl, 3rd Edition, R. L. Schwartz and T. Phoenix, O'Reilly & Associates, 2001 (ISBN 0596001320).

Perl in a Nutshell, 2nd Edition, S. Spainhour, E. Siever, and N. Patwardhan, O'Reilly & Associates, 2002 (ISBN 0596002416).

Programming Perl, 3rd Edition, L. Wall, T. Christiansen, and J. Orwant, O'Reilly & Associates, 2000 (ISBN 0596000278).

Advanced Perl Programming, S. Srinivasan, O'Reilly & Associates, 1997 (ISBN 1565922204).

A good book covering both the POSIX standard versions of awk and sed as well as the GNU versions:

Sed & Awk, 2nd Edition, D. Dougherty and A. Robbins, O'Reilly & Associates, 1997 (ISBN 1565922255).

Sams and Que

Learn the essentials of Unix shell programming from the ground up:

Sams Teach Yourself Shell Programming in 24 Hours, 2nd Edition, Sriranga Veeraraghaven, Sams Publishing, 2002 (ISBN 0672323583).

A good book for learning Unix and programming in C and Perl on a Unix system:

Sams Teach Yourself Unix in 24 Hours, 3rd Edition, Dave Taylor, Sams Publishing, 2001 (ISBN 0672321270).

This book offers a series of lectures written by several Unix experts who have years of experience to share with their audience:

Unix Unleashed, Robin Anderson and Andy Johnston, Sams Publishing, 2001 (ISBN 067232251X).

This book offers detailed information on a broad range of Red Hat Linux topics, from installation to multimedia:

Red Hat Linux 8 Unleashed, Billy Ball, Sams Publishing, 2002 (ISBN 067232458X).

Learn how to efficiently install Red Hat Linux 8 and then get the most out of your system:

Sams Teach Yourself Red Hat Linux 8.0 in 24 Hours, Aron Hsiao, Sams Publishing, 2003

(ISBN 067232475X).

This title offers a broad range of FreeBSD-related topics. It is detailed in its approach and offers information not found anywhere else:

FreeBSD Unleashed, Michael Urban and Brian Tiemann, Sams Publishing, 2001 (ISBN 0672322064).

Learn FreeBSD from the ground up. This book is the only beginning level tutorial that offers all the ins and outs of the FreeBSD operating system:

Sams Teach Yourself FreeBSD in 24 Hours, Michael Urban and Brian Tiemann, 2002 (ISBN 0672324245).

Other Publishers

This is the set of standard documentation for System V, Release 4 produced by AT&T. Although thorough, this two-book set dates from the early 1990s:

User's Reference Manual/System Administrator's Reference Manual, Prentice Hall, 1992 (ISBN 0139513108).

The following book contains complete coverage of the Korn shell, and is coauthored by its creator:

The New KornShell Command and Programming Language, 2nd Edition, D. Korn and M. Bolsky, Prentice Hall, 1995 (ISBN 0131827006).

An in-depth reference to the C shell:

The Unix C Shell Field Guide, G. Anderson and P. Anderson, Prentice Hall, 1986 (ISBN 013937468X).

A complete description of the awk language authored by its creators:

The AWK Programming Language, A. V. Aho, B. W. Kernighan, and P. J. Weinberger, Addison-Wesley, 1988 (ISBN 020107981X).

An advanced Unix programming book:

The Unix Programming Environment, B. W. Kernighan and R. Pike, Prentice Hall, 1984 (ISBN 013937681X).

An advanced Linux programming book:

Advanced Linux Programming, M. Mitchell, J. Oldham, and A. Samuel, New Riders Publishing, 2001 (ISBN 0735710430).

Index

Symbols

A

ALRM signal, 399

ampersand (&), 177-179, 364

AND operator, 158-159

apostrophe ('), 115-119, 371

archive files, 297-301

args program, 135, 187-189

arguments

    functions, 301

    passing, 133-134

        $# variable, 134-135

        $* variable, 135-136

        ${n} variable, 141

        phonebook file example, 136-141

        shift command, 141-142

    positional parameters

        defined, 133, 365

        left shifting, 141-142

        reassigning values to, 267, 276-277

arithmetic

    arithmetic expansion, 110-111

    arithmetic operators, 371-372

    arithmetically sorting files, 91-92

    integer arithmetic

        arithmetic bases, 342-343

        arithmetic expressions, 340-341

        integer types, 341-342

arithmetic expansion, 110-111

arithmetic expressions, 371-372

arithmetic operators, 371-372

$array construct, 352

${#array[i]} construct, 352

${array[*]} construct, 352

${array[i]} construct, 352-353

array[i]=val construct, 352

arrays, 346-352

    assigning elements to, 346

    retrieving elements from, 347

    subscripts, 346

asterisk (*), 24-26, 59-62, 171, 370-372

asynchronous execution, 289

automatically loaded functions, 340

awk command, 96

The AWK Programming Language, 406

B

b command (vi), 330-332

b conversion specification character, 229

\b escape character, 212, 380

-b option (set command), 394

background

    background processes, waiting for, 289-290

    executing jobs in, 199, 377, 353

    sending commands to, 36-37

backquote (`), 124-125, 371

backslash (\), 121-122, 364, 370-371

    backslash inside double quotes, 123-124

    line continuation character, 122-123

bases (arithmetic), 342-343

Bash shell, 325

beginning of line, matching, 55

bg command, 353-355, 377

books

    Advanced Linux Programming, 406

    Advanced Perl Programming, 405

    The AWK Programming Language, 406

naming conventions
  filenames, 7-9
  pathnames
    . pathname, 12
    .. pathname, 12
    full pathnames, 11
    relative pathnames, 11
  variables, 103
-ne operator, 155
negation operators
  logical AND operator (-a), 158-159
  logical negation operator (!), 158
  logical OR operator (-o), 159-160
The New Korn Shell Command and Programming Language, **406**
newgrp command, 391
newline characters, 47
nnn **escape characters, 212**
noclobber shell mode, 394
noexec shell mode, 394
noglob shell mode, 394
nolog shell mode, 394
nonzero exit status, 363
nounset shell mode, 394
null command (:), 177
null values, 107-108
number program, 226-227
number2 program, 282-283
numbers
  exit status
    $? variable, 146-149
    nonzero values, 145
    zero, 145
  job numbers, 37

line numbering program, 282-283
signal numbers, 291, 399

O

o conversion specification character, 229
-o (logical OR) operator, 159-160
+o option (set command), 394
-o option
  set command, 394
  sort command, 90-91
O'Reilly and Associates, 404-405
operators, 371-372
  file operators, 157-158
  integer operators, 155-157
  logical AND operator (-a), 158-159
  logical negation operator (!), 158
  logical OR operator (-o), 159-160
  string operators, 150-154
options (command), 8
OR operator (-o), 159-160
ordinary files, 6
output. *See* I/O (input/output)

P

P command (vi), 370
-p option (export command), 241
parameter substitution, 267, 270-273, 366
  ${*parameter*} construct, 268, 367
  ${#*parameter*} construct, 367

S

S command (vi), 369

s conversion specification character, 229

-s option
    fc command, 368
    paste command, 74
    sh command, 363
    tr command, 81-82

-s test operator, 157

Sams Teach Yourself FreeBSD in 24 Hours, 406

Sams Teach Yourself Red Hat Linux 8.0 in 24 Hours, 405

Sams Teach Yourself Shell Programming in 24 Hours, 405

Sams Teach Yourself Unix in 24 Hours, 405

saving matched characters, 64-66

search order, 359

searching. *See also* pattern matching
    files, 83-89
    phone book entries, 136-138, 312-313
    search order, 359

secondary prompts, 118

Sed & Awk, 405

sed command, 74-78

selecting shells, 326

semicolon (;), 363, 369

sending commands to background, 36-37

set command, 267, 280, 314, 393-395
    -- option, 277-280
    -x option, 274-275
    executing without arguments, 275-276
    reassigning positional parameters with, 276-277

sh command, 173-175

shell archive files, 297-301

shell variables. *See* variables

shells, 1-2, 41-42
    Bash, 325
    command execution, 46-48
    compatibility summary, 359-360
    defined, 1
    entering commands in, 45-46
    environmental control, 51
    filename substitution, 48-49
    input redirection, 49-51
    Korn, 325
    login shell, 42-45
        getty program, 42
        init program, 42-44
    output redirection, 49-51
    pipeline hookup, 51
    restricted shell (rsh), 355-356
    selecting, 326
    shell modes, 274-275, 394-395
    starting up, 363
    subshells, 236-237, 253-254, 373

shift command, 141-142, 395-396

How can we make this index more useful? Email us at indexes@samspublishing.com